# The Britannica Guide to
# Statistics and Probability

# MATH EXPLAINED

## The Britannica Guide to
# Statistics and Probability

EDITED BY ERIK GREGERSEN,
ASSOCIATE EDITOR, ASTRONOMY AND SPACE EXPLORATION

Britannica®
Educational Publishing

IN ASSOCIATION WITH

ROSEN
EDUCATIONAL SERVICES

Published in 2011 by Britannica Educational Publishing
(a trademark of Encyclopædia Britannica, Inc.)
in association with Rosen Educational Services, LLC
29 East 21st Street, New York, NY 10010.

First Edition

Britannica Educational Publishing
**Michael I. Levy: Executive Editor**
J.E. Luebering: Senior Manager
Marilyn L. Barton: Senior Coordinator, Production Control
Steven Bosco: Director, Editorial Technologies
Lisa S. Braucher: Senior Producer and Data Editor
Yvette Charboneau: Senior Copy Editor
Kathy Nakamura: Manager, Media Acquisition
Erik Gregersen: Associate Editor, Astronomy and Space Exploration

Rosen Educational Services
Heather M. Moore Niver: Editor
Nelson Sá: Art Director
Cindy Reiman: Photography Manager
Matthew Cauli: Designer, Cover Design
Introduction by John Strazzabosco

**Library of Congress Cataloging-in-Publication Data**

The Britannica guide to statistics and probability / edited by Erik Gregersen.—1st ed.
    p. cm.—(Math explained)
"In association with Britannica Educational Publishing, Rosen Educational Services."
Includes bibliographical references and index.
ISBN 978-1-61530-118-8 (library binding)
1. Probabilities—Popular works. 2. Mathematical statistics—Popular works. I. Gregersen, Erik.
QA273.15.B75 2011
519.2—dc22

                                                                        2010002546

*Manufactured in the United States of America*

# CONTENTS

96

109

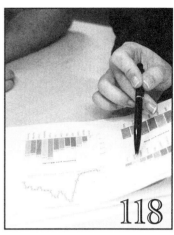

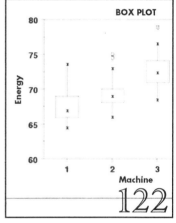

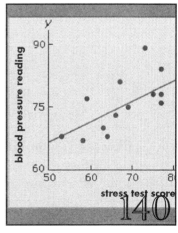

155

159

198

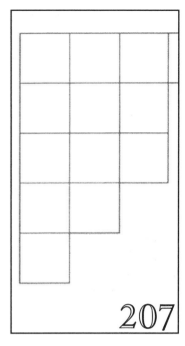

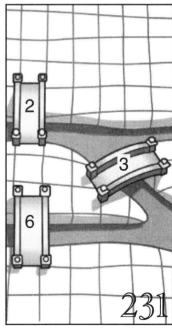

INTRODUCTION

This volume presents a multifaceted view of statistics and probability. Through the eyes of the discoverers we find the thrilling aspects of mathematical applications that changed the lives of the innovators themselves, as well as the world at large. The technology that speeds us through our modern age of discovery has depended upon statistical knowledge and probability theory for guidance. Within these pages readers will find the history of these important disciplines of mathematics: the geniuses of invention and theory, many practical applications of the math, as well as explanations of the major topics. Statistics and probability may seem forbidding terrain to some, but this collective branch of study has proven its practical usefulness everywhere from how to play a hand at a card table to evaluating SAT scores to ensuring the safety of rockets in outer space.

First, to space.

In 1960 an invitation was extended to select incoming engineering freshmen at a Midwestern university. These students could apply to participate in a scientific study that would provide necessary information for space travel. At the time, no one really knew how people locked in a space capsule would behave. Would crew members who were isolated and sequestered for a number of days at a stretch sleep well? Would they argue and get on each other's nerves? Would their dietary patterns be affected? Would they suffer anxiety attacks?

NASA was developing a program to send people into outer space. As there was no data on what happened to human beings once they left the confines of the planet, statistical data under simulated conditions was crucial. If several people were sequestered in a capsule under pressures of risk, the denial of home comforts, and with the added factor of personality differences, might they tend to push the wrong buttons on the control panel?

Not only was statistical data necessary, probability theory was crucial. These days, the common high school student who has watched the *World Series of Poker* tournaments on television knows that knowledge of the odds can and often does determine a player's stake. But poker, ruthless as it might be at times, is merely a game. Sending people off in a rocket for the first time ever is not.

Scientists and mathematicians, of course, were fairly sure of certain forces and events, such as gravitational pull, centrifugal force, friction, mathematical relationships governing ellipses and parabolas and such, to name a few. But add people—a rocket full of NASA crew members blasting off from the face of the earth—and could those scientists tell the pilots for sure—for *certain*—exactly what would happen? The answer was no. Everyone knew that risks existed. Mathematicians were called in to determine to the best of their abilities what those risks might be, and how confident one might be that the anticipated scientific responses and behaviours would indeed occur.

For example, during the all-important re-entry phase of the space journey, if the curvature of the flight path of a speeding spacecraft from one destination in space to a moving, spinning earth thousands of miles away was undertaken, what were the chances of a meteorite interfering? What were the odds of engine failure or abnormal frictional forces? What were the probabilities of the spacecraft and its occupants hitting the ocean instead of the Himalayas?

One must stand in awe of the mathematics that these theoreticians were asked to deliver. The results certainly eclipsed whether or not a straight flush would appear to assure a winning poker hand. To their best knowledge, these mathematicians were assessing the chances of life or death. Unlike the college classroom, partial credit on this exam would not be acceptable. And yet the mathematicians were not dealing with an exact science. They were hoping for probabilities that covered all related factors as far as they knew. What would *probably* happen? (And if the theorists had trouble sleeping at night, imagine the training space crew.)

Mathematical tension was rampant. In fact, news footage of NASA scientists in front of computers monitoring space flights showed them chain smoking, frequently rubbing their faces with their open palms, shifting with the jitters, and finally, ecstatic as football fans when a satisfactory mission ended and the words came: "Houston, we have recovery."

While probability and statistics look innocent, apparently composed of peaceful numbers and placid formulas about what might happen over the course of a certain event, we understand the inner turmoil beneath a calm exterior. And one isn't required to be a NASA mathematician to suffer from these statistical tensions. Take the average high school student trying to enter college, whose selection and application process might very well involve at least one fall Saturday morning spent taking the SAT test. One can feel one's blood pressure rising at the thought. It seems to the students that the culprits in student discomfort are the test questions. But the hidden instigators are actually statistical measures, standard deviations. After all, a student might miss many questions on the test and reach an acceptable score. The real concern is how far from the average student is the test taker? That is the measure college admissions officers would like to know. And the statistical standard deviation, converted to a score that is more understandable and easier to read and compare, is the cause of all that student agony. In any given SAT test, students are competing with the other students who are taking that same test. If every test taker were statistically average, no measurable standard deviation would exist, and nobody would score higher than anyone else. The college admissions people would have to find another way to make their decisions.

Making use of terms such as *agony* to discuss a mathematical tool seems melodramatic. Yet that term and others, including downright pejoratives, have been used to describe the applications of statistics. Recall author Darrell Huff's bestselling book, *How to Lie with Statistics*. If statistics can convince one to follow a certain path—a wrong path—then perhaps statistics alone are not enough for making a wise decision. Morality must be applied, as well. To use the term *sinister* when considering possible statistic applications might be reasonable, as will be explained shortly.

The math discipline often fondly referred to as "stats" by its students comes with an ingenious side, and also caveats. One wonders if Carl Friedrich Gauss (1777–1855) foresaw such developments when his probability distribution equations led to the still-popular bell curve, at the foundation of statistical measures.

The plotted curve demonstrates visually the distribution of a population, mean (or average), and standard deviation. The area under the curve can be made to illustrate the percents of the total population falling in certain standard deviation intervals. As the previous sentence shows, just the verbiage in describing this mathematical graph and its statistical measuring requires enormous amounts of detail held in the brain. By contrast, the rather beautiful curve itself gently relates its properties pictorially, aesthetically, and perhaps more effectively, especially for the novice.

The bell curve is also called the normal curve, or the curve showing normal distribution of the population members under study. This choice of expression, "normal," returns us to the caution required when entering the world of statistics. To study a population with the normal curve, one must be careful about assuming what is normal and what is not. The statistics being reached might just bleed off unintended inference: the bias, bigotry, political leanings, and even those sinister intentions mentioned earlier. On the positive side, statistics have helped pave the way for space travel, inoculations to wipe out polio, and even supplied sports information that helped the Boston Red Sox win a World Series title. This last advance (an advance depending on whom you root for, that is) came thanks to Red Sox statistician Bill James and his innovative view on what is important in baseball as opposed to what people had thought was important in baseball. On the negative side of statistics, consider a little Nazi statistical undertaking that involved a key Polish mathematician victim during the early 1940s.

Stefan Banach (1892–1945) founded functional analysis and helped develop the theory of topology, vector space, and normed linear spaces (which are now known as Banach spaces). These ingenious discoveries were all good things intended to help mankind and further human knowledge, our understanding of ourselves, and make life easier for succeeding generations. The 1920s and '30s were good years for Banach, but his life was destined to change quite abruptly. From 1941 to 1944, under the Nazi occupation, Banach was compelled to take work as a lice feeder, thereby becoming infested. For three years he was forced to become a virtual lice farm as the Nazis studied him, gathering statistics on infectious diseases. This brilliant mathematician died of lung cancer in 1945, the last years of his life spent not as a statistical analyst but rather as a subject. As previously mentioned, statistics can have a seamy side or a wonderfully illuminating side. How the stats are arrived at and how they are presented may make all the difference. Inferences are often crucial.

While the Nazis were taking statistics to a barbaric level, during another time in history in one of those complete twists of human nature that demonstrates caring and fair play, earlier statistical work from a brilliant German physicist helped unite previous rivals. The brilliancies in both discovery and collegiality are found in the work of Ludwig Eduard Boltzmann (1844–1906). Boltzmann's statistical mechanics helped explain and make available predictions of how the properties of atoms (their mass, charge, and structure) determine the properties of matter that become observable to scientists (for instance, viscosity, thermal conductivity, and diffusion). Boltzmann applied the theory of probability of the motions of atoms to the second law of thermodynamics. The second law was shown to be statistical. Its investigations led to the theorem of equipartition of energy (the Maxwell-Boltzmann distribution law). And perhaps the dual names in sponsorship of that equipartition law suggest traits of Boltzmann's character and ingenuity as well as the importance and benefits of a cooperative approach toward discovery. First a brief step back in time is required.

In the 1680s Isaac Newton (England) and Gottfried Wilhelm Leibniz (Germany) had simultaneously and independently discovered calculus. While both discoveries were accomplished in different ways, both were legitimate and provided a long-sought-after mathematical tool for future math discovery and scientific achievement. Unfortunately, a rivalry developed between the followers of Newton and Leibniz. The reticent Newton was content to achieve with rigor and with silence. Leibniz was a master of getting the word out about his work. Instant fame went to Leibniz. Leadership in mathematics discovery therefore shifted from England across the Channel to the Leibniz camp and the continent, remaining on the continent for quite some time.

Enter the aforementioned Ludwig Boltzmann in the late 1800s. He was one of the first continental scientists to recognize the importance of the electromagnetic theory proposed by James Clerk Maxwell of England. Maxwell's work had long been under attack. The support and recognition of Ludwig Boltzmann gave substance to belief in Maxwell's work. Discoveries in atomic physics now proved Maxwell correct. His Brownian motion investigations could be explained only by the statistical mechanics furthered by Boltzmann. (Brownian motion is the random movement of microscopic particles suspended in a fluid and is named for Scottish botanist Robert Brown, the first to study such fluctuations.) In reaching across the Channel, as Boltzmann did with Maxwell, we observe the growth of knowledge, discovery, innovation, and the achievements of modernity. One is left to wonder how much greater the discoveries might have been had Leibniz been able to reach out to Newton, if indeed that was even possible at the time, or if the Nazi regime had nurtured a Polish mathematician and encouraged discovery rather than generate statistics based upon the bite marks on his trunk and scalp. It seems we humans do best when we observe the achievements of past geniuses and grow from that. But we must be cautious in the process, such as statistically omitting from college ranks what a single test might point out as below normal, and from applying too strictly the numbers that arise from numbers.

We must admit that statistics can tell lies. We must make sure that they do not.

# CHAPTER I
## HISTORY OF STATISTICS AND PROBABILITY

Statistics and probability are the branches of mathematics concerned with the laws governing random events, including the collection, analysis, interpretation, and display of numerical data. Probability has its origin in the study of gambling and insurance in the 17th century, and it is now an indispensable tool of both social and natural sciences. Statistics may be said to have its origin in census counts taken thousands of years ago. As a distinct scientific discipline, however, it was developed in the early 19th century as the study of populations, economies, and moral actions and later in that century as the mathematical tool for analyzing such numbers.

## EARLY PROBABILITY

It is astounding that for a subject that has altered how humanity views nature and society, probability had its beginnings in frivolous gambling. How much should you bet on the turn of a card? An entirely new branch of mathematics developed from such questions.

### GAMES OF CHANCE

The modern mathematics of chance is usually dated to a correspondence between the French mathematicians Pierre de Fermat and Blaise Pascal in 1654. Their inspiration came from a problem about games of chance, proposed by a remarkably philosophical gambler, the chevalier de Méré. De Méré inquired about the proper

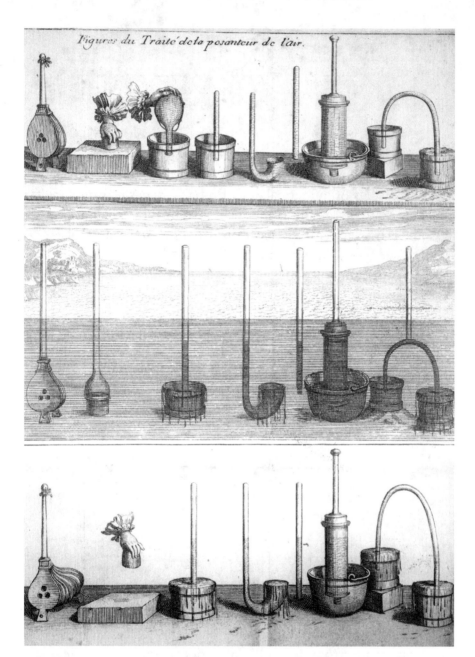

*Blaise Pascal invented the syringe and created the hydraulic press, an instrument based upon the principle that became known as Pascal's law.* Boyer/ Roger Viollet/Getty Images

division of the stakes when a game of chance is interrupted. Suppose two players, *A* and *B*, are playing a
three-point game, each having wagered 32 pistoles, and are
interrupted after *A* has two points and *B* has one. How
much should each receive?

Fermat and Pascal proposed somewhat different solutions, but they agreed about the numerical answer. Each
undertook to define a set of equal or symmetrical cases,
then to answer the problem by comparing the number for
*A* with that for *B*. Fermat, however, gave his answer in
terms of the chances, or probabilities. He reasoned that
two more games would suffice in any case to determine a
victory. There are four possible outcomes, each equally
likely in a fair game of chance. *A* might win twice, *AA*; or
first *A* then *B* might win; or *B* then *A*; or *BB*. Of these four
sequences, only the last would result in a victory for *B*.
Thus, the odds for *A* are 3:1, implying a distribution of 48
pistoles for *A* and 16 pistoles for *B*.

Pascal thought Fermat's solution unwieldy, and he proposed to solve the problem not in terms of chances but in
terms of the quantity now called "expectation." Suppose *B*
had already won the next round. In that case, the positions
of *A* and *B* would be equal, each having won two games,
and each would be entitled to 32 pistoles. *A* should receive
his portion in any case. *B*'s 32, by contrast, depend on the
assumption that he had won the first round. This first
round can now be treated as a fair game for this stake of 32
pistoles, so that each player has an expectation of 16.
Hence *A*'s lot is 32 + 16, or 48, and *B*'s is just 16.

Games of chance such as this one provided model
problems for the theory of chances during its early period,
and indeed they remain staples of the textbooks. A posthumous work of 1665 by Pascal on the "arithmetic triangle"
now linked to his name showed how to calculate numbers

of combinations and how to group them to solve elementary gambling problems. Fermat and Pascal were not the first to give mathematical solutions to problems such as these. More than a century earlier, the Italian mathematician, physician, and gambler Girolamo Cardano calculated odds for games of luck by counting up equally probable cases. His little book, however, was not published until 1663, by which time the elements of the theory of chances were already well known to mathematicians in Europe. It will never be known what would have happened had Cardano published in the 1520s. It cannot be assumed that probability theory would have taken off in the 16th century. When it began to flourish, it did so in the context of the "new science" of the 17th-century scientific revolution, when the use of calculation to solve tricky problems had gained a new credibility. Cardano, moreover, had no great faith in his own calculations of gambling odds, since he believed also in luck, particularly in his own. In the Renaissance world of monstrosities, marvels, and similitudes, chance—allied to fate—was not readily naturalized, and sober calculation had its limits.

## Risks, Expectations, and Fair Contracts

In the 17th century, Pascal's strategy for solving problems of chance became the standard. It was, for example, used by the Dutch mathematician Christiaan Huygens in his short treatise on games of chance, published in 1657. Huygens refused to define equality of chances as a fundamental presumption of a fair game but derived it instead from what he saw as a more basic notion of an equal exchange. Most questions of probability in the 17th century were solved, as Pascal solved his, by redefining the problem in terms of a series of games in which all players have equal expectations. The new theory of chances was not, in fact, simply about gambling but also about the legal notion of a fair contract. A fair contract implied equality of expectations, which served as the fundamental notion in these calculations. Measures of chance or probability were derived secondarily from these expectations.

Probability was tied up with questions of law and exchange in one other crucial respect. Chance and risk, in aleatory contracts, provided a justification for lending at interest, and hence a way of avoiding Christian prohibitions against usury. Lenders, the argument went, were like investors; having shared the risk, they deserved also to share in the gain. For this reason, ideas of chance had already been incorporated in a loose, largely nonmathematical way into theories of banking and marine insurance. From about 1670, initially in the Netherlands, probability began to be used to determine the proper rates at which to sell annuities. Jan de Wit, leader of the Netherlands from 1653 to 1672, corresponded in the 1660s with Huygens, and eventually he published a small treatise on the subject of annuities in 1671.

Annuities in early modern Europe were often issued by states to raise money, especially in times of war. They were generally sold according to a simple formula such as "seven years purchase," meaning that the annual payment to the annuitant, promised until the time of his or her death, would be one-seventh of the principal. This formula took no account of age at the time the annuity was purchased. Wit lacked data on mortality rates at different ages, but he understood that the proper charge for an annuity depended on the number of years that the purchaser could be expected to live and on the presumed rate of interest. Despite his efforts and those of other mathematicians, it remained rare even in the 18th century for rulers to pay much heed to such quantitative considerations. Life insurance, too, was connected only loosely to probability calculations and mortality records, though statistical data on death became increasingly available in the course of the 18th century. The first insurance society to price its policies on the basis of probability calculations was the Equitable, founded in London in 1762.

## Probability as the Logic of Uncertainty

The English clergyman Joseph Butler, in his very influential *Analogy of Religion* (1736), called probability "the very guide of life." The phrase did not refer to mathematical calculation, however, but merely to the judgments made where rational demonstration is impossible. The word *probability* was used in relation to the mathematics of chance in 1662 in the *Logic* of Port-Royal, written by Pascal's fellow Jansenists, Antoine Arnauld and Pierre Nicole. But from medieval times to the 18th century and even into the 19th, a probable belief was most often merely one that seemed plausible, came on good authority, or was worthy of approval. Probability, in this sense, was emphasized in England and France from the late 17th century as an answer to skepticism. Man may not be able to attain perfect knowledge but can know enough to make decisions about the problems of daily life. The new experimental natural philosophy of the later 17th century was associated with this more modest ambition, one that did not insist on logical proof.

Almost from the beginning, however, the new mathematics of chance was invoked to suggest that decisions could after all be made more rigorous. Pascal invoked it in the most famous chapter of his *Pensées*, "Of the Necessity of the Wager," in relation to the most important decision of all, whether to accept the Christian faith. One cannot know of God's existence with absolute certainty; there is no alternative but to bet ("il faut parier"). Perhaps, he supposed, the unbeliever can be persuaded by consideration of self-interest. If there is a God (Pascal assumed he must be the Christian God), to believe in him offers the prospect of an infinite reward for infinite time. However small the probability, provided only that it be finite, the mathematical expectation of this wager is infinite. For so great a benefit, one sacrifices rather little, perhaps a few paltry pleasures during one's brief life on Earth. It seemed plain which was the more reasonable choice.

The link between the doctrine of chance and religion remained an important one through much of the 18th century, especially in Britain. Another argument for belief in God relied on a probabilistic natural theology. The classic instance is a paper read by John Arbuthnot to the Royal Society of London in 1710 and published in its *Philosophical Transactions* in 1712. Arbuthnot presented there a table of christenings in London from 1629 to 1710. He observed that in every year there was a slight excess of male over female births. The proportion, approximately 14 boys for every 13 girls, was perfectly calculated, given the greater dangers to which young men are exposed in their search for food, to bring the sexes to an equality of numbers at the age of marriage. Could this excellent result have been produced by chance alone? Arbuthnot thought not, and he deployed a probability calculation to demonstrate the point. The probability that male births would by accident exceed female ones in 82 consecutive years is $(0.5)^{82}$. Considering further that this excess is found all over the world, he said, and within fixed limits of variation, the chance becomes almost infinitely small. This argument for the overwhelming probability of Divine Providence was repeated by many—and refined by a few. The Dutch natural philosopher Willem's Gravesande incorporated the limits of variation of these birth ratios into his mathematics and so attained a still more decisive vindication of Providence over chance. Nicolas Bernoulli, from the famous Swiss mathematical family, gave a more skeptical view. If the underlying probability of a male birth was assumed to be 0.5169 rather than 0.5, the data were quite in accord with probability theory. That is, no Providential direction was required.

Apart from natural theology, probability came to be seen during the 18th-century Enlightenment as a mathematical version of sound reasoning. In 1677 the German mathematician Gottfried Wilhelm Leibniz imagined a utopian world in which disagreements would be met by this challenge: "Let us calculate, sir." The French mathematician Pierre-Simon de Laplace, in the early 19th century, called probability "good sense reduced to calculation." This ambition, bold enough, was not quite so scientific as it may first appear. For there were some cases where a straightforward application of probability mathematics led to results that seemed to defy rationality. One example, proposed by Nicolas Bernoulli and made famous as the St. Petersburg paradox, involved a bet with an exponentially increasing payoff. A fair coin is to be tossed until the first time it comes up heads. If it comes up heads on the first toss, the payment is 2 ducats; if the first time it comes up heads is on the second toss, 4 ducats; and if on the $n$th toss, $2^n$ ducats. The mathematical expectation of this game is infinite, but no sensible person would pay a very large sum for the privilege of receiving the payoff from it. The disaccord between calculation and reasonableness created a problem, addressed by generations of mathematicians. Prominent among them was Nicolas's

*Pierre Simon de Laplace demonstrated the usefulness of probability for inter-preting scientific data.* Hulton Archive/Getty Images

cousin Daniel Bernoulli, whose solution depended on the idea that a ducat added to the wealth of a rich man benefits him much less than it does a poor man (a concept now known as decreasing marginal utility).

Probability arguments figured also in more practical discussions, such as debates during the 1750s and '60s about the rationality of smallpox inoculation. Smallpox was at this time widespread and deadly, infecting most and carrying off perhaps one in seven Europeans. Inoculation in these days involved the actual transmission of smallpox, not the cowpox vaccines developed in the 1790s by the English surgeon Edward Jenner, and was itself moderately risky. Was it rational to accept a small probability of an almost immediate death to greatly reduce a large probability of death by smallpox in the indefinite future? Calculations of mathematical expectation, as by Daniel Bernoulli, unambiguously led to a favourable answer. But some disagreed, most famously the eminent mathematician and perpetual thorn in the flesh of probability theorists, the French mathematician Jean Le Rond d'Alembert. One might, he argued, reasonably prefer a greater assurance of surviving in the near term to improved prospects late in life.

## THE PROBABILITY OF CAUSES

Many 18th-century ambitions for probability theory, including Arbuthnot's, involved reasoning from effects to causes. Jakob Bernoulli, uncle of Nicolas and Daniel, formulated and proved a law of large numbers to give formal structure to such reasoning. This was published in 1713 from a manuscript, the *Ars conjectandi*, left behind at his death in 1705. There he showed that the observed proportion of, say, tosses of heads or of male births will converge as the number of trials increases to the true probability $p$, supposing that it is uniform. His theorem was designed to give assurance that when $p$ is not known in advance, it can properly be inferred by someone with sufficient experience. He thought of disease and the weather as in some way like drawings from an urn. At bottom they are deterministic, but because one cannot know the causes in sufficient detail, one must be content to investigate the probabilities of events under specified conditions.

The English physician and philosopher David Hartley announced in his *Observations on Man* (1749) that a certain "ingenious Friend" had shown him a solution of the "inverse problem" of reasoning from the occurrence of an event $p$ times and its failure $q$ times to the "original Ratio" of causes. But Hartley named no names, and the first publication of the formula he promised occurred in 1763 in a posthumous paper of Thomas Bayes, communicated to the Royal Society by the British philosopher Richard Price. This has come to be known as Bayes's theorem. But it was the French, especially Laplace, who put the theorem to work as a calculus of induction, and it appears that Laplace's publication of the same mathematical result in 1774 was entirely independent. The result was perhaps more consequential in theory than in practice. An exemplary application was Laplace's probability that the sun will come up tomorrow, based on 6,000 years or so of experience in which it has come up every day.

Laplace and his more politically engaged fellow mathematicians, most notably Marie-Jean-Antoine-Nicolas de Caritat, marquis de Condorcet, hoped to make probability into the foundation of the moral sciences. This took the form principally of judicial and electoral probabilities, addressing thereby some of the central concerns of the Enlightenment philosophers and critics. Justice and elections were, for the French mathematicians, formally similar. In each, a crucial question was how to raise the probability that a jury or an electorate would decide correctly. One element involved testimonies, a classic topic of probability theory. In 1699 the British mathematician John Craig used probability to vindicate the truth of scripture and, more idiosyncratically, to forecast the end of time, when, because of the gradual attrition of truth through successive testimonies, the Christian religion would become no longer probable. The Scottish philosopher David Hume, more skeptically, argued in probabilistic but nonmathematical language beginning in 1748 that the testimonies supporting miracles were automatically suspect, deriving as they generally did from uneducated persons, lovers of the marvelous. Miracles, moreover, being violations of laws of nature, had such a low a priori probability that even excellent testimony could not make them probable. Condorcet also wrote on the probability of miracles, or at least *faits extraordinaires*, to the end of subduing the irrational. But he took a more sustained interest in testimonies at trials, proposing to weigh the credibility of the statements of any particular witness by considering the proportion of times that he had told the truth in the past, and then use inverse probabilities to combine the testimonies of several witnesses.

Laplace and Condorcet applied probability also to judgments. In contrast to English juries, French juries voted whether to convict or acquit without formal deliberations. The probabilists began by supposing that the jurors were independent and that each had a probability $p$ greater than $\frac{1}{2}$ of reaching a true verdict. There would be no injustice, Condorcet argued, in exposing innocent defendants to a risk of conviction equal to risks they voluntarily assume without fear, such as crossing the English

Channel from Dover to Calais. Using this number and considering also the interest of the state in minimizing the number of guilty who go free, it was possible to calculate an optimal jury size and the majority required to convict. This tradition of judicial probabilities lasted into the 1830s, when Laplace's student Siméon-Denis Poisson used the new statistics of criminal justice to measure some of the parameters. But by this time the whole enterprise had come to seem gravely doubtful, in France and elsewhere. In 1843 the English philosopher John Stuart Mill called it "the opprobrium of mathematics," arguing that one should seek more reliable knowledge rather than waste time on calculations that merely rearrange ignorance.

## THE RISE OF STATISTICS

During the 19th century, statistics grew up as the empirical science of the state and gained preeminence as a form of social knowledge. Population and economic numbers had been collected, but often not in a systematic way, since ancient times and in many countries.

### POLITICAL ARITHMETIC

In Europe, the late 17th century was an important time also for quantitative studies of disease, population, and wealth. In 1662 the English statistician John Graunt published a celebrated collection of numbers and observations pertaining to mortality in London, using records that had been collected to chart the advance and decline of the plague. In the 1680s the English political economist and statistician William Petty published a series of essays on a new science of "political arithmetic," which combined statistical records with bold—some thought fanciful—calculations, such as, for example, of the monetary value of all those living in Ireland. These studies accelerated in the 18th century and were increasingly supported by state activity, but ancien régime governments often kept the numbers secret. Administrators and savants used the numbers to assess and enhance state power but also as part of an emerging "science of man." The most assiduous, and perhaps the most renowned, of these political arithmeticians was the Prussian pastor Johann Peter Süssmilch, whose study of the divine order in human births and deaths was first published in 1741 and grew to three fat volumes by 1765. The decisive proof of Divine Providence in these demographic affairs was their regularity and order, perfectly arranged to promote man's fulfillment of what he called God's first commandment, to be fruitful and multiply. Still, he did not leave such matters to nature and to God, but rather he offered abundant advice about how kings and princes could promote the growth of their populations. He envisioned a rather spartan order of small farmers, paying modest rents and taxes, living without luxury, and practicing the Protestant faith. Roman Catholicism was unacceptable on account of priestly celibacy.

## SOCIAL NUMBERS

Lacking, as they did, complete counts of population, 18th-century practitioners of political arithmetic had to rely largely on conjectures and calculations. In France especially, mathematicians such as Laplace used probability to surmise the accuracy of population figures determined from samples. In the 19th century such methods of estimation fell into disuse, mainly because they were replaced by regular, systematic censuses. The census of the United States, required by the U.S. Constitution and conducted every 10 years beginning in 1790, was among the earliest. Sweden had begun earlier, and most leading nations of Europe followed by the mid-19th century. They were also eager to survey the populations of their colonial possessions, which indeed were among the first places counted. A variety of motives can be identified, ranging from the requirements of representative government to the need to raise armies. Some counting can scarcely be attributed to any purpose, and indeed the contemporary rage for numbers was by no means limited to counts of human populations. From the mid-18th century and especially after the conclusion of the Napoleonic Wars in 1815, the collection and publication of numbers proliferated in many domains, including experimental physics, land surveys, agriculture, and studies of the weather, tides, and terrestrial magnetism. Still, the management of human populations played a decisive role in the statistical enthusiasm of the early 19th century. Political instabilities associated with the French Revolution of 1789 and the economic changes of early industrialization made social science a great desideratum. A new field of moral statistics grew up to record and comprehend the problems of dirt, disease, crime, ignorance, and poverty.

Some investigations were conducted by public bureaus, but much was the work of civic-minded professionals, industrialists, and, especially after midcentury, women such as Florence Nightingale. One of the first serious statistical organizations arose in 1832 as section F of the new British Association for the Advancement of Science. The intellectual ties to natural science were uncertain at first, but there were some influential champions of statistics as a mathematical science. The most effective was the Belgian mathematician Adolphe Quetelet, who argued untiringly that mathematical probability was essential for social

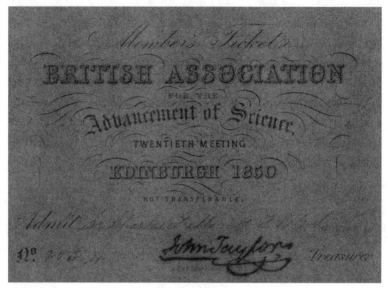

*Formed in 1832, section F of the British Association for the Advancement of Science was one of the first serious statistical organizations.* SSPL via Getty Images

statistics. Quetelet hoped to create from these materials a new science, which he called at first social mechanics and later social physics. He often wrote about the analogies linking this science to the most mathematical of the natural sciences, celestial mechanics. In practice, though, his methods were more like those of geodesy or meteorology, involving massive collections of data and the effort to detect patterns that might be identified as laws. These, in fact, seemed to abound. He found them in almost every collection of social numbers, beginning with some publications of French criminal statistics from the mid-1820s. The numbers, he announced, were essentially constant from year to year, so steady that one could speak here of statistical laws. If there was something paradoxical in these "laws" of crime, it was nonetheless comforting to find regularities underlying the manifest disorder of social life.

## A New Kind of Regularity

Even Quetelet was initially startled by the discovery of these statistical laws. Regularities of births and deaths belonged to the natural order and so were unsurprising, but here was constancy of moral and immoral acts, acts that would normally be attributed to human free will. Was there some mysterious fatalism that drove individuals, even against their will, to fulfill a budget of crimes? Were such actions beyond the reach of human intervention? Quetelet determined that they were not. Nevertheless, he continued to emphasize that the frequencies of such deeds should be understood in terms of causes acting at the level of society, not of choices made by individuals. His view was challenged by moralists, who insisted on complete individual responsibility for thefts, murders, and suicides. Quetelet was not so radical as to deny the legitimacy of punishment, because the system of justice was thought to help regulate crime rates. Yet he spoke of the murderer on the scaffold as himself a victim, part of the sacrifice that society requires for its own conservation. Individually, to be sure, it was perhaps within the power of the criminal to resist the inducements that drove him to his vile act. Collectively, however, crime is but trivially affected by these individual decisions. Not criminals but crime rates form the proper object of social investigation. Reducing them is to be achieved not at the level of the individual but at the level of the legislator, who can improve society by providing moral education or by improving systems of justice. Statisticians have a vital role as well. To them falls the task of studying the effects on society of legislative changes and of recommending measures that could bring about desired improvements.

Quetelet's arguments inspired a modest debate about the consistency of statistics with human free will. This intensified after 1857, when the English historian Henry Thomas Buckle recited his favourite examples of statistical law to support an uncompromising determinism in his immensely successful *History of Civilization in England*. Interestingly, probability had been linked to deterministic arguments from early in its history, at least since the time of Jakob Bernoulli. Laplace argued in his *Philosophical Essay on Probabilities* (1825) that man's dependence on probability was simply a consequence of imperfect knowledge. A being who could follow every particle in the universe, and who had unbounded powers of calculation, would be able to know the past and to predict the future with perfect certainty. The statistical determinism inaugurated by Quetelet had a quite different character. Now it was unnecessary to know things in infinite detail. At the micro-level, indeed, knowledge often fails, for who can penetrate the human soul so fully as to comprehend why a troubled individual has chosen to take his or her own life? Yet such uncertainty about individuals somehow dissolves in light of a whole society, whose regularities are often more perfect than those of physical systems such as the weather. Not real persons but *l'homme moyen*, the average man, formed the basis of social physics. This contrast between individual and collective phenomena was, in fact, hard to reconcile with an absolute determinism like Buckle's. Several critics of his book pointed this out, urging that the distinctive feature of statistical knowledge was precisely its neglect of individuals in favour of mass observations.

## STATISTICAL PHYSICS

The same issues were discussed also in physics. Statistical understandings first gained an influential role in physics at just this time, in consequence of papers by the German mathematical physicist Rudolf Clausius from the late 1850s and, especially, of one by the Scottish physicist James Clerk Maxwell published in 1860. Maxwell, at least, was familiar with the social statistical tradition, and he had been sufficiently impressed by Buckle's *History* and by the English astronomer John Herschel's influential essay on Quetelet's work in the *Edinburgh Review* (1850) to discuss them in letters. During the 1870s, Maxwell often introduced his gas theory using analogies from social statistics. The first and crucial point was that statistical regularities of vast numbers of molecules were quite sufficient to derive thermodynamic laws relating the pressure, volume, and temperature in gases. Some physicists, including, for a time, the German Max Planck, were troubled by the contrast between a molecular chaos at the microlevel and the very precise laws indicated by physical instruments. They wondered if it made sense to seek a molecular, mechanical grounding for thermodynamic laws. Maxwell invoked the regularities of crime and suicide as analogies to the statistical laws of thermodynamics and as evidence that local uncertainty can give way to large-scale predictability. At the same time, he insisted that statistical physics implied a certain imperfection of knowledge. In physics, as in social science, determinism was very much an issue in the 1850s and '60s. Maxwell argued that physical determinism could only be speculative, because human knowledge of events at the molecular level is necessarily imperfect. Many of the laws of physics, he said, are like those regularities detected by census officers: They are quite sufficient as a guide to practical life, but they lack the certainty characteristic of abstract dynamics.

## THE SPREAD OF STATISTICAL MATHEMATICS

Statisticians, wrote the English statistician Maurice Kendall in 1942, "have already overrun every branch of science with a rapidity of conquest rivaled only by Attila, Mohammed, and the Colorado beetle." The spread of statistical mathematics through the sciences began, in fact, at least a century before there were any professional statisticians. Even regardless of the use of probability to estimate populations and make insurance calculations, this history dates back at least to 1809. In that year, the German mathematician Carl Friedrich Gauss published a derivation of the new method of least squares incorporating a mathematical function that soon became known as the astronomer's curve of error, and later as the Gaussian or normal distribution.

The problem of combining many astronomical observations to give the best possible estimate of one or several parameters was discussed in the 18th century. The first publication of the method of least squares as a solution to this problem was inspired by a more practical problem, the analysis of French geodetic measures undertaken to fix the standard length of the metre. This was the basic measure of length in the new metric system, decreed by the French Revolution and defined as 1/40,000,000 of the longitudinal circumference of the Earth. In 1805 the French mathematician Adrien-Marie Legendre proposed to solve this problem by choosing values that minimize the sums of the squares of deviations of the observations from a point, line, or curve drawn through them. In the simplest case, where all observations were measures of a single point, this method was equivalent to taking an arithmetic mean.

Gauss soon announced that he had already been using least squares since 1795, a somewhat doubtful claim. After Legendre's publication, Gauss became interested in the mathematics of least squares, and he showed in 1809 that the method gave the best possible estimate of a parameter if the errors of the measurements were assumed to follow the normal distribution. This distribution, whose importance for mathematical probability and statistics was decisive, was first shown by the French mathematician Abraham de Moivre in the 1730s to be the limit (as the number of events increases) for the binomial distribution. In particular, this meant that a continuous function (the normal distribution) and the power of calculus could be substituted for a discrete function (the binomial distribution) and laborious numerical methods. Laplace used the normal distribution extensively as part of his strategy for applying probability to very large numbers of events. The most important problem of this kind in the 18th century involved estimating populations from smaller samples. Laplace also had an important role in reformulating the method of least squares as a problem of probabilities. For much of the 19th century, least squares was overwhelmingly the most important instance of statistics in its guise as a tool of estimation and the measurement of uncertainty. It had an important role in astronomy, geodesy, and related measurement disciplines, including even quantitative psychology. Later, about 1900, it provided a mathematical basis for a broader field of statistics that came to be used by a wide range of fields.

## STATISTICAL THEORIES IN THE SCIENCES

The role of probability and statistics in the sciences was not limited to estimation and measurement. Equally significant, and no less important for the formation of the mathematical field, were statistical theories of collective phenomena that bypassed the study of individuals. The social science bearing the name *statistics* was the prototype of this approach. Quetelet advanced its mathematical level by incorporating the normal distribution into it. He argued that human traits of every sort, from chest circumference and height to the distribution of propensities to marry or commit crimes, conformed to the astronomer's error law. The kinetic theory of gases of Clausius, Maxwell, and the Austrian physicist Ludwig Boltzmann was also a statistical one. Here it was not the imprecision or uncertainty of scientific measurements but the motions of the molecules themselves to which statistical understandings and probabilistic mathematics were applied. Once again, the error law played a crucial role. The Maxwell-Boltzmann distribution law of molecular velocities, as it has come to be known, is a three-dimensional version of this same function. In importing it into physics, Maxwell drew both on astronomical error theory and on Quetelet's social physics.

## BIOMETRY

The English biometric school developed from the work of the polymath Francis Galton, cousin of Charles Darwin. Galton admired Quetelet, but he was critical of the statistician's obsession with mean values rather than variation. The normal law, as he began to call it, was for him a way to measure and analyze variability. This was especially important for studies of biological evolution, because Darwin's theory was about natural selection acting on natural diversity. A figure from Galton's 1877 paper on breeding sweet peas shows a physical model, now known as the Galton board, that he employed to explain the normal distribution of inherited characteristics. In particular, he used his model to explain the tendency of progeny to have the same variance as their parents, a process he called

*Sir Francis Galton's Galton board helped explain the normal distribution of inherited characteristics.* SSPL via Getty Images

reversion, subsequently known as regression to the mean. Galton was also founder of the eugenics movement, which called for guiding the evolution of human populations the same way that breeders improve chickens or cows. He developed measures of the transmission of parental characteristics to their offspring: The children of exceptional parents were generally somewhat exceptional themselves, but there was always, on average, some reversion or regression toward the population mean. He developed the elementary mathematics of regression and correlation as a theory of hereditary transmission and thus as statistical biological theory rather than as a mathematical tool. Galton came to recognize that these methods could be applied to data in many fields, however, and by 1889, when he published his *Natural Inheritance*, he stressed the flexibility and adaptability of his statistical tools.

Still, evolution and eugenics remained central to the development of statistical mathematics. The most influential site for the development of statistics was the biometric laboratory set up at University College London by Galton's admirer, the applied mathematician Karl Pearson. From about 1892 he collaborated with the English biologist Walter F.R. Weldon on quantitative studies of evolution, and he soon began to attract an assortment of students from many countries and disciplines who hoped to learn the new statistical methods. Their journal, *Biometrika*, was for many years the most important venue for publishing new statistical tools and for displaying their uses.

Biometry was not the only source of new developments in statistics at the turn of the 19th century. German social statisticians such as Wilhelm Lexis had turned to more mathematical approaches some decades earlier. In England, the economist Francis Edgeworth became interested in statistical mathematics in the early 1880s. One of Pearson's earliest students, George Udny Yule, turned away from biometry and especially from eugenics in favour of the statistical investigation of social data. Nevertheless, biometry provided an important model, and many statistical techniques, for other disciplines. The 20th-century fields of psychometrics, concerned especially with mental testing, and econometrics, which focused on economic time-series, reveal this relationship in their very names.

## Samples and Experiments

Near the beginning of the 20th century, sampling regained its respectability in social statistics, for reasons that initially had little to do with mathematics. Early advocates, such as the first director of the Norwegian Central Bureau of Statistics, A.N. Kiaer, thought of their task primarily in terms of attaining representativeness in relation to the most important variables—for example, geographic region, urban and rural, rich and poor. The London statistician Arthur Bowley was among the first to urge that sampling should involve an element of randomness. Jerzy Neyman, a statistician from Poland who had worked for a time in Pearson's laboratory, wrote a particularly decisive mathematical paper on the topic in 1934. His method of stratified sampling incorporated a concern for representativeness across the most important variables, but it also required that the individuals sampled should be chosen randomly. This was designed to avoid selection biases but also to create populations to which probability theory could be applied to calculate expected errors. George Gallup achieved fame in 1936 when his polls, employing stratified sampling, successfully predicted the reelection of Franklin Delano Roosevelt, in defiance of the *Literary Digest*'s much larger but uncontrolled survey, which forecast a landslide for the Republican Alfred Landon.

The alliance of statistical tools and experimental design was also largely an achievement of the 20th century. Here, too, randomization came to be seen as central. The emerging protocol called for the establishment of experimental and control populations and for the use of chance where possible to decide which individuals would receive the experimental treatment. These experimental repertoires emerged gradually in educational psychology during the 1900s and '10s. They were codified and given a full mathematical basis in the next two decades by Ronald A. Fisher, the most influential of all the 20th-century statisticians. Through randomized, controlled experiments and statistical analysis, he argued, scientists could move beyond mere correlation to causal knowledge even in fields whose phenomena are highly complex and variable. His ideas of experimental design and analysis helped to reshape many disciplines, including psychology, ecology, and therapeutic research in medicine, especially during the triumphant era of quantification after 1945.

## THE MODERN ROLE OF STATISTICS

In some ways, statistics has finally achieved the Enlightenment aspiration to create a logic of uncertainty. Statistical tools are at work in almost every area of life, including agriculture, business, engineering, medicine, law, regulation, and social policy, as well as in the physical, biological, and social sciences and even in parts of the academic humanities. The replacement of human "computers" with mechanical and then electronic ones in the 20th century greatly lightened the immense burdens of calculation that statistical analysis once required. Statistical tests are used to assess whether observed results, such as increased harvests where fertilizer is applied, or improved earnings where early childhood education is provided, give reasonable assurance of causation, rather than merely random fluctuations. Following World War II, these significance levels virtually came to define an acceptable result in some of the sciences and also in policy applications.

From about 1930 there grew up in Britain and America—and a bit later in other countries—a profession of statisticians, experts in inference, who defined standards of experimentation as well as methods of analysis in many fields. To be sure, statistics in the various disciplines retained a fair degree of specificity. There were also divergent schools of statisticians, who disagreed, often vehemently, on some issues of fundamental importance. Fisher was highly critical of Pearson. Neyman and Egon Pearson, while unsympathetic to father Karl's methods, disagreed also with Fisher's. Under the banner of Bayesianism appeared yet another school, which, against its predecessors, emphasized the need for subjective assessments of prior probabilities. The most immoderate ambitions for statistics as the royal road to scientific inference depended on unacknowledged compromises that ignored or dismissed these disputes. Despite them, statistics has thrived as a somewhat heterogeneous but powerful set of tools, methods, and forms of expertise that continues to regulate the acquisition and interpretation of quantitative data.

# CHAPTER 2
## PROBABILITY THEORY

Probability theory is the branch of mathematics concerned with the analysis of random phenomena. The outcome of a random event cannot be determined before it occurs, but it may be any one of several possible outcomes. The actual outcome is considered to be determined by chance.

The word *probability* has several meanings in ordinary conversation, two of which are particularly important for the development and applications of the mathematical theory of probability. One is the interpretation of probabilities as relative frequencies, for which simple games involving coins, cards, dice, and roulette wheels provide examples. The distinctive feature of games of chance is that the outcome of a given trial cannot be predicted with certainty, but the collective results of a large number of trials display some regularity. For example, the statement that the probability of "heads" in tossing a coin equals one-half, according to the relative frequency interpretation, implies that in a large number of tosses the relative frequency with which "heads" actually occurs will be approximately one-half, but it contains no implication concerning the outcome of any given toss. There are many similar examples involving groups of people, molecules of a gas, genes, and so on. Actuarial statements about the life expectancy for persons of a certain age describe the collective experience of a large number of individuals but do not purport to say what will happen to any particular person. Similarly, predictions about the chance of a genetic disease occurring in a child of parents having a known genetic makeup are statements

*Probability theory is exemplified by roulette: players bet on within which red or black numbered compartment of a revolving wheel a small ball will come to rest.* Jeff T. Green/Getty Images about relative frequencies of occurrence in a large number of cases but are not predictions about a given individual.

# EXPERIMENTS, SAMPLE SPACE, EVENTS, AND EQUALLY LIKELY PROBABILITIES

Applications of probability theory inevitably involve simplifying assumptions that focus on some features of a problem at the expense of others. Thus, it is advantageous to begin by thinking about simple experiments, such as tossing a coin or rolling dice, and to see how these apparently frivolous investigations relate to important scientific questions.

## APPLICATIONS OF SIMPLE PROBABILITY EXPERIMENTS

The fundamental ingredient of probability theory is an experiment that can be repeated, at least hypothetically, under essentially identical conditions and that may lead to different outcomes on different trials. The set of all possible outcomes of an experiment is called a *sample space*. The experiment of tossing a coin once results in a sample space with two possible outcomes: heads and tails. Tossing two dice has a sample space with 36 possible outcomes, each of which can be identified with an ordered pair $(i, j)$, where $i$ and $j$ assume one of the values 1, 2, 3, 4, 5, 6 and denote the faces showing on the individual dice. It is important to think of the dice as identifiable (say by a difference in colour), so that the outcome (1, 2) is different from (2, 1). An *event* is a well-defined subset of the sample space. For example, the event "the sum of the faces showing on the two dice equals six" consists of the five outcomes (1, 5), (2, 4), (3, 3), (4, 2), and (5, 1).

A third example is to draw $n$ balls from an urn containing balls of various colours. A generic outcome to this experiment is an $n$-tuple, where the $i$th entry specifies the colour of the ball obtained on the $i$th draw ($i = 1, 2,..., n$). In spite of the simplicity of this experiment, a thorough understanding gives the theoretical basis for opinion polls and sample surveys. For example, individuals in a population favouring a particular candidate in an election may be identified with balls of a particular colour, those favouring a different candidate may be identified with a different colour, and so on. Probability theory provides the basis for learning about the contents of the urn from the sample of balls drawn from the urn. An application is to learn about the electoral preferences of a population on the basis of a sample drawn from that population.

Another application of simple urn models is to use clinical trials designed to determine whether a new treatment for a disease, a new drug, or a new surgical procedure is better than a standard treatment. In the simple case in which treatment can be regarded as either success or failure, the goal of the clinical trial is to discover whether the new treatment more frequently leads to success than does the standard treatment. Patients with the disease can be identified with balls in an urn. The red balls are those patients who are cured by the new treatment, and the black balls are those not cured. Usually there is a control group, who receive the standard treatment. They are represented by a second urn with a possibly different fraction of red balls. The goal of the experiment of drawing some number of balls from each urn is to discover on the basis of the sample which urn has the larger fraction of red balls. A variation of this idea can be used to test the efficacy of a new vaccine. Perhaps the largest and most famous example was the test of the Salk vaccine for poliomyelitis conducted in 1954. It was organized by the U.S.

Public Health Service and involved almost two million children. Its success has led to the almost complete elimination of polio as a health problem in the industrialized parts of the world. Strictly speaking, these applications are problems of statistics, for which the foundations are provided by probability theory.

In contrast to the experiments previously described, many experiments have infinitely many possible outcomes. For example, one can toss a coin until heads appears for the first time. The number of possible tosses is $n = 1, 2, \ldots$ Another example is to twirl a spinner. For an idealized spinner made from a straight line segment having no width and pivoted at its centre, the set of possible outcomes is the set of all angles that the final position of the spinner makes with some fixed direction, equivalently all real numbers in $[0, 2\pi)$. Many measurements in the natural and social sciences, such as volume, voltage, temperature, reaction time, marginal income, and so on, are made on continuous scales and at least in theory involve infinitely many possible values. If the repeated measurements on different subjects or at different times on the same subject can lead to different outcomes, probability theory is a possible tool to study this variability.

Because of their comparative simplicity, experiments with finite sample spaces are discussed first. In the early development of probability theory, mathematicians considered only those experiments for which it seemed reasonable, based on considerations of symmetry, to suppose that all outcomes of the experiment were "equally likely." Then in a large number of trials, all outcomes should occur with approximately the same frequency. The probability of an event is defined to be the ratio of the number of cases favourable to the event (i.e., the number of outcomes in the subset of the sample space defining the event) to the total number of cases. Thus, the 36 possible outcomes in the throw of two dice are assumed equally likely, and the probability of obtaining "six" is the number of favourable cases, 5, divided by 36, or 5/36.

Now suppose that a coin is tossed $n$ times, and consider the probability of the event "heads does not occur" in the $n$ tosses. An outcome of the experiment is an $n$-tuple, the $k$th entry of which identifies the result of the $k$th toss. Because there are two possible outcomes for each toss, the number of elements in the sample space is $2^n$. Of these, only one outcome corresponds to having no heads, so the required probability is $1/2^n$.

It is only slightly more difficult to determine the probability of "at most one head." In addition to the single case in which no head occurs, there are $n$ cases in which exactly one head occurs, because it can occur on the first, second, ..., or $n$th toss. Hence, there are $n + 1$ cases favourable to obtaining at most one head, and the desired probability is $(n + 1)/2^n$.

## THE PRINCIPLE OF ADDITIVITY

This last example illustrates the fundamental principle that if the event whose probability is sought can be represented as the union of several other events that have no outcomes in common ("at most one head" is the union of "no heads" and "exactly one head"), then the probability of the union is the sum of the probabilities of the individual events making up the union. To describe this situation symbolically, let $S$ denote the sample space. For two events $A$ and $B$, the intersection of $A$ and $B$ is the set of all experimental outcomes belonging to both $A$ and $B$ and is denoted $A \cap B$; the union of $A$ and $B$ is the set of all experimental outcomes belonging to $A$ or $B$ (or both) and is denoted $A \cup B$. The impossible event (i.e., the event containing no outcomes) is denoted by $\emptyset$. The probability of an event $A$

is written $P(A)$. The principle of addition of probabilities is that, if $A_1, A_2, \ldots, A_n$ are events with $A_i \cap A_j = \emptyset$ for all pairs $i \neq j$, then

$$P(A_1 \cup A_2 \cup \cdots \cup A_n) = P(A_1) + P(A_2) + \cdots + P(A_n). \quad (1)$$

Equation (1) is consistent with the relative frequency interpretation of probabilities. For, if $A_i \cap A_j = \emptyset$ for all $i \neq j$, the relative frequency with which at least one of the $A_i$ occurs equals the sum of the relative frequencies with which the individual $A_i$ occur.

Equation (1) is fundamental for everything that follows. Indeed, in the modern axiomatic theory of probability, which eschews a definition of probability in terms of "equally likely outcomes" as being hopelessly circular, an extended form of equation (1) plays a basic role.

An elementary, useful consequence of equation (1) is the following. With each event $A$ is associated the complementary event $A^c$ consisting of those experimental outcomes that do not belong to $A$. Because $A \cap A^c = \emptyset$, $A \cup A^c = S$, and $P(S) = 1$ (where $S$ denotes the sample space), it follows from equation (1) that $P(A^c) = 1 - P(A)$. For example, the probability of "at least one head" in $n$ tosses of a coin is one minus the probability of "no head," or $1 - 1/2^n$.

## MULTINOMIAL PROBABILITY

A basic problem first solved by Jakob Bernoulli is to find the probability of obtaining exactly $i$ red balls in the experiment of drawing $n$ times at random with replacement from an urn containing $b$ black and $r$ red balls. To draw at random means that, on a single draw, each of the $r + b$ balls is equally likely to be drawn and, because each ball is replaced before the next draw, there are $(r + b) \times \cdots \times (r + b) = (r + b)^n$ possible outcomes to the experiment. Of these possible outcomes, the number that is favourable to obtaining $i$ red balls and $n - i$ black balls in any one particular order is

$$\overbrace{r \times r \times \cdots \times r}^{i} \times \overbrace{b \times b \times \cdots \times b}^{n-i} = r^i \times b^{n-i}.$$

The number of possible orders in which $i$ red balls and $n - i$ black balls can be drawn from the urn is the binomial coefficient

$$\binom{n}{i} = \frac{n!}{i!\,(n-i)!}, \qquad (2)$$

where $k! = k \times (k - 1) \times \cdots \times 2 \times 1$ for positive integers $k$, and $0! = 1$. Hence, the probability in question, which equals the number of favourable outcomes divided by the number of possible outcomes, is given by the binomial distribution

$$\binom{n}{i} \frac{r^i b^{n-i}}{(r+b)^n} = \binom{n}{i} p^i q^{n-i} \qquad (i = 0, 1, 2, \ldots, n), \qquad (3)$$

where $p = r/(r + b)$ and $q = b/(r + b) = 1 - p$.

For example, suppose $r = 2b$ and $n = 4$. According to equation (3), the probability of "exactly two red balls" is

$$\binom{4}{2}\left(\frac{2}{3}\right)^2\left(\frac{1}{3}\right)^2 = 6 \times \frac{4}{81} = \frac{8}{27}.$$

In this case the

$$\binom{4}{2} = 6$$

possible outcomes are easily enumerated: (*rrbb*), (*rbrb*), (*brrb*), (*rbbr*), (*brbr*), (*bbrr*). (For a derivation of equation (2), observe that to draw exactly *i* red balls in *n* draws one must either draw *i* red balls in the first *n* - 1 draws and a black ball on the *n*th draw or draw *i* - 1 red balls in the first *n* - 1 draws followed by the *i*th red ball on the *n*th draw. Hence,

$$\binom{n}{i} = \binom{n-1}{i} + \binom{n-1}{i-1},$$

from which equation (2) can be verified by induction on *n*.)

Two related examples are (i) drawing without replacement from an urn containing *r* red and *b* black balls and (ii) drawing with or without replacement from an urn containing balls of *s* different colours. If *n* balls are drawn without replacement from an urn containing *r* red and *b* black balls, the number of possible outcomes is

$$\binom{r+b}{n},$$

of which the number favourable to drawing *i* red and *n* - *i* black balls is

$$\binom{r}{i}\binom{b}{n-1}.$$

Hence, the probability of drawing exactly $i$ red balls in $n$ draws is the ratio

$$\frac{\binom{r}{i}\binom{b}{n-i}}{\binom{r+b}{n}}.$$

If an urn contains balls of $s$ different colours in the ratios $p_1{:}p_2{:}\ldots{:}ps$, where $p_1 + \cdots + ps = 1$ and if $n$ balls are drawn with replacement, then the probability of obtaining $i_1$ balls of the first colour, $i_2$ balls of the second colour, and so on is the multinomial probability

$$\frac{n!}{i_1!\,i_2!\ldots i_s!}\,p_1^{i_1}\,p_2^{i_2}\ldots p_s^{i_s}.$$

The evaluation of equation (3) with pencil and paper grows increasingly difficult with increasing $n$. It is even more difficult to evaluate related cumulative probabilities—for example the probability of obtaining "at most $j$ red balls" in the $n$ draws, which can be expressed as the sum of equation (3) for $i = 0, 1, \ldots, j$. The problem of approximate computation of probabilities that are known in principle is a recurrent theme throughout the history of probability theory and will be discussed in more detail in the following text.

## THE BIRTHDAY PROBLEM

An entertaining example is to determine the probability that in a randomly selected group of $n$ people at least two have the same birthday. If one assumes for simplicity that a year contains 365 days and that each day is equally likely to be the birthday of a randomly selected person, then in a group of $n$ people there are $365^n$ possible combinations of birthdays. The simplest solution is to determine the probability of no matching birthdays and then subtract this probability from 1. Thus, for no matches, the first person may have any of the 365 days for his birthday, the second any of the remaining 364 days for his birthday, the third any of the remaining 363 days, ..., and the $n$th any of the remaining $365 - n + 1$. The number of ways that all $n$ people can have different birthdays is then $365 \times 364 \times \cdots \times (365 - n + 1)$, so that the probability that at least two have the same birthday is

$$P = 1 - \frac{365 \times 364 \times \cdots \times (365 - n + 1)}{365^n}.$$

Numerical evaluation shows, rather surprisingly, that for $n = 23$ the probability that at least two people have the same birthday is about 0.5 (half the time). For $n = 42$ the probability is about 0.9 (90 percent of the time).

This example illustrates that applications of probability theory to the physical world are facilitated by assumptions that are not strictly true, but they should be approximately true. Thus, the assumptions that a year has 365 days and that all days are equally likely to be the birthday of a random individual are false, because one year in four has 366 days and because birth dates are irregularly distributed throughout the year. Moreover, if one attempts to apply this result to an actual group of individuals, it is necessary to ask what it means for these to be "randomly selected." Naturally, it would be unreasonable to apply it to a group known to contain twins. In spite of the obvious failure of the assumptions to be literally true, as a classroom example, it rarely disappoints instructors of classes having more than 40 students.

## CONDITIONAL PROBABILITY

Suppose two balls are drawn sequentially without replacement from an urn containing $r$ red and $b$ black balls. The probability of getting a red ball on the first draw is $r/(r + b)$. If, however, one is told that a red ball was obtained on the first draw, then the conditional probability of getting a red ball on the second draw is $(r - 1)/(r + b - 1)$, because for the second draw there are $r + b - 1$ balls in the urn, of which $r - 1$ are red. Similarly, if one is told that the first ball drawn is black, then the conditional probability of getting red on the second draw is $r/(r + b - 1)$.

In a number of trials the relative frequency with which $B$ occurs among those trials in which $A$ occurs is just the frequency of occurrence of $A \cap B$ divided by the frequency of occurrence of $A$. This suggests that the conditional probability of $B$ given $A$ (denoted $P(B|A)$) should be defined by

$$P(B|A) = \frac{P(A \cap B)}{P(A)}. \qquad (4)$$

If $A$ denotes a red ball on the first draw and $B$ a red ball on the second draw in the experiment of the preceding paragraph, $P(A) = r/(r + b)$ and

$$P(A \cap B) = \frac{r(r - 1)}{[(r + b)(r + b - 1)]},$$

which is consistent with the "obvious" answer derived above.

Rewriting equation (4) as $P(A \cap B) = P(A)P(B|A)$ and adding to this expression the same expression with $A$ replaced by $A^c$ ("not $A$") leads via equation (1) to the equality

$$P(B) = P(A \cap B) + P(A^c \cap B)$$

$$= P(A)P(B|A) + P(A^c)P(B|A^c).$$

More generally, if $A_1, A_2, \ldots, An$ are mutually exclusive events and their union is the entire sample space, so that exactly one of the $Ak$ must occur, essentially the same argument gives a fundamental relation, which is frequently called the law of total probability:

$$P(B) = P(A_1)P(B|A_1) + P(A_2)P(B|A_2) + \cdots + P(A_n)P(B|A_n).$$

## APPLICATIONS OF CONDITIONAL PROBABILITY

An application of the law of total probability to a problem originally posed by Christiaan Huygens is to find the probability of "gambler's ruin." Suppose two players, often called Peter and Paul, initially have $x$ and $m - x$ dollars, respectively. A ball, which is red with probability $p$ and black with probability $q = 1 - p$, is drawn from an urn. If a red ball is drawn, then Paul must pay Peter one dollar, while Peter must pay Paul one dollar if the ball drawn is black. The ball is replaced, and the game continues until one player is ruined. It is quite difficult to determine the probability of Peter's ruin by a direct analysis of all possible cases. But let $Q(x)$ denote that probability as a function of Peter's initial fortune $x$ and observe that after one draw the structure of the rest of the game is exactly as it was before the first draw, except that Peter's fortune is now either $x + 1$ or $x - 1$ according to the results of the first draw. The law of total probability with $A$ = {red ball on first draw} and $A^c$ = {black ball on first draw} shows that

$$Q(x) = pQ(x+1) + qQ(x-1). \tag{5}$$

This equation holds for $x = 2, 3, \ldots, m - 2$. It also holds for $x = 1$ and $m - 1$ if one adds the boundary conditions $Q(0) = 1$ and $Q(m) = 0$, which say that if Peter initially has 0 dollars, his probability of ruin is 1, whereas if he has all $m$ dollars, he is certain to win.

It can be verified by direct substitution that equation (5) together with the indicated boundary conditions are satisfied by

$$Q(x) = \frac{\left(\frac{q}{p}\right)^x - \left(\frac{q}{p}\right)^m}{1 - \left(\frac{q}{p}\right)^m} \qquad \left(p \neq \frac{1}{2}\right)$$

$$= 1 - \frac{x}{m} \qquad \left(p = \frac{1}{2}\right). \tag{6}$$

Additional analysis shows that these give the only solutions and hence must be the desired probabilities.

Suppose $m = 10x$, so that Paul initially has nine times as much money as Peter. If $p = 1/2$, the probability of Peter's ruin is 0.9 regardless of the values of $x$ and $m$. If $p = 0.51$, so that each trial slightly favours Peter, then the situation is quite different. For $x = 1$ and $m = 10$, the probability of

Peter's ruin is 0.88, only slightly less than before. However, for $x$ = 100 and $m$ = 1,000, Peter's slight advantage on each trial becomes so important that the probability of his ultimate ruin is now less than 0.02.

Generalizations of the problem of gambler's ruin play an important role in statistical sequential analysis, developed by the Hungarian-born American statistician Abraham Wald in response to the demand for more efficient methods of industrial quality control during World War II. They also enter into insurance risk theory.

The following example shows that, even when it is given that $A$ occurs, it is important in evaluating $P(B|A)$ to recognize that $A^c$ might have occurred, and hence in principle it must be possible also to evaluate $P(B|A^c)$. By lot, two out of three prisoners—Sam, Jean, and Chris—are chosen to be executed. There are

$$\binom{3}{2} = 6$$

possible pairs of prisoners to be selected for execution, of which two contain Sam, so the probability that Sam is slated for execution is 2/3. Sam asks the guard which of the others is to be executed. Because at least one must be, it appears that the guard would give Sam no information by answering. After hearing that Jean is to be executed, Sam reasons that, because either he or Chris must be the other one, the conditional probability that he will be executed is 1/2. Thus, it appears that the guard has given Sam some information about his own fate. However, the experiment is incompletely defined, because it is not specified how the guard chooses whether to answer "Jean" or "Chris" in case both are to be executed. If the guard answers "Jean" with probability $p$, then the conditional probability of the event "Sam will be executed" given "the guard says Jean will be executed" is

$$\frac{\frac{1}{3}}{\frac{1}{3} + \frac{p}{3}} = \frac{1}{1 + p}.$$

Only in the case $p = 1$ is Sam's reasoning correct. If $p = 1/2$, then the guard in fact gives no information about Sam's fate.

## INDEPENDENCE

One of the most important concepts in probability theory is that of "independence." The events $A$ and $B$ are said to be (stochastically) independent if $P(B|A) = P(B)$, or equivalently if

$$P(A \cap B) = P(A)P(B). \qquad (7)$$

The intuitive meaning of the definition in terms of conditional probabilities is that the probability of $B$ is not changed by knowing that $A$ has occurred. Equation (7) shows that the definition is symmetric in $A$ and $B$.

It is intuitively clear that, in drawing two balls with replacement from an urn containing $r$ red and $b$ black balls, the event "red ball on the first draw" and the event "red ball on the second draw" are independent. (This statement presupposes that the balls are thoroughly mixed before each draw.) An analysis of the $(r + b)^2$ equally likely outcomes of the experiment shows that the formal definition is indeed satisfied.

In terms of the concept of independence, the experiment leading to the binomial distribution can be described

as follows. On a single trial, a particular event has probability $p$. An experiment consists of $n$ independent
repetitions of this trial. The probability that the particular
event occurs exactly $i$ times is given by equation (3).
Independence plays a central role in the law of large numbers, the central limit theorem, the Poisson distribution,
and Brownian motion.

## BAYES'S THEOREM

Consider now the defining relation for the conditional
probability $P(A_n|B)$, where the $A_i$ are mutually exclusive
and their union is the entire sample space. Substitution of
$P(A_n)P(B|A_n)$ in the numerator of equation (4)

$$P(B|A) = \frac{P(A \cap B)}{P(A)} \qquad (4)$$

and substitution of the right-hand side of the law of total
probability in the denominator yields a result known as
Bayes's theorem (after the 18th-century English clergyman Thomas Bayes) or the law of inverse probability:

$$P(A_n|B) = \frac{P(A_n)P(B|A_n)}{\sum_i P(A_i)P(B|A_i)}.$$

As an example, suppose that two balls are drawn without replacement from an urn containing $r$ red and $b$ black
balls. Let $A$ be the event "red on the first draw" and $B$ the
event "red on the second draw." From the obvious rela-
tions $P(A) = r/(r + b) = 1 - P(A^c)$, $P(B|A) = (r - 1)/(r + b - 1)$,
$P(B|A^c) = r/(r + b - 1)$, and Bayes's theorem, it follows that

the probability of a red ball on the first draw given that the second one is known to be red equals $(r - 1)/(r + b - 1)$. A more interesting and important use of Bayes's theorem appears in the following text in the discussion of subjective probabilities.

# RANDOM VARIABLES, DISTRIBUTIONS, EXPECTATION, AND VARIANCE

## RANDOM VARIABLES

Usually, it is more convenient to associate numerical values with the outcomes of an experiment than to work directly with a nonnumerical description such as "red ball on the first draw." For example, an outcome of the experiment of drawing $n$ balls with replacement from an urn containing black and red balls is an $n$-tuple that tells us whether a red or a black ball was drawn on each of the draws. This $n$-tuple is conveniently represented by an $n$-tuple of ones and zeros, where the appearance of a one in the $k$th position indicates that a red ball was drawn on the $k$th draw. A quantity of particular interest is the number of red balls drawn, which is just the sum of the entries in this numerical description of the experimental outcome. Mathematically a rule that associates with every element of a given set a unique real number is called a "(real-valued) function." In the history of statistics and probability, real-valued functions defined on a sample space have traditionally been called "random variables." Thus, if a sample space $S$ has the generic element $e$, the outcome of an experiment, then a random variable is a real-valued function $X = X(e)$. Customarily one omits the argument $e$ in the notation for a random variable. For the experiment of drawing balls from an urn containing black and red balls, $R$, the number of red balls drawn, is a random variable. A particularly useful random variable is $1[A]$, the indicator variable of the event $A$, which equals 1 if $A$ occurs and 0 otherwise. A "constant" is a trivial random variable that always takes the same value regardless of the outcome of the experiment.

## PROBABILITY DISTRIBUTION

Suppose $X$ is a random variable that can assume one of the values $x_1, x_2, \ldots, x_m$, according to the outcome of a random experiment, and consider the event $\{X = x_i\}$, which is a shorthand notation for the set of all experimental outcomes $e$ such that $X(e) = x_i$. The probability of this event, $P\{X = x_i\}$, is itself a function of $x_i$, called the probability distribution function of $X$. Thus, the distribution of the random variable $R$ defined in the preceding section is the function of $i = 0, 1, \ldots, n$ given in the binomial equation. Introducing the notation $f(x_i) = P\{X = x_i\}$, one sees from the basic properties of probabilities that

$$f(x_i) \geq 0 \text{ for all } i, \qquad \sum_i f(x_i) = 1,$$

and

$$P\{a < X \leq b\} = \sum_{a < x_i \leq b} f(x_i),$$

for any real numbers $a$ and $b$. If $Y$ is a second random variable defined on the same sample space as $X$ and taking the values $y_1, y_2, \ldots, y_n$, then the function of two variables

$h(x_i, y_j) = P\{X = x_i, Y = y_j\}$ is called the joint distribution of $X$ and $Y$. Because $\{X = x_i\} = \cup_j \{X = x_i, Y = y_j\}$, and this union consists of disjoint events in the sample space,

$$f(x_i) = \sum_j h(x_i, y_j), \quad \text{for all } i. \qquad (8)$$

Often $f$ is called the marginal distribution of $X$ to emphasize its relation to the joint distribution of $X$ and $Y$. Similarly, $g(y_j) = \Sigma_i h(x_i, y_j)$ is the (marginal) distribution of $Y$. The random variables $X$ and $Y$ are defined to be independent if the events $\{X = x_i\}$ and $\{Y = y_j\}$ are independent for all $i$ and $j$, such as if $h(x_i, y_j) = f(x_i)g(y_j)$ for all $i$ and $j$. The joint distribution of an arbitrary number of random variables is similarly defined.

Suppose two dice are thrown. Let $X$ denote the sum of the numbers appearing on the two dice, and let $Y$ denote the number of even numbers appearing. The possible values of $X$ are 2, 3, ..., 12, while the possible values of $Y$ are 0, 1, 2. Because there are 36 possible outcomes for the two dice, the accompanying table giving the joint

| JOINT DISTRIBUTION OF X AND Y | | | | | | | | | | | | |
|---|---|---|---|---|---|---|---|---|---|---|---|---|
| | | | | | i | | | | | | | row sum = g(j) |
| | | 2 | 3 | 4 | 5 | 6 | 7 | 8 | 9 | 10 | 11 | 12 | |
| j | 0 | 1/36 | 0 | 1/18 | 0 | 1/12 | 0 | 1/18 | 0 | 1/36 | 0 | 0 | 1/4 |
| | 1 | 0 | 1/18 | 0 | 1/9 | 0 | 1/6 | 0 | 1/9 | 0 | 1/18 | 0 | 1/2 |
| | 2 | 0 | 0 | 1/36 | 0 | 1/18 | 0 | 1/12 | 0 | 1/18 | 0 | 1/36 | 1/4 |
| column sum = f(i) | | 1/36 | 1/18 | 1/12 | 1/9 | 5/36 | 1/6 | 5/36 | 1/9 | 1/12 | 1/18 | 1/36 | |

distribution $h(i, j)$ ($i$ = 2, 3, . . . , 12; $j$ = 0, 1, 2) and the marginal distributions $f(i)$ and $g(j)$ is easily computed by direct enumeration.

For more complex experiments, determination of a complete probability distribution usually requires a combination of theoretical analysis and empirical experimentation and is often difficult. Consequently, it is desirable to describe a distribution insofar as possible by a small number of parameters that are comparatively easy to evaluate and interpret. The most important are the mean and the variance. These are both defined in terms of the "expected value" of a random variable.

## EXPECTED VALUE

Given a random variable $X$ with distribution $f$, the expected value of $X$, denoted $E(X)$, is defined by $E(X) = \sum_i x_i f(x_i)$. In words, the expected value of $X$ is the sum of each of the possible values of $X$ multiplied by the probability of obtaining that value. The expected value of $X$ is also called the mean of the distribution $f$. The basic property of $E$ is that of linearity: If $X$ and $Y$ are random variables and if $a$ and $b$ are both constants, then $E(aX + bY) = aE(X) + bE(Y)$. To see why this is true, note that $aX + bY$ is itself a random variable, which assumes the values $ax_i + by_j$ with the probabilities $h(x_i, y_j)$. Hence,

$$E(aX + bY) = \sum_{i,j} (ax_i + by_j)h(x_i, y_j)$$

$$= a\sum_{i,j} x_i h(x_i, y_j) + b\sum_{i,j} y_j h(x_i, y_j).$$

If the first sum on the right-hand side is summed over $j$ while holding $i$ fixed, by equation (8)

$$f(x_i) = \sum_j h(x_i, y_j), \quad \text{for all } i \qquad (8)$$

the result is

$$\sum_i x_i f(x_i),$$

which by definition is $E(X)$. Similarly, the second sum equals $E(Y)$.

If $\mathbf{1}[A]$ denotes the "indicator variable" of $A$ (i.e., a random variable equal to $1$ if $A$ occurs and equal to $0$ otherwise), then $E\{1[A]\} = 1 \times P(A) + 0 \times P(A^c) = P(A)$. This shows that the concept of expectation includes that of probability as a special case.

As an illustration, consider the number $R$ of red balls in $n$ draws with replacement from an urn containing a proportion $p$ of red balls. From the definition and the binomial distribution of $R$,

$$E(R) = \sum_i i \binom{n}{i} p^i q^{n-i},$$

which can be evaluated by algebraic manipulation and found to equal $np$. It is easier to use the representation $R = 1[A_1] + \cdots + 1[An]$, where $Ak$ denotes the event "the $k$th draw results in a red ball." Since $E\{1[Ak]\} = p$ for all $k$, by linearity $E(R) = E\{1[A_1]\} + \cdots + E\{1[An]\} = np$. This argument illustrates the principle that one can often compute the expected value of a random variable without first computing its distribution. For another example, suppose $n$ balls are dropped at random into $n$ boxes. The number of empty boxes, $Y$, has the representation $Y = 1[B_1] + \cdots + 1[Bn]$, where $Bk$ is the event that "the $k$th box is empty." Because the $k$th box is empty if and only if each of the $n$ balls went into one of the other $n - 1$ boxes, $P(Bk) = [(n - 1)/n]n$ for all $k$, and consequently $E(Y) = n(1 - 1/n)n$. The exact distribution of $Y$ is very complicated, especially if $n$ is large.

Many probability distributions have small values of $f(x_i)$ associated with extreme (large or small) values of $x_i$ and larger values of $f(x_i)$ for intermediate $x_i$. For example, both marginal distributions in the table are symmetrical about a midpoint that has relatively high probability, and the probability of other values decreases as one moves away from the midpoint. Insofar as a distribution $f(x_i)$ follows this kind of pattern, one can interpret the mean of $f$ as a rough measure of location of the bulk of the probability distribution, because in the defining sum the values $x_i$ associated with large values of $f(x_i)$ more or less define the centre of the distribution. In the extreme case, the expected value of a constant random variable is just that constant.

## VARIANCE

It is also of interest to know how closely packed about its mean value a distribution is. The most important measure of concentration is the variance, denoted by Var($X$) and defined by Var($X$) = $E\{[X - E(X)]^2\}$. By linearity of expectations, one has equivalently Var($X$) = $E(X^2) - \{E(X)\}^2$. The standard deviation of $X$ is the square root of its variance. It has a more direct interpretation than the variance because it is in the same units as $X$. The variance of a constant random variable is 0. Also, if $c$ is a constant, Var($cX$) = $c^2$Var($X$).

There is no general formula for the expectation of a product of random variables. If the random variables $X$ and $Y$ are independent, then $E(XY) = E(X)E(Y)$. This can be used to show that if $X_1, \ldots, X_n$ are independent random variables, the variance of the sum $X_1 + \cdots + X_n$ is just the sum of the individual variances, $\text{Var}(X_1) + \cdots + \text{Var}(X_n)$. If the $X$s have the same distribution and are independent, then the variance of the average $(X_1 + \cdots + X_n)/n$ is $\text{Var}(X_1)/n$. Equivalently, the standard deviation of $(X_1 + \cdots + X_n)/n$ is the standard deviation of $X_1$ divided by $\sqrt{n}$. This quantifies the intuitive notion that the average of repeated observations is less variable than the individual observations. More precisely, it says that the variability of the average is inversely proportional to the square root of the number of observations. This result is tremendously important in problems of statistical inference.

Consider again the binomial distribution given by equation (3). As in the calculation of the mean value, one can use the definition combined with some algebraic manipulation to show that if $R$ has the binomial distribution, then $\text{Var}(R) = npq$. From the representation $R = 1[A_1] + \cdots + 1[A_n]$ defined earlier, and the observation that the events $A_k$ are independent and have the same probability, it follows that

$$\text{Var}(R) = \text{Var}\{1[A_1]\} + \cdots + n\,\text{Var}\{1[A_n]\} = \text{Var}\{1[A_1]\}.$$

Moreover,

$$\text{Var}\{1[A_1]\} = E\{1[A_1]^2\} - [E\{1[A_n]\}]^2 = p - p^2 = pq,$$

so $\text{Var}(R) = npq$.

The conditional distribution of $Y$ given $X = x_i$ is defined by:

$$P\{Y = y_j | X = x_i\} = \frac{h(x_i, y_j)}{f(x_i)}$$

(compare equation [4]), and the conditional expectation of $Y$ given $X = x_i$ is

$$E(Y | X = x_i) = \sum_j \frac{y_j\, h(x_i, y_j)}{f(x_i)}. \qquad (9)$$

One can regard $E(Y|X)$ as a function of $X$. Because $X$ is a random variable, this function of $X$ must itself be a random variable. The conditional expectation $E(Y|X)$ considered as a random variable has its own (unconditional) expectation $E\{E(Y|X)\}$, which is calculated by multiplying equation (9) by $f(x_i)$ and summing over $i$ to obtain the important formula

$$E\{E(Y|X)\} = E(Y). \qquad (10)$$

Properly interpreted, equation (10) is a generalization of the law of total probability.

For a simple example of the use of equation (10), recall the problem of the gambler's ruin and let $e(x)$ denote the expected duration of the game if Peter's fortune is initially equal to $x$. The reasoning leading to equation (5) in conjunction with equation (10) shows that $e(x)$ satisfies the equations $e(x) = 1 + pe(x + 1) + qe(x - 1)$ for $x = 1, 2, \ldots, m - 1$ with the boundary conditions $e(0) = e(m) = 0$. The solution for $p \neq 1/2$ is rather complicated; for $p = 1/2$, $e(x) = x(m - x)$.

## AN ALTERNATIVE INTERPRETATION OF PROBABILITY

In ordinary conversation the word *probability* is applied not only to variable phenomena but also to propositions of uncertain veracity. The truth of any proposition concerning the outcome of an experiment is uncertain before the

experiment is performed. Many other uncertain propositions cannot be defined in terms of repeatable experiments.
An individual can be uncertain about the truth of a scientific theory, a religious doctrine, or even about the
occurrence of a specific historical event when inadequate
or conflicting eyewitness accounts are involved. Using
probability as a measure of uncertainty enlarges its domain
of application to phenomena that do not meet the require-
ment of repeatability. The concomitant disadvantage is
that probability as a measure of uncertainty is subjective
and varies from one person to another.

According to one interpretation, to say that someone
has subjective probability $p$ that a proposition is true
means that for any integers $r$ and $b$ with $r/(r + b) < p$, if that
individual is offered an opportunity to bet the same
amount on the truth of the proposition or on "red in a
single draw" from an urn containing $r$ red and $b$ black balls,
then he or she prefers the first bet, whereas if $r/(r + b) > p$,
then the second bet is preferred.

An important stimulus to modern thought about subjective probability has been an attempt to understand
decision making in the face of incomplete knowledge. It is
assumed that an individual, when faced with the necessity
of making a decision that may have different consequences
depending on situations about which he or she has incomplete knowledge, can express personal preferences and
uncertainties in a way consistent with certain axioms of
rational behaviour. It can then be deduced that the individual has a utility function, which measures the value to him
or her of each course of action when each of the uncertain
possibilities is the true one, and a "subjective probability
distribution," which quantitatively expresses the individual's beliefs about the uncertain situations. The individual's
optimal decision is the one that maximizes his or her
expected utility with respect to subjective probability. The

concept of utility goes back at least to Daniel Bernoulli (Jakob Bernoulli's nephew) and was developed in the 20th century by John von Neumann and Oskar Morgenstern, Frank P. Ramsey, and Leonard J. Savage, among others. Ramsey and Savage stressed the importance of subjective probability as a concomitant ingredient of decision making in the face of uncertainty. An alternative approach to subjective probability without the use of utility theory was developed by Bruno de Finetti.

The mathematical theory of probability is the same regardless of one's interpretation of the concept, but the importance attached to various results can heavily depend on the interpretation. In particular, in the theory and applications of subjective probability, Bayes's theorem plays an important role.

For example, suppose that an urn contains $N$ balls, $r$ of which are red and $b = N - r$ of which are black, but $r$ (hence $b$) is unknown. One is permitted to learn about the value of $r$ by performing the experiment of drawing with replacement $n$ balls from the urn. Suppose also that one has a subjective probability distribution giving the probability $f(r)$ that the number of red balls is in fact $r$ where $f(0) + \cdots + f(N) = 1$. This distribution is called an a priori distribution because it is specified prior to the experiment of drawing balls from the urn. The binomial distribution is now a conditional probability, given the value of $r$. Finally, one can use Bayes's theorem to find the conditional probability that the unknown number of red balls in the urn is $r$, given that the number of red balls drawn from the urn is $i$. The result is

$$\frac{f(r) r^i b^{n-i}}{\displaystyle\sum_{r_0=0}^{n} f(r_0) r_0^i b_0^{n-i}}, \qquad \text{where } b_0 = N - r_0.$$

This distribution, derived by using Bayes's theorem to combine the a priori distribution with the conditional distribution for the outcome of the experiment, is called the *a posteriori distribution*.

The virtue of this calculation is that it makes possible a probability statement about the composition of the urn, which is not directly observable, in terms of observable data, from the composition of the sample taken from the urn. The weakness, as previously indicated, is that different people may choose different subjective probabilities for the composition of the urn a priori and hence reach different conclusions about its composition a posteriori.

To see how this idea might apply in practice, consider a simple urn model of opinion polling to predict which of two candidates will win an election. The red balls in the urn are identified with voters who will vote for candidate *A* and the black balls with those voting for candidate *B*. Choosing a sample from the electorate and asking their preferences is a well-defined random experiment, which in theory and in practice is repeatable. The composition of the urn is uncertain and is not the result of a well-defined random experiment. Nevertheless, to the extent that a vote for a candidate is a vote for a political party, other elections provide information about the content of the urn, which, if used judiciously, should be helpful in supplementing the results of the actual sample to make a prediction. Exactly how to use this information is a difficult problem in which individual judgment plays an important part. One possibility is to incorporate the prior information into an a priori distribution about the electorate, which is then combined via Bayes's theorem with the outcome of the sample and summarized by an a posteriori distribution.

# THE LAW OF LARGE NUMBERS, THE CENTRAL LIMIT THEOREM, AND THE POISSON APPROXIMATION

## THE LAW OF LARGE NUMBERS

The relative frequency interpretation of probability is that if an experiment is repeated a large number of times under identical conditions and independently, then the relative frequency with which an event $A$ actually occurs and the probability of $A$ should be approximately the same. A mathematical expression of this interpretation is the law of large numbers. This theorem says that if $X_1$, $X_2$, ..., $X_n$ are independent random variables having a common distribution with mean $\mu$, then for any number $\varepsilon > 0$, no matter how small, as $n \to \infty$,

$$ P\{|n^{-1}(X_1 + \cdots + X_n) - \mu| < \varepsilon\} \to 1. \qquad (11) $$

The law of large numbers was first proved by Jakob Bernoulli in the special case where $X_k$ is 1 or 0 according as the $k$th draw (with replacement) from an urn containing $r$ red and $b$ black balls is red or black. Then $E(X_k) = r/(r + b)$, and the last equation says that the probability that "the difference between the empirical proportion of red balls in $n$ draws and the probability of red on a single draw is less than $\varepsilon$" converges to 1 as $n$ becomes infinitely large.

Insofar as an event that has probability close to 1 is practically certain to happen, this result justifies the relative frequency interpretation of probability. Strictly speaking, however, the justification is circular because the probability in the preceding equation, which is very close to but not equal to 1, requires its own relative frequency interpretation. Perhaps it is better to say that the weak law of large numbers is consistent with the relative frequency interpretation of probability.

The following simple proof of the law of large numbers is based on Chebyshev's inequality, which illustrates the sense in which the variance of a distribution measures how the distribution is dispersed about its mean. If $X$ is a random variable with distribution $f$ and mean $\mu$, then by definition $\text{Var}(X) = \Sigma_i (x_i - \mu)^2 f(x_i)$. Because all terms in this sum are positive, the sum can only decrease if some terms are omitted. Suppose one omits all terms with $|x_i - \mu| < b$, where $b$ is an arbitrary given number. Each term remaining in the sum has a factor of the form $(x_i - \mu)^2$, which is greater than or equal to $b^2$. Hence, $\text{Var}(X) \geq b^2 \Sigma' f(x_i)$, where the prime on the summation sign indicates that only terms with $|x_i - \mu| \geq b$ are included in the sum. Chebyshev's inequality is this expression rewritten as

$$P\{|X - \mu| \geq b\} \leq \frac{\text{Var}(X)}{b^2}.$$

This inequality can be applied to the complementary event of that appearing in equation (11), with $b = \varepsilon$. The $X$s are independent and have the same distribution, $E[n^{-1}(X_1 + \cdots + X_n)] = \mu$ and $\text{Var}[(X_1 + \cdots + X_n)/n] = \text{Var}(X_1)/n$, so that

$$P\{|\frac{(X_1 + \cdots + X_n)}{n} - \mu| < \varepsilon\} \geq 1 - \frac{\text{Var}(X_1)}{n\varepsilon^2}.$$

This not only proves equation (11), but it also says quantitatively how large $n$ should be so that the empirical average, $n^{-1}(X_1 + \cdots + X_n)$, approximate its expectation to any required degree of precision.

Suppose, for example, that the proportion $p$ of red balls in an urn is unknown and is to be estimated by the empirical proportion of red balls in a sample of size $n$ drawn from the urn with replacement. Chebyshev's inequality with $X_k = 1\{$red ball on the $k$th draw$\}$ implies that for the observed proportion to be within $\varepsilon$ of the true proportion $p$ with probability at least 0.95, it suffices that $n$ be at least $20 \times \mathrm{Var}(X_1)/\varepsilon^2$. Because $\mathrm{Var}(X_1) = p(1 - p) \le 1/4$ for all $p$, for $\varepsilon = 0.03$ it suffices that $n$ be at least 5,555. The following text shows that this value of $n$ is much larger than necessary, because Chebyshev's inequality is insufficiently precise to be useful in numerical calculations.

Although Jakob Bernoulli did not know Chebyshev's inequality, the inequality he derived was also imprecise. Perhaps because of his disappointment in not having a quantitatively useful approximation, he did not publish the result during his lifetime. It appeared in 1713, eight years after his death.

## THE CENTRAL LIMIT THEOREM

The desired useful approximation is given by the central limit theorem, which in the special case of the binomial distribution was first discovered by Abraham de Moivre about 1730. Let $X_1, \ldots, X_n$ be independent random variables having a common distribution with expectation $\mu$ and variance $\sigma^2$. The law of large numbers implies that the distribution of the random variable $X^-_n = n^{-1}(X_1 + \cdots + X_n)$ is essentially just the degenerate distribution of the constant $\mu$, because $E(X^-_n) = \mu$ and $\mathrm{Var}(X^-_n) = \sigma^2/n \to 0$ as $n \to \infty$. The standardized random variable $(X^-_n - \mu)/(\sigma/\sqrt{n})$ has mean 0 and variance 1. The central limit theorem gives the remarkable result that, for any real numbers $a$ and $b$, as $n \to \infty$,

$$P\{a < \frac{(\overline{X}_n - \mu)}{(\sigma/n^{1/2})} \le b\} \to G(b) - G(a), \qquad (12)$$

where

$$G(z) = \frac{1}{\sqrt{2\pi}} \int_{-\infty}^{z} \exp(\frac{-t^2}{2})dt.$$

Thus, if $n$ is large, then the standardized average has a distribution that is approximately the same, regardless of the original distribution of the $X$s. The equation also illustrates clearly the square root law: The accuracy of $\overline{X}_n$ as an estimator of $\mu$ is inversely proportional to the square root of the sample size $n$.

Use of equation (12) to evaluate approximately the probability on the left-hand side of equation (11), by setting $b = -a = \varepsilon\sqrt{n}/\sigma$, yields the approximation $G(\varepsilon\sqrt{n}/\sigma) - G(-\varepsilon\sqrt{n}/\sigma)$. Because $G(2) - G(-2)$ is approximately 0.95, $n$ must be about $4\sigma^2/\varepsilon^2$ in order that the difference $|\overline{X}_n - \mu|$ will be less than $\varepsilon$ with probability 0.95. For the special case of the binomial distribution, one can again use the inequality $\sigma^2 = p(1 - p) \le 1/4$ and now conclude that about 1,100 balls must be drawn from the urn in order that the empirical proportion of red balls drawn will be within 0.03 of the true proportion of red balls with probability about 0.95. The frequently appearing statement in U.S. newspapers that a given opinion poll involving a sample of about 1,100 persons has a sampling error of no more than 3 percent is based on this kind of calculation. The qualification that this 3 percent sampling error may be exceeded in about 5 percent of the cases is often omitted.

The actual situation in opinion polls or sample surveys generally is more complicated. The sample is drawn without replacement, so, strictly speaking, the binomial distribution is not applicable. However, the "urn" (i.e., the population from which the sample is drawn) is extremely large, in many cases infinitely large for practical purposes. Hence, the composition of the urn is effectively the same throughout the sampling process, and the binomial distribution applies as an approximation. Also, the population is usually stratified into relatively homogeneous groups, and the survey is designed to take advantage of this stratification. To pursue the analogy with urn models, imagine the balls to be in several urns in varying proportions, and decide how to allocate the $n$ draws from the various urns so as to estimate efficiently the overall proportion of red balls.

Considerable effort has been put into generalizing both the law of large numbers and the central limit theorem. Thus, it is unnecessary for the variables to be either independent or identically distributed.

The law of large numbers previously discussed is often called the "weak law of large numbers," to distinguish it from the "strong law," a conceptually different result discussed in the following text in the section on infinite probability spaces.

## THE POISSON APPROXIMATION

The weak law of large numbers and the central limit theorem give information about the distribution of the proportion of successes in a large number of independent trials when the probability of success on each trial is $p$. In the mathematical formulation of these results, it is assumed that $p$ is an arbitrary, but fixed, number in the interval (0, 1) and $n \to \infty$, so that the expected number of successes in the $n$ trials, $np$, also increases toward $+\infty$ with $n$. A rather different kind of approximation is of interest when $n$ is large and the probability $p$ of success on a single trial is inversely proportional to $n$, so that $np = \mu$ is a fixed number even though $n \to \infty$. An example is the following simple model of radioactive decay of a source consisting of a large number of atoms, which independently of one another decay by spontaneously emitting a particle. The time scale is divided into a large number of small intervals of equal lengths. In each interval, independently of what happens in the other intervals, the source emits one or no particle with probability $p$ or $q = 1 - p$, respectively. It is assumed that the intervals are so small that the probability of two or more particles being emitted in a single interval is negligible. One now imagines that the size of the intervals shrinks to 0, so that the number of trials up to any fixed time $t$ becomes infinite. It is reasonable to assume that the probability of emission during a short time interval is proportional to the length of the interval. The result is a different kind of approximation to the binomial distribution, called the Poisson distribution (after the French mathematician Siméon-Denis Poisson) or the law of small numbers.

Assume, then, that a biased coin having probability $p = \mu\delta$ of heads is tossed once in each time interval of length $\delta$, so that by time $t$ the total number of tosses is an integer $n$ approximately equal to $t/\delta$. Introducing these values into the binomial equation and passing to the limit as $\delta \to 0$ gives as the distribution for $N(t)$ the number of radioactive particles emitted in time $t$:

$$P\{N(t) = i\} = \frac{(\mu t)^i \exp(-\mu t)}{i!} \qquad (i = 0, 1, \ldots). \qquad (13)$$

The right-hand side of this equation is the Poisson distribution. Its mean and variance are both equal to $\mu t$. Although the Poisson approximation is not comparable to the central limit theorem in importance, it nevertheless provides one of the basic building blocks in the theory of stochastic processes.

# INFINITE SAMPLE SPACES AND AXIOMATIC PROBABILITY

## INFINITE SAMPLE SPACES

The experiments described in the preceding discussion involve finite sample spaces for the most part, although the central limit theorem and the Poisson approximation involve limiting operations and hence lead to integrals and infinite series. In a finite sample space, calculation of the probability of an event $A$ is conceptually straightforward because the principle of additivity tells one to calculate the probability of a complicated event as the sum of the probabilities of the individual experimental outcomes whose union defines the event.

Experiments having a continuum of possible outcomes (e.g., that of selecting a number at random from the interval $[r, s]$) involve subtle mathematical difficulties that were not satisfactorily resolved until the 20th century. If one chooses a number at random from $[r, s]$, then the probability that the number falls in any interval $[x, y]$ must be proportional to the length of that interval. Because the probability of the entire sample space $[r, s]$ equals 1, the constant of proportionality equals $1/(s - r)$. Hence, the probability of obtaining a number in the interval $[x, y]$ equals $(y - x)/(s - r)$. From this and the principle of additivity one can determine the probability of any event that can be expressed as a finite union of intervals. There are, however, rather complicated sets having no simple relation to the intervals (e.g., the rational numbers), and it is not immediately clear what the probabilities of these sets should be. Also, the probability of selecting exactly the number $x$ must be 0, because the set consisting of $x$ alone is contained in the interval $[x, x + 1/n]$ for all $n$ and hence must have no larger probability than $1/[n(s - r)]$, no matter how large $n$ is. Consequently, it makes no sense to attempt computing the probability of an event by "adding" the probabilities of the individual outcomes making up the event, because each individual outcome has probability 0.

A closely related experiment, although at first there appears to be no connection, arises as follows. Suppose that a coin is tossed $n$ times, and let $X_k$ = 1 or 0 according as the outcome of the $k$th toss is heads or tails. The weak law of large numbers given above says that a certain sequence of numbers — namely the sequence of probabilities given in equation (11) and defined in terms of these $n$ $X$s — converges to 1 as $n \to \infty$. To formulate this result, it is only necessary to imagine that one can toss the coin $n$ times and that this finite number of tosses can be arbitrarily large. In other words, there is a sequence of experiments, but each one involves a finite sample space. It is also natural to ask whether the sequence of random variables $(X_1 + \cdots + X_n)/n$ converges as $n \to \infty$. However, this question cannot even be formulated mathematically unless infinitely many $X$s can be defined on the same sample space, which in turn requires that the underlying experiment involve an actual infinity of coin tosses.

For the conceptual experiment of tossing a fair coin infinitely many times, the sequence of zeros and ones, $(X_1, X_2, \ldots)$, can be identified with that real number that has the $X$s as the coefficients of its expansion in the base 2, namely $X_1/2^1 + X_2/2^2 + X_3/2^3 + \cdots$. For example, the outcome of getting heads on the first two tosses and tails thereafter corresponds to the real number $1/2 + 1/4 + 0/8 + \cdots = 3/4$. (There are some technical mathematical difficulties that arise from the fact that some numbers have two representations. Obviously $1/2 = 1/2 + 0/4 + \cdots$, and the formula for the sum of an infinite geometric series shows that it also equals $0/2 + 1/4 + 1/8 + \cdots$. It can be shown that these difficulties do not pose a serious problem, and they are ignored in the subsequent discussion.) For any particular specification $i_1, i_2, \ldots, i_n$ of zeros and ones, the event $\{X_1 = i_1, X_2 = i_2, \ldots, X_n = i_n\}$ must have probability $1/2^n$ to be consistent with the experiment of tossing the coin only $n$ times. Moreover, this event corresponds to the interval of real numbers $[i_1/2^1 + i_2/2^2 + \cdots + i_n/2^n, i_1/2^1 + i_2/2^2 + \cdots + i_n/2^n + 1/2^n]$ of length $1/2^n$, because any continuation $X_{n+1}, X_{n+2}, \ldots$ corresponds to a number that is at least 0 and at most $1/2^{n+1} + 1/2^{n+2} + \cdots = 1/2^n$ by the formula for an infinite geometric series. It follows that the mathematical model for choosing a number at random from $[0, 1]$ and that of tossing a fair coin infinitely many times assign the same probabilities to all intervals of the form $[k/2^n, 1/2^n]$.

## THE STRONG LAW OF LARGE NUMBERS

The mathematical relation between these two experiments was recognized in 1909 by the French mathematician Émile Borel, who used the then new ideas of measure theory to give a precise mathematical model and to formulate what is now called the strong law of large numbers for fair coin tossing. His results can be described as follows. Let $e$ denote a number chosen at random from $[0, 1]$, and let

$X_k(e)$ be the $k$th coordinate in the expansion of $e$ to the base 2. Then $X_1, X_2, \ldots$ are an infinite sequence of independent random variables taking the values 0 or 1 with probability 1/2 each. Moreover, the subset of [0, 1] consisting of those $e$ for which the sequence $n^{-1}[X_1(e) + \cdots + X_n(e)]$ tends to 1/2 as $n \to \infty$ has probability 1. Symbolically:

$$P\left\{ \lim_{n \to \infty} [n^{-1}(X_1 + \cdots + X_n)] = \frac{1}{2} \right\} = 1. \qquad (14)$$

The weak law of large numbers given in equation (11) says that for any $\varepsilon > 0$, for each sufficiently large value of $n$, there is only a small probability of observing a deviation of $\overline{X}_n = n^{-1}(X_1 + \cdots + X_n)$ from 1/2 which is larger than $\varepsilon$; nevertheless, it leaves open the possibility that sooner or later this rare event will occur if one continues to toss the coin and observe the sequence for a sufficiently long time. The strong law, however, asserts that the occurrence of even one value of $XRU_k$ for $k \geq n$ that differs from 1/2 by more than $\varepsilon$ is an event of arbitrarily small probability provided $n$ is large enough. The proof of equation (14) and various subsequent generalizations is much more difficult than that of the weak law of large numbers. The adjectives "strong" and "weak" refer to the fact that the truth of a result such as equation (14) implies the truth of the corresponding version of equation (11), but not conversely.

## MEASURE THEORY

During the two decades following 1909, measure theory was used in many concrete problems of probability theory, notably in the American mathematician Norbert Wiener's treatment (1923) of the mathematical theory of Brownian motion, but the notion that all problems of probability theory could be formulated in terms of measure is customarily attributed to the Soviet mathematician Andrey Nikolayevich Kolmogorov in 1933.

The fundamental quantities of the measure theoretic foundation of probability theory are the sample space $S$, which as before is just the set of all possible outcomes of an experiment, and a distinguished class $M$ of subsets of $S$, called events. Unlike the case of finite $S$, in general not every subset of $S$ is an event. The class $M$ must have certain properties described in the following text. Each event is assigned a probability, which means mathematically that a probability is a function $P$ mapping $M$ into the real numbers that satisfies certain conditions derived from one's physical ideas about probability.

The properties of $M$ are as follows: (i) $S \in M$; (ii) if $A \in M$, then $A^c \in M$; (iii) if $A_1, A_2, \ldots \in M$, then $A_1 \cup A_2 \cup \cdots \in M$. Recalling that $M$ is the domain of definition of the probability $P$, one can interpret (i) as saying that $P(S)$ is defined, (ii) as saying that, if the probability of $A$ is defined, then the probability of "not $A$" is also defined, and (iii) as saying that, if one can speak of the probability of each of a sequence of events $A_n$ individually, then one can speak of the probability that at least one of the $A_n$ occurs. A class of subsets of any set that has properties (i)–(iii) is called a σ-field. From these properties one can prove others. For example, it follows at once from (i) and (ii) that Ø (the empty set) belongs to the class $M$. Because the intersection of any class of sets can be expressed as the complement of the union of the complements of those sets (DeMorgan's law), it follows from (ii) and (iii) that, if $A_1, A_2, \ldots \in M$, then $A_1 \cap A_2 \cap \cdots \in M$.

Given a set $S$ and a σ-field $M$ of subsets of $S$, a probability measure is a function $P$ that assigns to each set $A \in M$ a nonnegative real number and that has the following properties: (a) $P(S) = 1$ and (b) if $A_1, A_2, \ldots \in M$ and $A_i \cap A_j = \emptyset$ for all $i \neq j$, then $P(A_1 \cup A_2 \cup \cdots) = P(A_1) + P(A_2) + \cdots$. Property (b) is called the axiom of countable additivity. It is clearly motivated by equation (1), which suffices for finite sample spaces because there are only finitely many events. In infinite sample spaces it implies, but is not implied by, equation (1). There is, however, nothing in one's intuitive notion of probability that requires the acceptance of this property. Indeed, a few mathematicians have developed probability theory with only the weaker axiom of finite additivity, but the absence of interesting models that fail to satisfy the axiom of countable additivity has led to its virtually universal acceptance.

To get a better feeling for this distinction, consider the experiment of tossing a biased coin having probability $p$ of heads and $q = 1 - p$ of tails until heads first appears. To be consistent with the idea that the tosses are independent, the probability that exactly $n$ tosses are required equals $q^{n-1}p$, because the first $n - 1$ tosses must be tails, and they must be followed by a head. One can imagine that this experiment never terminates (i.e., that the coin continues to turn up tails forever). By the axiom of countable additivity, however, the probability that heads occurs at some finite value of $n$ equals $p + qp + q^2p + \cdots = p/(1 - q) = 1$, by the formula for the sum of an infinite geometric series. Hence, the probability that the experiment goes on forever equals 0. Similarly, one can compute the probability that the number of tosses is odd, as $p + q^2p + q^4p + \cdots = p/(1 - q^2) = 1/(1 + q)$. Conversely, if only finite additivity were required, then it would be possible to define the following admittedly bizarre probability. The sample space $S$ is the set of all natural numbers, and the $\sigma$-field $M$ is the class of all subsets of $S$. If an event $A$ contains finitely many elements, then $P(A) = 0$, and if the complement of $A$ contains finitely many elements, then $P(A) = 1$. As a consequence of the deceptively innocuous axiom of choice (which says that, given any collection $C$ of nonempty sets, there exists a rule for selecting a unique point from each set in $C$), one can show that many finitely additive probabilities consistent with these requirements exist. However, one cannot be certain what the probability of getting an odd number is, because that set is neither finite nor its complement finite, nor can it be expressed as a finite disjoint union of sets whose probability is already defined.

It is a basic problem, and by no means a simple one, to show that the intuitive notion of choosing a number at random from [0, 1], as described above, is consistent with the preceding definitions. Because the probability of an interval is to be its length, the class of events $M$ must contain all intervals. To be a σ-field it must contain other sets, however, many of which are difficult to describe simply. One example is the event in equation (14), which must belong to $M$ in order that one can talk about its probability. Also, although it seems clear that the length of a finite disjoint union of intervals is just the sum of their lengths, a rather subtle argument is required to show that length has the property of countable additivity. A basic theorem says that there is a suitable σ-field containing all the intervals and a unique probability defined on this σ-field for which the probability of an interval is its length. The σ-field is called the class of Lebesgue-measurable sets, and the probability is called the Lebesgue measure, after the French mathematician and principal architect of measure theory, Henri-Léon Lebesgue.

In general, a σ-field need not be all subsets of the sample space $S$. The question of whether all subsets of [0, 1] are Lebesgue-measurable turns out to be a difficult problem that is intimately connected with the foundations of mathematics and in particular with the axiom of choice.

## PROBABILITY DENSITY FUNCTIONS

For random variables having a continuum of possible values, the function that plays the same role as the probability distribution of a discrete random variable is called a probability density function. If the random variable is denoted by $X$, then its probability density function $f$ has the property that

$$P\{a < X \le b\} = \int_a^b f(x)\,dx$$

for every interval $(a, b]$. For example, the probability that $X$ falls in $(a, b]$ is the area under the graph of $f$ between $a$ and $b$. For example, if $X$ denotes the outcome of selecting a number at random from the interval $[r, s]$, then the probability density function of $X$ is given by $f(x) = 1/(s - r)$ for $r < x < s$ and $f(x) = 0$ for $x < r$ or $x > s$. The function $F(x)$ defined by $F(x) = P\{X \le x\}$ is called the distribution function, or cumulative distribution function, of $X$. If $X$ has a probability density function $f(x)$, then the relation between $f$ and $F$ is $F'(x) = f(x)$ or equivalently

$$F(x) = \int_{-\infty}^{x} f(t)\,dt.$$

The distribution function $F$ of a discrete random variable should not be confused with its probability distribution $f$. In this case the relation between $F$ and $f$ is

$$F(x) = \sum_{x_i \leq x} f(x_i).$$

If a random variable $X$ has a probability density function $f(x)$, then its "expectation" can be defined by

$$E(X) = \int_{-\infty}^{\infty} x f(x)\, dx, \qquad (15)$$

provided that this integral is convergent. It turns out to be simpler, however, not only to use Lebesgue's theory of measure to define probabilities but also to use his theory of integration to define expectation. Accordingly, for any random variable $X$, $E(X)$ is defined to be the Lebesgue integral of $X$ with respect to the probability measure $P$, provided that the integral exists. In this way it is possible to provide a unified theory in which all random variables, both discrete and continuous, can be treated simultaneously. To follow this path, it is necessary to restrict the class of those functions $X$ defined on $S$ that are to be called random variables, just as it was necessary to restrict the class of subsets of $S$ that are called events. The appropriate restriction is that a random variable must be a measurable function. The definition is taken over directly from the Lebesgue theory of integration and will not be discussed here. It can be shown that, whenever $X$ has a probability density function, its expectation (provided it exists) is given by equation (15),

$$E(X) = \int_{-\infty}^{\infty} x f(x)\, dx, \qquad (15)$$

which remains a useful formula for calculating $E(X)$.

Some important probability density functions are the following:

(i) Normal: $f(x) = (2\pi\sigma^2)^{-1/2} \exp\left[\dfrac{-(x-\mu)^2}{2\sigma^2}\right]$

$\quad (-\infty < x < +\infty); \qquad E(X) = \mu, \operatorname{Var}(X) = \sigma^2.$

(ii) Exponential: $f(x) = \mu \exp(-\mu x) \qquad (0 \le x < +\infty),$

$\quad f(x) = 0 \qquad (x < 0); \qquad E(X) = \dfrac{1}{\mu}.$

(iii) Cauchy: $f(x) = \dfrac{1}{[\pi(1+x^2)]} \qquad (-\infty < x < +\infty);$

$\quad E(X)$ does not exist.

The cumulative distribution function of the normal distribution with mean o and variance ı has already appeared as the function $G$ defined following equation (12). The law of large numbers and the central limit theorem continue to hold for random variables on infinite sample spaces. A useful interpretation of the central limit theorem stated formally in equation (12) is as follows: The probability that the average (or sum) of a large number of independent, identically distributed random variables with finite variance falls in an interval $(c_1, c_2]$ approximately equals the area between $c_1$ and $c_2$ underneath the graph of a normal density function chosen to have the same expectation and variance as the given average (or sum).

The exponential distribution arises naturally in the study of the Poisson distribution introduced in equation (13). If $T_k$ denotes the time interval between the emission of the $k$ - ıst and $k$th particle, then $T_1, T_2, \ldots$ are independent random variables having an exponential distribution with parameter μ. This is obvious for $T_1$ from the observation that $\{T_1 > t\} = \{N(t) = 0\}$. Hence, $P\{T_1 \le t\} = 1 - P$ $\{N(t) = 0\} = 1 - \exp(-\mu t)$, and by differentiation one obtains the exponential density function.

The Cauchy distribution does not have a mean value or a variance, because the integral (15) does not converge. As a result, it has a number of unusual properties. For example, if $X_1, X_2, \ldots, X_n$ are independent random variables having a Cauchy distribution, then the average $(X_1 + \cdots + X_n)/n$ also has a Cauchy distribution. The variability of the average is exactly the same as that of a single observation. Another random variable that does not have an expectation is the waiting time until the number of heads first equals the number of tails in tossing a fair coin.

## CONDITIONAL EXPECTATION AND LEAST SQUARES PREDICTION

An important problem of probability theory is to predict the value of a future observation $Y$ given knowledge of a related observation $X$ (or, more generally, given several related observations $X_1, X_2, \ldots$). Examples are to predict the future course of the national economy or the path of a rocket, given its present state.

Prediction is often just one aspect of a "control" problem. For example, in guiding a rocket, measurements of the rocket's location, velocity, and so on are made almost continuously. At each reading, the rocket's future course is predicted, and a control is then used to correct its future course. The same ideas are used to steer automatically large tankers transporting crude oil, for which even slight gains in efficiency result in large financial savings.

Given $X$, a predictor of $Y$ is just a function $H(X)$. The problem of "least squares prediction" of $Y$ given the observation $X$ is to find that function $H(X)$ that is closest to $Y$ in the sense that the mean square error of prediction,

$E\{[Y - H(X)]^2\}$, is minimized. The solution is the conditional expectation $H(X) = E(Y|X)$.

In applications a probability model is rarely known exactly and must be constructed from a combination of theoretical analysis and experimental data. It may be quite difficult to determine the optimal predictor, $E(Y|X)$, particularly if instead of a single $X$ a large number of predictor variables $X_1, X_2, \ldots$ are involved. An alternative is to restrict the class of functions $H$ over which one searches to minimize the mean square error of prediction, in the hope of finding an approximately optimal predictor that is much easier to evaluate. The simplest possibility is to restrict consideration to linear functions $H(X) = a + bX$. The coefficients $a$ and $b$ that minimize the restricted mean square prediction error $E\{(Y - a - bX)^2\}$ give the best linear least squares predictor. Treating this restricted mean square prediction error as a function of the two coefficients $(a, b)$ and minimizing it by methods of the calculus yield the optimal coefficients: $\hat{b} = E\{[X - E(X)][Y - E(Y)]\}/\mathrm{Var}(X)$ and $\hat{a} = E(Y) - \hat{b}E(X)$. The numerator of the expression for $\hat{b}$ is called the covariance of $X$ and $Y$ and is denoted $\mathrm{Cov}(X, Y)$. Let $\hat{Y} = \hat{a} + \hat{b}X$ denote the optimal linear predictor. The mean square error of prediction is $E\{(Y - \hat{Y})^2\} = \mathrm{Var}(Y) - [\mathrm{Cov}(X, Y)]^2/\mathrm{Var}(X)$.

If $X$ and $Y$ are independent, $\mathrm{Cov}(X, Y) = 0$, the optimal predictor is just $E(Y)$, and the mean square error of prediction is $\mathrm{Var}(Y)$. Hence, $|\mathrm{Cov}(X, Y)|$ is a measure of the value $X$ has in predicting $Y$. In the extreme case that $[\mathrm{Cov}(X, Y)]^2 = \mathrm{Var}(X)\mathrm{Var}(Y)$, $Y$ is a linear function of $X$, and the optimal linear predictor gives error-free prediction.

In one important case the optimal mean square predictor actually is the same as the optimal linear predictor. If $X$ and $Y$ are jointly normally distributed, then the conditional expectation of $Y$ given $X$ is just a linear function of $X$, and hence the optimal predictor and the optimal linear predictor are the same. The form of the bivariate normal distribution as well as expressions for the coefficients $\hat{a}$ and $\hat{b}$ and for the minimum mean square error of prediction were discovered by the English eugenicist Sir Francis Galton in his studies of the transmission of inheritable characteristics from one generation to the next. They form the foundation of the statistical technique of linear regression.

# THE POISSON PROCESS AND THE BROWNIAN MOTION PROCESS

The theory of stochastic processes attempts to build probability models for phenomena that evolve over time. A primitive example is the problem of gambler's ruin.

## THE POISSON PROCESS

An important stochastic process described implicitly in the discussion of the Poisson approximation to the binomial distribution is the Poisson process. Modeling the emission of radioactive particles by an infinitely large number of tosses of a coin having infinitesimally small probability for heads on each toss led to the conclusion that the number of particles $N(t)$ emitted in the time interval $[0, t]$ has the Poisson distribution given in equation (13) with expectation $\mu t$. The primary concern of the theory of stochastic processes is not this marginal distribution of $N(t)$ at a particular time but rather the evolution of $N(t)$ over time. Two properties of the Poisson process that make it attractive to deal with theoretically are as follows: (i) The times between emission of particles are independent and exponentially distributed with expected value $1/\mu$; (ii) given that $N(t) = n$, the times at which the $n$ particles are emitted have the same joint distribution as $n$ points distributed independently and uniformly on the interval $[0, t]$.

As a consequence of property (i), a picture of the function $N(t)$ is easily constructed. Originally $N(0) = 0$. At an exponentially distributed time $T_1$, the function $N(t)$ jumps from 0 to 1. It remains at 1 another exponentially distributed random time, $T_2$, which is independent of $T_1$, and at time $T_1 + T_2$ it jumps from 1 to 2, and so on.

Examples of other phenomena for which the Poisson process often serves as a mathematical model are the number of customers arriving at a counter and requesting service, the number of claims against an insurance company, or the number of malfunctions in a computer system. The importance of the Poisson process consists in (a) its simplicity as a test case for which the mathematical theory, and hence the implications, are more easily understood than for more realistic models and (b) its use as a building block in models of complex systems.

## BROWNIAN MOTION PROCESS

The most important stochastic process is the Brownian motion or Wiener process. It was first discussed by Louis Bachelier (1900), who was interested in modeling fluctuations in prices in financial markets, and by Albert Einstein (1905), who gave a mathematical model for the irregular motion of colloidal particles first observed by the Scottish botanist Robert Brown in 1827. The first mathematically rigorous treatment of this model was given by Wiener (1923). Einstein's results led to an early, dramatic confirmation of the molecular theory of matter in the French physicist Jean Perrin's experiments to determine Avogadro's number, for which Perrin was awarded a Nobel Prize in 1926. Today somewhat different models for physical Brownian motion are deemed more appropriate than

*Scottish botanist Robert Brown is best known for his description of the natural continuous motion of minute particles in solution, known as Brownian movement.* Hulton Archive/Getty Images

Einstein's, but the original mathematical model continues to play a central role in the theory and application of stochastic processes.

Let $B(t)$ denote the displacement (in one dimension for simplicity) of a colloidally suspended particle, which is buffeted by the numerous much smaller molecules of the medium in which it is suspended. This displacement will be obtained as a limit of a random walk occurring in discrete time as the number of steps becomes infinitely large and the size of each individual step infinitesimally small. Assume that at times $k\delta, k = 1, 2, \ldots$, the colloidal particle is displaced a distance $hX_k$, where $X_1, X_2, \ldots$ are +1 or -1 according as the outcomes of tossing a fair coin are heads or tails. By time $t$ the particle has taken $m$ steps, where $m$ is the largest integer $\leq t/\delta$, and its displacement from its original position is $B_m(t) = h(X_1 + \cdots + X_m)$. The expected value of $B_m(t)$ is 0, and its variance is $h^2m$, or approximately $h^2t/\delta$. Now suppose that $\delta \to 0$, and at the same time $h \to 0$ in such a way that the variance of $B_m(1)$ converges to some positive constant, $\sigma^2$. This means that $m$ becomes infinitely large, and $h$ is approximately $\sigma(t/m)^{1/2}$. It follows from the central limit theorem (equation [12])

$$P\{a < \frac{(\overline{X}_n - \mu)}{(\sigma/n^{1/2})} \leq b\} \to G(b) - G(a), \qquad (12)$$

that $\lim P\{B_m(t) \leq x\} = G(x/\sigma t^{1/2})$, where $G(x)$ is the standard normal cumulative distribution function defined just below equation (12). The Brownian motion process $B(t)$ can be defined to be the limit in a certain technical sense of the $B_m(t)$ as $\delta \to 0$ and $h \to 0$ with $h^2/\delta \to \sigma^2$.

The process $B(t)$ has many other properties, which in principle are all inherited from the approximating random walk $B_m(t)$. For example, if $(s_1, t_1)$ and $(s_2, t_2)$ are disjoint intervals, then the increments $B(t_1) - B(s_1)$ and $B(t_2) - B(s_2)$ are independent random variables that are normally distributed with expectation 0 and variances equal to $\sigma^2(t_1 - s_1)$ and $\sigma^2(t_2 - s_2)$, respectively.

Einstein took a different approach and derived various properties of the process $B(t)$ by showing that its probability density function, $g(x, t)$, satisfies the diffusion equation $\partial g/\partial t = D\partial^2 g/\partial x^2$, where $D = \sigma^2/2$. The important implication of Einstein's theory for subsequent experimental research was that he identified the diffusion constant $D$ in terms of certain measurable properties of the particle (its radius) and of the medium (its viscosity and temperature), which allowed one to make predictions and hence to confirm or reject the hypothesized existence of the unseen molecules that were assumed to be the cause of the irregular Brownian motion. Because of the beautiful blend of mathematical and physical reasoning involved, a brief summary of the successor to Einstein's model is given in the following text.

Unlike the Poisson process, it is impossible to "draw" a picture of the path of a particle undergoing mathematical Brownian motion. Wiener (1923) showed that the functions $B(t)$ are continuous, as one expects, but nowhere differentiable. Thus, a particle undergoing mathematical Brownian motion does not have a well-defined velocity, and the curve $y = B(t)$ does not have a well-defined tangent at any value of $t$. To see why this might be so, recall that the derivative of $B(t)$, if it exists, is the limit as $h \to 0$ of the ratio $[B(t + h) - B(t)]/h$. Because $B(t + h) - B(t)$ is normally distributed with mean 0 and standard deviation $h^{1/2}\sigma$, in rough terms $B(t + h) - B(t)$ can be expected to equal some multiple (positive or negative) of $h^{1/2}$. But the limit as $h \to 0$ of $h^{1/2}/h = 1/h^{1/2}$ is infinite. A related fact that illustrates the extreme irregularity of $B(t)$ is that in every interval of time, no matter how small, a particle undergoing mathematical Brownian motion travels an infinite distance. Although these properties contradict the common sense idea of a function—and indeed it is quite difficult to write down explicitly a single example of a continuous, nowhere-differentiable function—they turn out to be typical of a large class of stochastic processes, called *diffusion processes*, of which Brownian motion is the most prominent member. Especially notable contributions to the mathematical theory of Brownian motion and diffusion processes were made by Paul Lévy and William Feller during the years 1930–60.

A more sophisticated description of physical Brownian motion can be built on a simple application of Newton's second law: $F = ma$. Let $V(t)$ denote the velocity of a colloidal particle of mass $m$. It is assumed that

$$m\,dV(t) = -f V(t)\,dt + dA(t) \qquad (16)$$

The quantity $f$ retarding the movement of the particle is caused by friction resulting from the surrounding medium. The term $dA(t)$ is the contribution of the frequent collisions of the particle with unseen molecules of the medium. It is assumed that $f$ can be determined by classical fluid mechanics, in which the molecules making up the surrounding medium are so many and so small that the medium can be considered smooth and homogeneous. Then by Stokes's law, for a spherical particle in a gas, $f = 6\pi a\eta$, where $a$ is the radius of the particle and $\eta$ the coefficient of viscosity of the medium. Hypotheses concerning $A(t)$ are less specific, because the molecules making up the surrounding medium cannot be observed directly. For example, it is assumed that for $t \neq s$, the infinitesimal random increments $dA(t) = A(t + dt) - A(t)$ and $A(s + ds) - A(s)$ caused by collisions of the particle with molecules of the surrounding medium are independent random variables having distributions with mean o and unknown variances $\sigma^2 dt$ and $\sigma^2 ds$ and that $dA(t)$ is independent of $dV(s)$ for $s < t$.

The differential equation (16)

$$m \, dV(t) = -f V(t) \, dt + dA(t) \qquad (16)$$

has the solution

$$V(t) = V(0)\exp(-\beta t) + m^{-1} \int_0^t \exp[-\beta(t - s)] \, dA(s), \qquad (17)$$

where $\beta = f/m$. From this equation and the assumed properties of $A(t)$, it follows that $E[V^2(t)] \to \sigma^2/(2mf)$ as $t \to \infty$. Now assume that, in accordance with the principle of equipartition of energy, the steady-state average kinetic energy of the particle, $m \lim_{t \to \infty} E[V^2(t)]/2$, equals the average kinetic energy of the molecules of the medium. According to the kinetic theory of an ideal gas, this is $RT/2N$, where $R$ is the ideal gas constant, $T$ is the temperature of the gas in kelvins, and $N$ is Avogadro's number, the number of molecules in one gram molecular weight of the gas. It follows that the unknown value of $\sigma^2$ can be determined: $\sigma^2 = 2RTf/N$.

If one also assumes that the functions $V(t)$ are continuous, which is certainly reasonable from physical considerations, it follows by mathematical analysis that $A(t)$ is a Brownian motion process as previously defined. This conclusion poses questions about the meaning of the initial equation (16), because for mathematical Brownian motion the term $dA(t)$ does not exist in the usual sense of a derivative. Some additional mathematical analysis shows that the stochastic differential equation (16) and its solution equation (17) have a precise mathematical interpretation. The process $V(t)$ is called the Ornstein-Uhlenbeck process, after the physicists Leonard Salomon Ornstein and George Eugene Uhlenbeck. The logical outgrowth of these attempts to differentiate and integrate with respect to a Brownian motion process is the Ito (named for the Japanese mathematician Itō Kiyosi) stochastic calculus, which plays an important role in the modern theory of stochastic processes.

The displacement at time $t$ of the particle whose velocity is given by equation (17) is

$$X(t) - X(0) = \int_0^t V(u)du = \beta^{-1}V(0)[1 - \exp(-\beta t)] +$$
$$f^{-1}A(t) - f^{-1}\int_0^t \exp[-\beta(t-u)]dA(u).$$

For $t$ large compared with $\beta$, the first and third terms in this expression are small compared with the second. Hence, $X(t) - X(0)$ is approximately equal to $A(t)/f$, and the mean square displacement, $E\{[X(t) - X(0)]^2\}$, is approximately $\sigma^2/f^2 = RT/(3\pi a \eta N)$. These final conclusions are consistent with Einstein's model, but here they arise as an approximation to the model obtained from equation (17). Because it is primarily the conclusions that have observational consequences, there are essentially no new experimental implications. However, the analysis arising directly out of Newton's second law, which yields a process having a well-defined velocity at each point, seems more satisfactory theoretically than Einstein's original model.

## STOCHASTIC PROCESSES

A stochastic process is a family of random variables $X(t)$ indexed by a parameter $t$, which usually takes values in the discrete set $T = \{0, 1, 2, \ldots\}$ or the continuous set $T = [0, +\infty)$. In many cases $t$ represents time, and $X(t)$ is a random variable observed at time $t$. Examples are the Poisson process, the Brownian motion process, and the Ornstein-Uhlenbeck process described in the preceding section. Considered as a totality, the family of random variables $\{X(t), t \in T\}$ constitutes a "random function."

### STATIONARY PROCESSES

The mathematical theory of stochastic processes attempts to define classes of processes for which a unified theory can be developed. The most important classes are stationary processes and Markov processes. A stochastic process is called stationary if, for all $n$, $t_1 < t_2 < \cdots < t_n$, and $h > 0$, then the joint distribution of $X(t_1 + h), \ldots, X(t_n + h)$ does not depend on $h$. This means that in effect there is no origin on the time axis. The stochastic behaviour of a stationary process is the same no matter when the process is observed. A sequence of independent identically distributed random variables is an example of a stationary process. A rather different example is defined as follows: $U(0)$ is uniformly distributed on $[0, 1]$; for each $t = 1, 2, \ldots$, $U(t) = 2U(t - 1)$ if $U(t - 1) \leq 1/2$, and $U(t) = 2U(t - 1) - 1$ if $U(t - 1) > 1/2$. The marginal distributions of $U(t)$, $t = 0, 1, \ldots$ are uniformly distributed on $[0, 1]$, but, in contrast to the case of independent identically distributed random variables, the entire sequence can be predicted from knowledge of $U(0)$. A third example of a stationary process is

$$X(t) = \sum_k c_k [Y_k \cos(\theta_k t) + Z_k \sin(\theta_k t)],$$

where the $Y$s and $Z$s are independent normally distributed random variables with mean 0 and unit variance, and the $c$s and $\theta$s are constants. Processes of this kind can help model seasonal or approximately periodic phenomena.

A remarkable generalization of the strong law of large numbers is the ergodic theorem: If $X(t)$, $t = 0, 1, \ldots$ for the discrete case or $0 \leq t < \infty$ for the continuous case, is a stationary process such that $E[X(0)]$ is finite, then with probability 1 the average

$$s^{-1}\sum_{t=0}^{s-1} X(t), \text{if } t \text{ is discrete, or } s^{-1}\int_{0}^{s} X(t)dt,$$

if $t$ is continuous, converges to a limit as $s \to \infty$. In the special case that $t$ is discrete and the $X$s are independent and identically distributed, the strong law of large numbers is also applicable and shows that the limit must equal $E\{X(0)\}$. However, the example that $X(0)$ is an arbitrary random variable and $X(t) = {}^{-} X(0)$ for all $t > 0$ shows that this cannot be true in general. The limit does equal $E\{X(0)\}$ under an additional rather technical assumption to the effect that there is no subset of the state space, having probability strictly between 0 and 1, in which the process can get stuck and never escape. This assumption is not fulfilled by the example $X(t) \equiv X(0)$ for all $t$, which immediately gets stuck at its initial value. It is satisfied by the sequence $U(t)$ previously defined, so by the ergodic theorem the average of these variables converges to 1/2 with probability 1. The ergodic theorem was first conjectured by the American chemist J. Willard Gibbs in the early 1900s in the context of statistical mechanics and was proved in a corrected, abstract formulation by the American mathematician George David Birkhoff in 1931.

## MARKOVIAN PROCESSES

A stochastic process is called Markovian (after the Russian mathematician Andrey Andreyevich Markov) if at any time $t$ the conditional probability of an arbitrary future event given the entire past of the process, i.e., given $X(s)$ for all $s \leq t$, equals the conditional probability of that future event given only $X(t)$. Thus, to make a probabilistic statement about the future behaviour of a Markov process, it is no more helpful to know the entire history of the process than it is to know only its current state. The conditional distribution of $X(t + h)$ given $X(t)$ is called the transition probability of the process. If this conditional distribution does not depend on $t$, then the process is said to have "stationary" transition probabilities. A Markov process with stationary transition probabilities may or may not be a stationary process in the sense of the preceding paragraph. If $Y_1, Y_2, \ldots$ are independent random variables and $X(t) = Y_1 + \cdots + Y_t$, then the stochastic process $X(t)$ is a Markov process. Given $X(t) = x$, the conditional probability that $X(t + h)$ belongs to an interval $(a, b)$ is just the probability that $Y_{t+1} + \cdots + Y_{t+h}$ belongs to the translated interval $(a - x, b - x)$. Because of independence this conditional probability would be the same if the values of $X(1)$, . . ., $X(t - 1)$ were also given. If the $Y$s are identically distributed as well as independent, this transition probability does not depend on $t$, and then $X(t)$ is a Markov process with stationary transition probabilities. Sometimes $X(t)$ is called a random walk, but this terminology is not completely standard. Because both the Poisson process and Brownian motion are created from random walks by simple limiting processes, they, too, are Markov processes with stationary transition probabilities. The Ornstein-Uhlenbeck process defined as the solution (19) to the stochastic differential equation (18) is also a Markov process with stationary transition probabilities.

The Ornstein-Uhlenbeck process and many other Markov processes with stationary transition probabilities behave like stationary processes as $t \to \infty$. Generally, the conditional distribution of $X(t)$ given $X(0) = x$ converges as $t \to \infty$ to a distribution, called the stationary distribution, that does not depend on the starting value $X(0) = x$. Moreover, with probability 1, the proportion of time the process spends in any subset of its state space converges to the stationary probability of that set. If $X(0)$ is given the stationary distribution to begin with, then the process becomes a stationary process. The Ornstein-Uhlenbeck process defined in equation (19) is stationary if $V(0)$ has a normal distribution with mean 0 and variance $\sigma^2/(2mf)$.

At another extreme are absorbing processes. An example is the Markov process describing Peter's fortune during the game of gambler's ruin. The process is absorbed whenever either Peter or Paul is ruined. Questions of interest involve the probability of being absorbed in one state rather than another and the distribution of the time until absorption occurs. Some additional examples of stochastic processes follow.

## THE EHRENFEST MODEL OF DIFFUSION

The Ehrenfest model of diffusion (named after the Austrian Dutch physicist Paul Ehrenfest) was proposed in the early 1900s to illuminate the statistical interpretation of the second law of thermodynamics, that the entropy of a closed system can only increase. Suppose $N$ molecules of a gas are in a rectangular container divided into two equal parts by a permeable membrane. The state of the system at time $t$ is $X(t)$, the number of molecules on the left-hand side of the membrane. At each time $t = 1, 2, \ldots$ a molecule is chosen at random (i.e., each molecule has probability $1/N$ to be chosen) and is moved from its present location to the other side of the membrane. Hence, the system evolves according to the transition probability $p(i, j) = P\{X(t + 1) = j | X(t) = i\}$, where

$$p(i, i+1) = 1 - \frac{i}{N}, \qquad p(i, i-1) = \frac{i}{N},$$

$$p(i, j) = 0 \quad \text{for} \quad j \neq i+1, i-1.$$

The long-run behaviour of the Ehrenfest process can be inferred from general theorems about Markov processes in discrete time with discrete state space and stationary transition probabilities. Let $T(j)$ denote the first time $t \geq 1$ such that $X(t) = j$ and set $T(j) = \infty$ if $X(t) \neq j$ for all $t$. Assume that for all states $i$ and $j$ it is possible for the process to go from $i$ to $j$ in some number of steps, i.e., $P\{T(j) < \infty | X(0) = i\} > 0$. If the equations

$$Q(j) = \sum_i Q(i) p(i, j) \qquad (19)$$

have a solution $Q(j)$ that is a probability distribution, i.e., $Q(j) \geq 0$, and $\Sigma Q(j) = 1$, then that solution is unique and is the stationary distribution of the process. Moreover, $Q(j) = 1/E\{T(j) | X(0) = j\}$. For any initial state $j$, the proportion of time $t$ that $X(t) = i$ converges with probability 1 to $Q(i)$.

For the special case of the Ehrenfest process, assume that $N$ is large and $X(0) = 0$. According to the deterministic prediction of the second law of thermodynamics, the entropy of this system can only increase, which means that

$X(t)$ will steadily increase until half the molecules are on each side of the membrane. Indeed, according to the stochastic model described earlier, there is overwhelming probability that $X(t)$ does increase initially. However, because of random fluctuations, the system occasionally moves from configurations having large entropy to those of smaller entropy and eventually even returns to its starting state, in defiance of the second law of thermodynamics.

The accepted resolution of this contradiction is that the length of time such a system must operate so an observable decrease of entropy may occur is so enormously long that a decrease could never be verified experimentally. To consider only the most extreme case, let $T$ denote the first time $t \geq 1$ at which $X(t) = 0$ (i.e., the time of first return to the starting configuration having all molecules on the right-hand side of the membrane). It can be verified by substitution in equation (18) that the stationary distribution of the Ehrenfest model is the binomial distribution

$$ Q(j) = \binom{n}{j} 2^{-N}, $$

and hence $E(T) = 2^{N}$. For example, if $N$ is only 100 and transitions occur at the rate of $10^{6}$ per second, then $E(T)$ is of the order of $10^{15}$ years. Hence, on the macroscopic scale, on which experimental measurements can be made, the second law of thermodynamics holds.

## The Symmetric Random Walk

A Markov process that behaves in quite different and surprising ways is the symmetric random walk. A particle occupies a point with integer coordinates in $d$-dimensional Euclidean space. At each time $t = 1, 2, \ldots$ it moves from its present location to one of its $2d$ nearest neighbours with equal probabilities $1/(2d)$, independently of its past moves. For $d = 1$ this corresponds to moving a step to the right or left according to the outcome of tossing a fair coin. It may be shown that for $d = 1$ or $2$ the particle returns with probability $1$ to its initial position and hence to every possible position infinitely many times, if the random walk continues indefinitely. In three or more dimensions, at any time $t$ the number of possible steps that increase the distance of the particle from the origin is much larger than the number decreasing the distance, with the result that the particle eventually moves away from the origin and never returns. Even in one or two dimensions, although the particle eventually returns to its initial position, the expected waiting time until it returns is infinite, there is no stationary distribution, and the proportion of time the particle spends in any state converges to 0!

## QUEUING MODELS

The simplest service system is a single-server queue, where customers arrive, wait their turn, are served by a single server, and depart. Related stochastic processes are the waiting time of the $n$th customer and the number of customers in the queue at time $t$. For example, suppose that customers arrive at times $0 = T_0 < T_1 < T_2 < \cdots$ and wait in a queue until their turn. Let $V_n$ denote the service time required by the $n$th customer, $n = 0, 1, 2,...$, and set $U_n = T_n - T_{n-1}$. The waiting time, $W_n$, of the $n$th customer satisfies the relation $W_0 = 0$ and, for $n \geq 1$, $W_n = \max(0, W_{n-1} + V_{n-1} - U_n)$. To see this, observe that the $n$th customer must wait for the same length of time as the $(n - 1)$th customer plus the service time of the $(n - 1)$th customer minus the time between the arrival of the $(n - 1)$th and $n$th customer, during which the $(n - 1)$th customer is already waiting but the $n$th customer is not. An exception occurs if this quantity is negative, and then the waiting time of the $n$th customer is 0. Various assumptions can be made about the input and service mechanisms. One possibility is that customers arrive according to a Poisson process and their service times are independent, identically distributed random variables that are also independent of the arrival process. Then, in terms of $Y_n = V_{n-1} - U_n$, which are independent, identically distributed random variables, the recursive relation defining $W_n$ becomes $W_n = \max(0, W_{n-1} + Y_n)$. This process is a Markov process. It is often called a random walk with reflecting barrier at 0, because it behaves like a random walk whenever it is positive and is pushed up to be equal to 0 whenever it tries to become negative. Quantities of interest are the mean and variance of the waiting time of the $n$th customer and, because these are difficult to determine exactly, the mean and variance of the stationary distribution. More realistic queuing models try to accommodate systems with

*In the single-server queue, as depicted by patients waiting for a vaccine, customers arrive, wait their turn, are served by a single server, and depart.*
Andrew Caballero-Reynolds/Getty Images

several servers and different classes of customers, who are served according to certain priorities. In most cases, it is impossible to give a mathematical analysis of the system, which must be simulated on a computer in order to obtain numerical results. The insights gained from theoretical analysis of simple cases can be helpful in performing these simulations. Queuing theory had its origins in attempts to understand traffic in telephone systems. Present-day research is stimulated, among other things, by problems associated with multiple-user computer systems.

Reflecting barriers arise in other problems as well. For example, if $B(t)$ denotes Brownian motion, then $X(t) = B(t) + ct$ is called Brownian motion with drift $c$. This model is appropriate for Brownian motion of a particle under the influence of a constant force field such as gravity. One can add a reflecting barrier at 0 to account for reflections of the Brownian particle off the bottom of its container. The result is a model for sedimentation, which for $c < 0$ in the steady state as $t \to \infty$ gives a statistical derivation of the law of pressure as a function of depth in an isothermal atmosphere. Just as ordinary Brownian motion can be obtained as the limit of a rescaled random walk as the number of steps becomes large and the size of individual steps small, Brownian motion with a reflecting barrier at 0 can be obtained as the limit of a rescaled random walk with reflection at 0. In this way, Brownian motion with a reflecting barrier plays a role in the analysis of queuing systems. In fact, in modern probability theory one of the most important uses of Brownian motion and other diffusion processes is as approximations to more complicated stochastic processes. The exact mathematical description of these approximations gives remarkable generalizations of the central limit theorem from sequences of random variables to sequences of random functions.

## INSURANCE RISK THEORY

The ruin problem of insurance risk theory is closely related to the problem of gambler's ruin described earlier and, rather surprisingly, to the single-server queue as well. Suppose the amount of capital at time $t$ in one portfolio of an insurance company is denoted by $X(t)$. Initially $X(0) = x > 0$. During each unit of time, the portfolio receives an amount $c > 0$ in premiums. At random times claims are made against the insurance company, which must pay the amount $V_n > 0$ to settle the $n$th claim. If $N(t)$ denotes the number of claims made in time $t$, then

$$X(t) = x + ct - \sum_1^{N(t)} V_n,$$

provided that this quantity has been positive at all earlier times $s < t$. At the first time $X(t)$ becomes negative, however, the portfolio is ruined. A principal problem of insurance risk theory is to find the probability of ultimate ruin. If one imagines that the problem of gambler's ruin is modified so that Peter's opponent has an infinite amount of capital and can never be ruined, then the probability that Peter is ultimately ruined is similar to the ruin probability of insurance risk theory. In fact, with the artificial assumptions that (i) $c = 1$, (ii) time proceeds by discrete units, say $t = 1, 2,...$, (iii) $V_n$ is identically equal to 2 for all $n$, and (iv) at each time $t$ a claim occurs with probability $p$ or does not occur with probability $q$ independently of what occurs at other times, then the process $X(t)$ is the same stochastic process as Peter's fortune, which is absorbed if it ever reaches the state 0. The probability of Peter's ultimate ruin against an infinitely rich adversary is easily obtained by taking the limit of equation

(6) as $m \to \infty$. The answer is $(q/p)^x$ if $p > q$ (i.e., the game is favourable to Peter) and $1$ if $p \le q$. More interesting assumptions for the insurance risk problem are that the number of claims $N(t)$ is a Poisson process and the sizes of the claims $V_1$, $V_2$,... are independent, identically distributed positive random variables. Rather surprisingly, under these assumptions the probability of ultimate ruin as a function of the initial fortune $x$ is exactly the same as the stationary probability that the waiting time in the single-server queue with Poisson input exceeds $x$. Unfortunately, neither problem is easy to solve exactly, however, there is an excellent approximate solution originally derived by the Swedish mathematician Harald Cramér.

## MARTINGALE THEORY

As a final example, it seems appropriate to mention one of the dominant ideas of modern probability theory, which at the same time springs directly from the relation of probability to games of chance. Suppose that $X_1$, $X_2$,... is any stochastic process and, for each $n = 0, 1,...,$ $f_n = f_n(X_1,..., X_n)$ is a (Borel-measurable) function of the indicated observations. The new stochastic process $f_n$ is called a martingale if $E(f_n|X_1,..., X_{n-1}) = f_{n-1}$ for every value of $n > 0$ and all values of $X_1,..., X_{n-1}$. If the sequence of $X$s are outcomes in successive trials of a game of chance and $f_n$ is the fortune of a gambler after the $n$th trial, then the martingale condition says that the game is absolutely fair in the sense that, no matter what the past history of the game, the gambler's conditional expected fortune after one more trial is exactly equal to his present fortune. For example, let $X_0 = x$, and for $n \ge 1$ let $X_n$ equal $1$ or $-1$ according as a coin having probability $p$ of heads and $q = 1 - p$ of tails turns up heads or tails on the $n$th toss.

Let $S_n = X_0 + \cdots + X_n$. Then $f_n = S_n - n(p - q)$ and $f_n = (q/p)^{S_n}$ are martingales. One basic result of martingale theory is that, if the gambler is free to quit the game at any time using any strategy whatsoever, provided only that this strategy does not foresee the future, then the game remains fair. This means that, if $N$ denotes the stopping time at which the gambler's strategy tells him to quit the game, so that his final fortune is $f_N$, then

$$E(f_N | f_0) = f_0 \qquad (19)$$

Strictly speaking, this result is not true without some additional conditions that must be verified for any particular application. To see how efficiently it works, consider once again the problem of gambler's ruin and let $N$ be the first value of $n$ such that $S_n = 0$ or $m$. For example, $N$ denotes the random time at which ruin first occurs and the game ends. In the case $p = 1/2$, application of

$$E(f_N | f_0) = f_0 \qquad (19)$$

to the martingale $f_n = S_n$, together with the observation that $f_N =$ either $0$ or $m$, yields the equalities $x = f_0 = E(f_N | f_0 = x) = m[1 - Q(x)]$, which can be immediately solved to give the answer in equation (6)

$$Q(x) = \frac{\left(\frac{q}{p}\right)^x - \left(\frac{q}{p}\right)^m}{1 - \left(\frac{q}{p}\right)^m} \qquad \left(p \neq \frac{1}{2}\right)$$

$$\qquad (6)$$

$$= 1 - \frac{x}{m} \qquad \left(p = \frac{1}{2}\right).$$

For $p \neq 1/2$, one uses the martingale $f_n = (q/p)^{S_n}$ and similar reasoning to obtain

$$\left(\frac{q}{p}\right)^x = E(f_N \mid f_0 = x) = 1 Q(x) + \left(\frac{q}{p}\right)^m [1 - Q(x)],$$

from which the first equation in (6)

$$Q(x) = \frac{\left(\frac{q}{p}\right)^x - \left(\frac{q}{p}\right)^m}{1 - \left(\frac{q}{p}\right)^m} \qquad \left(p \neq \frac{1}{2}\right)$$

$$= 1 - \frac{x}{m} \qquad \left(p = \frac{1}{2}\right)$$

(6)

easily follows. The expected duration of the game is obtained by a similar argument.

A particularly beautiful and important result is the martingale convergence theorem, which implies that a nonnegative martingale converges with probability 1 as $n \to \infty$. This means that if a gambler's successive fortunes form a (nonnegative) martingale, then they cannot continue to fluctuate indefinitely but must approach some limiting value.

Basic martingale theory and many of its applications were developed by the American mathematician Joseph Leo Doob during the 1940s and '50s following some earlier results due to Paul Lévy. Subsequently, it has become one of the most powerful tools available to study stochastic processes.

# CHAPTER 3
## STATISTICS

Statistics is the science of collecting, analyzing, presenting, and interpreting data. Governmental needs for census data as well as information about a variety of economic activities provided much of the early impetus for the field of statistics. Currently, the need to turn the large amounts of data available in many applied fields into useful information has stimulated both theoretical and practical developments in statistics.

Data are the facts and figures that are collected, analyzed, and summarized for presentation and interpretation. Data may be classified as either quantitative or qualitative. Quantitative data measure either how much or how many of something, and qualitative data provide labels, or names, for categories of like items. For example, suppose that a particular study is interested in characteristics such as age, gender, marital status, and annual income for a sample of 100 individuals. These characteristics would be called the variables of the study, and data values for each of the variables would be associated with each individual. Thus, the data values of 28, male, single, and $30,000 would be recorded for a 28-year-old single male with an annual income of $30,000. With 100 individuals and 4 variables, the data set would have $100 \times 4 = 400$ items. In this example, age and annual income are quantitative variables; the corresponding data values indicate how many years and how much money for each individual. Gender and marital status are qualitative variables. The labels male and female provide the qualitative data for gender, and the labels single, married, divorced, and widowed indicate marital status.

Sample survey methods are used to collect data from observational studies, and experimental design methods are used to collect data from experimental studies. The area of descriptive statistics is concerned primarily with methods of presenting and interpreting data using graphs, tables, and numerical summaries. Whenever statisticians use data from a sample (i.e., a subset of the population) to make statements about a population, they are performing statistical inference. Estimation and hypothesis testing are procedures used to make statistical inferences. Fields such as health care, biology, chemistry, physics, education, engineering, business, and economics make extensive use of statistical inference.

Methods of probability were developed initially for the analysis of gambling games. Probability plays a key role in statistical inference. It is used to provide measures of the quality and precision of the inferences. Many methods of statistical inference are described in this chapter. Some are used primarily for single-variable studies, whereas others, such as regression and correlation analysis, are used to make inferences about relationships among two or more variables.

## DESCRIPTIVE STATISTICS

Descriptive statistics are tabular, graphical, and numerical summaries of data. The purpose of descriptive statistics is to facilitate the presentation and interpretation of data. Most statistical presentations appearing in newspapers and magazines are descriptive in nature. Univariate methods of descriptive statistics use data to enhance the understanding of a single variable. Multivariate methods focus on using statistics to understand the relationships among two or more variables. To illustrate methods of descriptive statistics, the previous example in which data were collected on the age, gender, marital status, and annual income of 100 individuals will be examined.

## TABULAR METHODS

The most commonly used tabular summary of data for a single variable is a frequency distribution. A frequency distribution shows the number of data values in each of several nonoverlapping classes. Another tabular summary, called a relative frequency distribution, shows the fraction, or percentage, of data values in each class. The most common tabular summary of data for two variables is a cross tabulation, a two-variable analogue of a frequency distribution.

For a qualitative variable, a frequency distribution shows the number of data values in each qualitative category. For instance, the variable gender has two categories: male and female. Thus, a frequency distribution for gender would have two nonoverlapping classes to show the number of males and females. A relative frequency distribution for this variable would show the fraction of individuals that are male and the fraction of individuals that are female.

Constructing a frequency distribution for a quantitative variable requires more care in defining the classes and the division points between adjacent classes. For instance, if the age data of the example above ranged from 22 to 78 years, then the following six nonoverlapping classes could be used: 20–29, 30–39, 40–49, 50–59, 60–69, and 70–79. A frequency distribution would show the number of data values in each of these classes, and a relative frequency distribution would show the fraction of data values in each.

A cross tabulation is a two-way table with the rows of the table representing the classes of one variable and the columns of the table representing the classes of another variable. To construct a cross tabulation using the variables gender and age, gender could be shown with two rows, male and female, and age could be shown with six columns corresponding to the age classes 20–29, 30–39, 40–49, 50–59, 60–69, and 70–79. The entry in each cell of the table would specify the number of data values with the gender given by the row heading and the age given by the column heading. Such a cross tabulation could help understand the relationship between gender and age.

## GRAPHICAL METHODS

Many graphical methods are available for describing data. A bar graph is a graphical device for depicting qualitative data that have been summarized in a frequency distribution. Labels for the categories of the qualitative variable are shown on the horizontal axis of the graph. A bar

*If an independent variable is not expressly temporal, a bar graph may be used to show discrete numerical quantities in relation to each other.* Brand New Images/Stone/Getty Images

above each label is constructed such that the height of each bar is proportional to the number of data values in the category. A pie chart is another graphical device for summarizing qualitative data. The size of each slice of the pie is proportional to the number of data values in the corresponding class.

A histogram is the most common graphical presentation of quantitative data that have been summarized in a frequency distribution. The values of the quantitative variable are shown on the horizontal axis. A rectangle is drawn above each class such that the base of the rectangle is equal to the width of the class interval and its height is proportional to the number of data values in the class.

## Numerical Measures

A variety of numerical measures are used to summarize data. The proportion, or percentage, of data values in each category is the primary numerical measure for qualitative data. The mean, median, mode, percentiles, range, variance, and standard deviation are the most commonly used numerical measures for quantitative data. The mean, often called the average, is computed by adding all the data values for a variable and dividing the sum by the number of data values. The mean is a measure of the central location for the data. The median is another measure of central location that, unlike the mean, is not affected by extremely large or extremely small data values. When determining the median, the data values are first ranked in order from the smallest value to the largest value. If there is an odd number of data values, then the median is the middle value. If there is an even number of data values, then the median is the average of the two middle values. The third measure of central tendency is the mode, the data value that occurs with greatest frequency.

Percentiles provide an indication of how the data values are spread over the interval from the smallest value to the largest value. Approximately $p$ percent of the data values fall below the $p$th percentile, and roughly $100 - p$ percent of the data values are above the $p$th percentile. Percentiles are reported, for example, on most standardized tests. Quartiles divide the data values into four parts; the first quartile is the 25th percentile, the second quartile is the 50th percentile (also the median), and the third quartile is the 75th percentile.

The range, the difference between the largest value and the smallest value, is the simplest measure of variability in the data. The range is determined by only the two extreme data values. The variance ($s^2$) and the standard deviation ($s$), however, are measures of variability that are based on all the data and are more commonly used. Equation 1 shows the formula for computing the variance of a sample consisting of $n$ items. In applying equation 1, the deviation (difference) of each data value from the sample mean is computed and squared. The squared deviations are then summed and divided by $n - 1$ to provide the sample variance.

$$s^2 = \frac{\sum_{i=1}^{n} \left(x_i - \bar{x}\right)^2}{n - 1} \qquad (1)$$

The standard deviation is the square root of the variance. Because the unit of measure for the standard deviation is the same as the unit of measure for the data, many individuals prefer to use the standard deviation as the descriptive measure of variability.

OUTLIERS

Sometimes data for a variable will include one or more values that appear unusually large or small and out of place when compared with the other data values. These values are known as outliers and often have been erroneously included in the data set. Experienced statisticians take steps to identify outliers and then review each one carefully for accuracy and the appropriateness of its inclusion in the data set. If an error has been made, then corrective action, such as rejecting the data value in question, can be taken. The mean and standard deviation are used to identify outliers. A $z$-score can be computed for each data value. With $x$ representing the data value, $x^-$ the sample mean, and $s$ the sample standard deviation, the $z$-score is given by $z = (x - x^-)/s$. The $z$-score represents the relative position of the data value by indicating the number of standard deviations it is from the mean. A rule of thumb is that any value with a $z$-score less than -3 or greater than +3 should be considered an outlier.

## EXPLORATORY DATA ANALYSIS

Exploratory data analysis provides a variety of tools for quickly summarizing and gaining insight about a set of data. Two such methods are the five-number summary and the box plot. A five-number summary simply consists of the smallest data value, the first quartile, the median, the third quartile, and the largest data value. A box plot is a graphical device based on a five-number summary. A rectangle (i.e., the box) is drawn with the ends of the rectangle located at the first and third quartiles. The rectangle represents the middle 50 percent of the data. A vertical line is drawn in the rectangle to locate the median. Finally lines, called *whiskers*, extend from one end of the rectangle to the smallest data value and from the other end of the rectangle to the largest data value. If outliers are present, then the whiskers generally extend only to the smallest and largest data values that are not outliers.

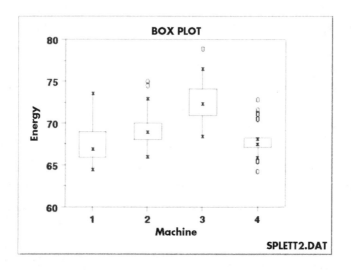

*Based on a five-number summary, a box plot quickly summarizes and provides insight about a set of data.* NIST/SEMATECH e-Handbook of Statistical Methods (http://www.itl.nist.gov/div898/handbook/eda/section3/boxplot.htm). Rendered by Rosen Educational Services

Dots, or asterisks, are then placed outside the whiskers to denote the presence of outliers.

## PROBABILITY

Probability is a subject that deals with uncertainty. In everyday terminology, probability can be thought of as a numerical measure of the likelihood that a particular event will occur. Probability values are assigned on a scale from 0 to 1, with values near 0 indicating that an event is unlikely to occur and those near 1 indicating that an event is likely to take place. A probability of 0.50 means that an event is equally likely to occur as not to occur.

## EVENTS AND THEIR PROBABILITIES

Oftentimes probabilities need to be computed for related events. For instance, advertisements are developed for the purpose of increasing sales of a product. If seeing the advertisement increases the probability of a person buying the product, then the events "seeing the advertisement" and "buying the product" are said to be dependent. If two events are independent, then the occurrence of one event does not affect the probability of the other event taking place. When two or more events are independent, the probability of their joint occurrence is the product of their individual probabilities. Two events are said to be mutually exclusive if the occurrence of one event means that the other event cannot occur. In this case, when one event takes place, the probability of the other event occurring is zero.

## RANDOM VARIABLES AND PROBABILITY DISTRIBUTIONS

A random variable is a numerical description of the outcome of a statistical experiment. A random variable that may assume only a finite number or an infinite sequence of values is said to be discrete. One that may assume any value in some interval on the real number line is said to be continuous. For instance, a random variable representing the number of automobiles sold at a particular dealership on one day would be discrete, while a random variable representing the weight of a person in kilograms (or pounds) would be continuous.

The probability distribution for a random variable describes how the probabilities are distributed over the values of the random variable. For a discrete random variable, $x$, the probability distribution is defined by a probability mass function, denoted by $f(x)$. This function provides the probability for each value of the random variable. In the development of the probability function for a discrete random variable, two conditions must be satisfied: (1) $f(x)$ must be nonnegative for each value of the random variable, and (2) the sum of the probabilities for each value of the random variable must equal one.

A continuous random variable may assume any value in an interval on the real number line or in a collection of intervals. Because there is an infinite number of values in any interval, it is not meaningful to talk about the probability that the random variable will take on a specific value. Instead, the probability that a continuous random variable will lie within a given interval is considered.

In the continuous case, the counterpart of the probability mass function is the probability density function, also denoted by $f(x)$. For a continuous random variable, the probability density function provides the height or value of the function at any particular value of $x$. It does not directly give the probability of the random variable taking on a specific value. However, the area under the graph of $f(x)$ corresponding to some interval, obtained by computing the integral of $f(x)$ over that interval, provides the probability that the variable will take on a value within that interval. A probability density function must satisfy two requirements: (1) $f(x)$ must be nonnegative for each value of the random variable, and (2) the integral over all values of the random variable must equal one.

The expected value, or mean, of a random variable— denoted by $E(x)$ or $\mu$—is a weighted average of the values the random variable may assume. In the discrete case the weights are given by the probability mass function, and in the continuous case the weights are given by the probability density function. The formulas for computing the expected values of discrete and continuous random variables are given by equations (2) and (3), respectively.

$$E(x) = \Sigma x f(x) \qquad (2)$$

$$E(x) = \int x f(x) dx \qquad (3)$$

The variance of a random variable, denoted by $Var(x)$ or $\sigma^2$, is a weighted average of the squared deviations from the mean. In the discrete case the weights are given by the probability mass function, and in the continuous case the weights are given by the probability density function. The formulas for computing the variances of discrete and continuous random variables are given by equations (4) and (5), respectively. The standard deviation, denoted $\sigma$, is the positive square root of the variance. Because the standard deviation is measured in the same units as the random variable and the variance is measured in squared units, the standard deviation is often the preferred measure.

$$Var(x) = \sigma^2 = \Sigma(x - \mu)^2 f(x) \qquad (4)$$

$$Var(x) = \sigma^2 = \int(x - \mu)^2 f(x) dx \qquad (5)$$

## SPECIAL PROBABILITY DISTRIBUTIONS

### THE BINOMIAL DISTRIBUTION

Two of the most widely used discrete probability distributions are the binomial and Poisson. The binomial probability mass function in equation (6) provides the probability that $x$ successes will occur in $n$ trials of a binomial experiment.

$$f(x) = \left(\frac{n}{x}\right)p^x(1-p)^{(n-x)} \qquad (6)$$

A binomial experiment has four properties: (1) It consists of a sequence of $n$ identical trials; (2) two outcomes, success or failure, are possible on each trial; (3) the probability of success on any trial, denoted $p$, does not change from trial to trial; and (4) the trials are independent. For example, suppose that it is known that 10 percent of the owners of two-year old automobiles have had problems with their automobile's electrical system. To compute the probability of finding exactly 2 owners who have had electrical system problems out of a group of 10 owners, the binomial probability mass function can be used by setting $n$ = 10, $x$ = 2, and $p$ = 0.1 in equation (6). For this case the probability is 0.1937.

## The Poisson Distribution

The Poisson probability distribution is often used as a model of the number of arrivals at a facility within a given period of time. For instance, a random variable might be defined as the number of telephone calls coming into an airline reservation system during a period of 15 minutes. If the mean number of arrivals during a 15-minute interval is known, then the Poisson probability mass function can be used to compute the probability of $x$ arrivals.

$$f(x) = \frac{\mu^x e^{-\mu}}{x!} \qquad (7)$$

For example, suppose that the mean number of calls arriving in a 15-minute period is 10. To compute the probability that 5 calls come in within the next 15 minutes, $\mu$ = 10 and $x$ = 5 are substituted in equation (7), giving a probability of 0.0378.

## THE NORMAL DISTRIBUTION

The most widely used continuous probability distribution in statistics is the normal probability distribution. Like all normal distribution graphs, it is a bell-shaped curve. Probabilities for the normal probability distribution can be computed using statistical tables for the standard normal probability distribution, which is a normal probability distribution with a mean of zero and a standard deviation of one. A simple mathematical formula is used to convert any value from a normal probability distribution with mean $\mu$ and a standard deviation $\sigma$ into a corresponding value for a standard normal distribution. The tables for the standard normal distribution are then used to compute the appropriate probabilities.

There are many other discrete and continuous probability distributions. Other widely used discrete distributions include the geometric, the hypergeometric, and the negative binomial. Other commonly used continuous distributions include the uniform, exponential, gamma, chi-square, beta, $t$, and F.

## ESTIMATION

It is often of interest to learn about the characteristics of a large group of elements such as individuals, households, buildings, products, parts, customers, and so on. All the elements of interest in a particular study form the population. Because of time, cost, and other considerations, data often cannot be collected from every element of the population. In such cases, a subset of the population, called a sample, is used to provide the data. Data from the sample are then used to develop estimates of the characteristics of the larger population. The process of using a sample to make inferences about a population is called statistical inference.

Characteristics such as the population mean, the population variance, and the population proportion are called parameters of the population. Characteristics of the sample such as the sample mean, the sample variance, and the sample proportion are called sample statistics. There are two types of estimates: point and interval. A point estimate is a value of a sample statistic that is used as a single estimate of a population parameter. No statements are made about the quality or precision of a point estimate. Statisticians prefer interval estimates because interval estimates are accompanied by a statement concerning the degree of confidence that the interval contains the population parameter being estimated. Interval estimates of population parameters are called confidence intervals.

## SAMPLING AND SAMPLING DISTRIBUTIONS

It should be noted here that the methods of statistical inference, and estimation in particular, are based on the notion that a probability sample has been taken. The key characteristic of a probability sample is that each element in the population has a known probability of being included in the sample. The most fundamental type is a simple random sample.

For a population of size $N$, a simple random sample is a sample selected such that each possible sample of size $n$ has the same probability of being selected. Choosing the elements from the population one at a time so that each element has the same probability of being selected will provide a simple random sample. Tables of random numbers, or computer-generated random numbers, can be used to guarantee that each element has the same probability of being selected.

A sampling distribution is a probability distribution for a sample statistic. Knowledge of the sampling distribution is necessary for the construction of an interval estimate for a population parameter, which is why a probability sample is needed. Without a probability sample, the sampling distribution cannot be determined and an interval estimate of a parameter cannot be constructed.

## ESTIMATION OF A POPULATION MEAN

The most fundamental point and interval estimation process involves the estimation of a population mean. Suppose it is of interest to estimate the population mean, $\mu$, for a quantitative variable. Data collected from a simple random sample can be used to compute the sample mean, $x^-$, where the value of $x^-$ provides a point estimate of $\mu$.

When the sample mean is used as a point estimate of the population mean, some error can be expected owing to the fact that a sample, or subset of the population, is used to compute the point estimate. The absolute value of the difference between the sample mean, $x^-$, and the population mean, $\mu$, written $|x^- - \mu|$, is called the sampling error. Interval estimation incorporates a probability statement about the magnitude of the sampling error. The sampling distribution of $x^-$ provides the basis for such a statement.

Statisticians have shown that the mean of the sampling distribution of $x^-$ is equal to the population mean, $\mu$, and that the standard deviation is given by $\sigma/\sqrt{n}$, where $\sigma$ is the population standard deviation. The standard deviation of a sampling distribution is called the standard error. For large sample sizes, the central limit theorem indicates that the sampling distribution of $x^-$ can be approximated by a normal probability distribution. As a matter of practice, statisticians usually consider samples of size 30 or more to be large.

In the large-sample case, a 95% confidence interval estimate for the population mean is given by $x^- \pm 1.96\sigma/\sqrt{n}$.

When the population standard deviation, $\sigma$, is unknown, the sample standard deviation is used to estimate $\sigma$ in the confidence interval formula. The quantity $1.96\sigma/\sqrt{n}$ is often called the margin of error for the estimate. The quantity $\sigma/\sqrt{n}$ is the standard error, and $1.96$ is the number of standard errors from the mean necessary to include 95% of the values in a normal distribution. The interpretation of a 95% confidence interval is that 95% of the intervals constructed in this manner will contain the population mean. Thus, any interval computed in this manner has a 95% confidence of containing the population mean. By changing the constant from $1.96$ to $1.645$, a 90% confidence interval can be obtained. It should be noted from the formula for an interval estimate that a 90% confidence interval is narrower than a 95% confidence interval and as such has a slightly smaller confidence of including the population mean. Lower levels of confidence lead to even more narrow intervals. In practice, a 95% confidence interval is the most widely used.

Owing to the presence of the $n^{1/2}$ term in the formula for an interval estimate, the sample size affects the margin of error. Larger sample sizes lead to smaller margins of error. This observation forms the basis for procedures used to select the sample size. Sample sizes can be chosen such that the confidence interval satisfies any desired requirements about the size of the margin of error.

The procedure just described for developing interval estimates of a population mean is based on the use of a large sample. In the small-sample case (i.e., where the sample size $n$ is less than 30) the $t$ distribution is used when specifying the margin of error and constructing a confidence interval estimate. For example, at a 95% level of confidence, a value from the $t$ distribution, determined by the value of $n$, would replace the $1.96$ value obtained from the normal distribution. The $t$ values will always be larger, leading to wider confidence intervals, but, as the sample size becomes larger, the $t$ values get closer to the corresponding values from a normal distribution. With a sample size of 25, the $t$ value used would be 2.064, as compared with the normal probability distribution value of 1.96 in the large-sample case.

## ESTIMATION OF OTHER PARAMETERS

For qualitative variables, the population proportion is a parameter of interest. A point estimate of the population proportion is given by the sample proportion. With knowledge of the sampling distribution of the sample proportion, an interval estimate of a population proportion is obtained in much the same fashion as for a population mean. Point and interval estimation procedures such as these can be applied to other population parameters as well. For instance, interval estimation of a population variance, standard deviation, and total can be required in other applications.

## ESTIMATION PROCEDURES FOR TWO POPULATIONS

The estimation procedures can be extended to two populations for comparative studies. For example, suppose a study is being conducted to determine differences between the salaries paid to a population of men and a population of women. Two independent simple random samples, one from the population of men and one from the population of women, would provide two sample means, $\bar{x}_1$ and $\bar{x}_2$. The difference between the two sample means, $\bar{x}_1 - \bar{x}_2$, would be used as a point estimate of the difference between the two population means. The sampling distribution of $\bar{x}_1 - \bar{x}_2$ would provide the basis for a confidence interval estimate of the difference between the two population means. For qualitative variables, point and interval estimates of the difference between population proportions can be constructed by considering the difference between sample proportions.

## HYPOTHESIS TESTING

Hypothesis testing is a form of statistical inference that uses data from a sample to draw conclusions about a population parameter or a population probability distribution. First, a tentative assumption is made about the parameter or distribution. This assumption is called the null hypothesis and is denoted by $H_o$. An alternative hypothesis (denoted $H_a$), which is the opposite of what is stated in the null hypothesis, is then defined. The hypothesis-testing procedure involves using sample data to determine whether or not $H_o$ can be rejected. If $H_o$ is rejected, then the statistical conclusion is that the alternative hypothesis $H_a$ is true.

For example, assume that a radio station selects the music it plays based on the assumption that the average age of its listening audience is 30 years. To determine whether this assumption is valid, a hypothesis test could be conducted with the null hypothesis given as $H_o$: $\mu = 30$ and the alternative hypothesis given as $H_a$: $\mu \neq 30$. Based on a sample of individuals from the listening audience, the sample mean age, $x^-$, can be computed and used to determine whether there is sufficient statistical evidence to reject $H_o$. Conceptually, a value of the sample mean that is "close" to 30 is consistent with the null hypothesis, while a value of the sample mean that is "not close" to 30 provides support for the alternative hypothesis. What is considered "close" and "not close" is determined by using the sampling distribution of $x^-$.

Ideally, the hypothesis-testing procedure leads to the acceptance of $H_o$ when $H_o$ is true and the rejection of $H_o$

when $H_0$ is false. Unfortunately, because hypothesis tests are based on sample information, the possibility of errors must be considered. A type I error corresponds to rejecting $H_0$ when $H_0$ is actually true, and a type II error corresponds to accepting $H_0$ when $H_0$ is false. The probability of making a type I error is denoted by α, and the probability of making a type II error is denoted by β.

In using the hypothesis-testing procedure to determine if the null hypothesis should be rejected, the person

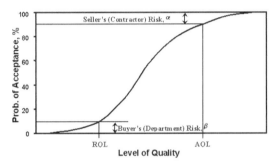

Figure 3 - Typical Operating Characteristic (OC) Curve for an Accept/Reject Acceptance

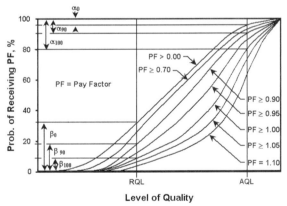

Figure 4 - Typical Operating Characteristic (OC) Curves for an Acceptance Plan with Pay Adjustments

*Operating-characacteristic curves, like these from a U.S. federal government report, can be constructed to show how changes in sample size can affect the probability of a type II error.* U.S. Dept. of Transportation Federal Highway Administration Technical Advisory (http://www.fhwa.dot.gov/Construction/t61203.cfm). Rendered by Rosen Educational Services

conducting the hypothesis test specifies the maximum allowable probability of making a type I error, called the level of significance for the test. Common choices for the level of significance are $\alpha = 0.05$ and $\alpha = 0.01$. Although most applications of hypothesis testing control the probability of making a type I error, they do not always control the probability of making a type II error. A graph known as an operating-characteristic curve can be constructed to show how changes in the sample size affect the probability of making a type II error.

A concept known as the $p$-value provides a convenient basis for drawing conclusions in hypothesis-testing applications. The $p$-value is a measure of how likely the sample results are, assuming the null hypothesis is true; the smaller the $p$-value, the less likely the sample results. If the $p$-value is less than $\alpha$, then the null hypothesis can be rejected. Otherwise, the null hypothesis cannot be rejected. The $p$-value is often called the observed level of significance for the test.

A hypothesis test can be performed on parameters of one or more populations as well as in a variety of other situations. In each instance, the process begins with the formulation of null and alternative hypotheses about the population. In addition to the population mean, hypothesis-testing procedures are available for population parameters such as proportions, variances, standard deviations, and medians.

Hypothesis tests are also conducted in regression and correlation analysis to determine if the regression relationship and the correlation coefficient are statistically significant. A goodness-of-fit test refers to a hypothesis test in which the null hypothesis is that the population has a specific probability distribution, such as a normal probability distribution. Nonparametric statistical methods also involve a variety of hypothesis-testing procedures.

# BAYESIAN METHODS

The methods of statistical inference previously described are often referred to as classical methods. Bayesian methods (named after the English mathematician Thomas Bayes) provide alternatives that allow one to combine prior information about a population parameter with information contained in a sample to guide the statistical inference process. A prior probability distribution for a parameter of interest is specified first. Sample information is then obtained and combined through an application of Bayes's theorem to provide a posterior probability distribution for the parameter. The posterior distribution provides the basis for statistical inferences concerning the parameter.

A key, and somewhat controversial, feature of Bayesian methods is the notion of a probability distribution for a population parameter. According to classical statistics, parameters are constants and cannot be represented as random variables. Bayesian proponents argue that if a parameter value is unknown, then it makes sense to specify a probability distribution that describes the possible values for the parameter as well as their likelihood. The Bayesian approach permits the use of objective data or subjective opinion in specifying a prior distribution. With the Bayesian approach, different individuals might specify different prior distributions. Classical statisticians argue that for this reason Bayesian methods suffer from a lack of objectivity. Bayesian proponents argue that the classical methods of statistical inference have built-in subjectivity (through the choice of a sampling plan) and that the advantage of the Bayesian approach is that the subjectivity is made explicit.

Bayesian methods have been used extensively in statistical decision theory. In this context, Bayes's theorem provides a mechanism for combining a prior probability distribution for the states of nature with sample information to provide a revised (posterior) probability distribution about the states of nature. These posterior probabilities are then used to make better decisions.

# EXPERIMENTAL DESIGN

Data for statistical studies are obtained by conducting either experiments or surveys. Experimental design is the branch of statistics that deals with the design and analysis of experiments. The methods of experimental design are widely used in the fields of agriculture, medicine, biology, marketing research, and industrial production.

Variables of interest are identified in an experimental study. One or more of these variables, referred to as the factors of the study, are controlled so that data may be obtained about how the factors influence another variable referred to as the response variable, or simply the response. As a case in point, consider an experiment designed to determine the effect of three different exercise programs on the cholesterol level of patients with elevated cholesterol. Each patient is referred to as an experimental unit, the response variable is the cholesterol level of the patient at the completion of the program, and the exercise program is the factor whose effect on cholesterol level is being investigated. Each of the three exercise programs is referred to as a treatment.

Three of the more widely used experimental designs are the completely randomized design, the randomized block design, and the factorial design. In a completely randomized experimental design, the treatments are randomly assigned to the experimental units. For instance, applying this design method to the cholesterol level study, the three types of exercise program (treatment) would be randomly assigned to the experimental units (patients).

The use of a completely randomized design yields less precise results when factors not accounted for by the experimenter affect the response variable. Consider, for example, an experiment designed to study the effect of two different gasoline additives on the fuel efficiency, measured in miles per gallon (mpg), of full-size automobiles produced by three manufacturers. Suppose that 30 automobiles, 10 from each manufacturer, were available for the experiment. In a completely randomized design, the two gasoline additives (treatments) would be randomly assigned to the 30 automobiles, with each additive being assigned to 15 different cars. Suppose that manufacturer 1 has developed an engine that gives its full-size cars a higher fuel efficiency than those produced by manufacturers 2 and 3. A completely randomized design could, by chance, assign gasoline additive 1 to a larger proportion of cars from manufacturer 1. In such a case, gasoline additive 1 might be judged as more fuel efficient when in fact the difference observed is actually a result of the better engine design of automobiles produced by manufacturer 1. To prevent this from occurring, a statistician could design an experiment in which both gasoline additives are tested using five cars produced by each manufacturer. In this way, any effects caused by the manufacturer would not affect the test for significant differences resulting from the gasoline additive. In this revised experiment, each manufacturer is referred to as a block, and the experiment is called a randomized block design. In general, blocking is used to enable comparisons among the treatments to be made within blocks of homogeneous experimental units.

Factorial experiments are designed to draw conclusions about more than one factor, or variable. The term factorial is used to indicate that all possible combinations of the factors are considered. For instance, if there are two factors with $a$ levels for factor 1 and $b$ levels for factor 2, then the experiment will involve collecting data on *ab* treatment combinations. The factorial design can be extended to experiments involving more than two factors and experiments involving partial factorial designs.

## ANALYSIS OF VARIANCE AND SIGNIFICANCE TESTING

A computational procedure frequently used to analyze the data from an experimental study employs a statistical procedure known as the analysis of variance. For a single-factor experiment, this procedure uses a hypothesis test concerning equality of treatment means to determine if the factor has a statistically significant effect on the response variable. For experimental designs involving multiple factors, a test for the significance of each individual factor as well as interaction effects caused by one or more factors acting jointly can be made. Further discussion of the analysis of variance procedure is contained in the subsequent section.

## REGRESSION AND CORRELATION ANALYSIS

Regression analysis involves identifying the relationship between a dependent variable and one or more independent variables. A model of the relationship is hypothesized, and estimates of the parameter values are used to develop an estimated regression equation. Various tests are then employed to determine if the model is satisfactory. If the model is deemed satisfactory, then the estimated regression equation can be used to predict the value of the dependent variable given values for the independent variables.

### REGRESSION MODEL

In simple linear regression, the model used to describe the relationship between a single dependent variable $y$ and a single independent variable $x$ is $y = \beta_0 + \beta_1 x + \varepsilon$. $\beta_0$ and $\beta_1$ are referred to as the model parameters, and $\varepsilon$ is a probabilistic error term that accounts for the variability in $y$ that cannot be explained by the linear relationship with $x$. If the error term were not present, then the model would be deterministic. In that case, knowledge of the value of $x$ would be sufficient to determine the value of $y$.

In multiple regression analysis, the model for simple linear regression is extended to account for the relationship between the dependent variable $y$ and $p$ independent variables $x_1, x_2, \ldots, x_p$. The general form of the multiple regression model is $y = \beta_0 + \beta_1 x_1 + \beta_2 x_2 + \ldots + \beta_p x_p + \varepsilon$. The parameters of the model are the $\beta_0, \beta_1, \ldots, \beta_p$, and $\varepsilon$ is the error term.

## LEAST SQUARES METHOD

Either a simple or multiple regression model is initially posed as a hypothesis concerning the relationship among the dependent and independent variables. The least squares method is the most widely used procedure for developing estimates of the model parameters. For simple linear regression, the least squares estimates of the model parameters $\beta_0$ and $\beta_1$ are denoted $b_0$ and $b_1$. Using these estimates, an estimated regression equation is constructed: $\hat{y} = b_0 + b_1 x$. The graph of the estimated regression equation for simple linear regression is a straight line approximation to the relationship between $y$ and $x$.

As an illustration of regression analysis and the least squares method, suppose a university medical centre is investigating the relationship between stress and blood pressure. Assume that both a stress test score and a blood pressure reading have been recorded for a sample of 20 patients. The data can be shown graphically in a scatter diagram. Values of the independent variable, stress test score, are given on the horizontal axis, and values of the dependent variable, blood pressure, are shown on the vertical axis. The line passing through the data points is the graph of the estimated regression equation: $\hat{y}$ = 42.3 + 0.49$x$. The parameter estimates, $b_o$ = 42.3 and $b_1$ = 0.49, were obtained using the least squares method.

A primary use of the estimated regression equation is to predict the value of the dependent variable when values for the independent variables are given. For instance, given a patient with a stress test score of 60, the predicted blood pressure is 42.3 + 0.49(60) = 71.7. The values predicted by the estimated regression equation are the points on the line, and the actual blood pressure readings are represented by the points scattered about the line. The difference between the observed value of $y$ and the value of $y$ predicted by the estimated regression equation is called a residual. The least squares method chooses the

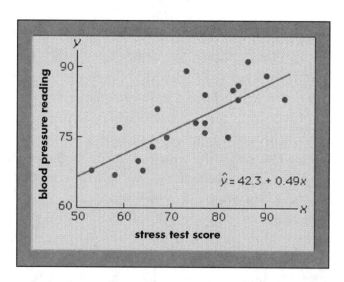

*In this scatter diagram, stress test scores are the independent variable (x axis), and blood pressure values are the dependent variable (y axis). Copyright Encyclopædia Britannica; rendering for this edition by Rosen Educational Services*

parameter estimates such that the sum of the squared residuals is minimized.

## ANALYSIS OF VARIANCE AND GOODNESS OF FIT

A commonly used measure of the goodness of fit provided by the estimated regression equation is the coefficient of determination. Computation of this coefficient is based on the analysis of variance procedure that partitions the total variation in the dependent variable, denoted SST, into two parts: the part explained by the estimated regression equation, denoted SSR, and the part that remains unexplained, denoted SSE.

The measure of total variation, SST, is the sum of the squared deviations of the dependent variable about its mean: $\Sigma(y - \bar{y})^2$. This quantity is known as the total sum of squares. The measure of unexplained variation, SSE, is referred to as the residual sum of squares. SSE is the sum of the squared distances from each point in the scatter diagram to the estimated regression line: $\Sigma(y - \hat{y})^2$. SSE is also commonly referred to as the error sum of squares. A key result in the analysis of variance is that SSR + SSE = SST.

The ratio $r^2$ = SSR/SST is called the coefficient of determination. If the data points are clustered closely about the estimated regression line, then the value of SSE will be small and SSR/SST will be close to 1. Using $r^2$, whose values lie between 0 and 1, provides a measure of goodness of fit. Values closer to 1 imply a better fit. A value of $r^2$ = 0 implies that there is no linear relationship between the dependent and independent variables.

When expressed as a percentage, the coefficient of determination can be interpreted as the percentage of the total sum of squares that can be explained using the estimated regression equation. For the stress-level research study, the value of $r^2$ is 0.583. Thus, 58.3% of the total sum of squares can be explained by the estimated regression equation $\hat{y} = 42.3 + 0.49x$. For typical data found in the social sciences, values of $r^2$ as low as 0.25 are often considered useful. For data in the physical sciences, $r^2$ values of 0.60 or greater are frequently found.

## Significance Testing

In a regression study, hypothesis tests are usually conducted to assess the statistical significance of the overall relationship represented by the regression model and to test for the statistical significance of the individual parameters. The statistical tests used are based on the following four assumptions concerning the error term: (1) $\varepsilon$ is a random variable with an expected value of 0, (2) the variance of $\varepsilon$ is the same for all values of $x$, (3) the values of $\varepsilon$ are independent, and (4) $\varepsilon$ is a normally distributed random variable.

The mean square caused by regression, denoted MSR, is computed by dividing SSR by a number referred to as its degrees of freedom. Similarly, the mean square caused by error, MSE, is computed by dividing SSE by its degrees of freedom. An F-test based on the ratio MSR/MSE can be used to test the statistical significance of the overall relationship between the dependent variable and the set of independent variables. In general, large values of F = MSR/MSE support the conclusion that the overall relationship is statistically significant. If the overall model is deemed statistically significant, statisticians usually conduct hypothesis tests on the individual parameters to determine if each independent variable makes a significant contribution to the model.

## Residual Analysis

The analysis of residuals plays an important role in validating the regression model. If the error term in the regression model satisfies the four assumptions noted earlier, then the model is considered valid. Because the statistical tests for significance are also based on these assumptions, the conclusions resulting from these significance tests are called into question if the assumptions regarding $\varepsilon$ are not satisfied.

The $i$th residual is the difference between the observed value of the dependent variable, $y_i$, and the value predicted by the estimated regression equation, $\hat{y}_i$. These residuals, computed from the available data, are treated as estimates of the model error, $\varepsilon$. As such, they are used by statisticians to validate the assumptions concerning $\varepsilon$. Good judgment and experience play key roles in residual analysis.

Graphical plots and statistical tests concerning the residuals are examined carefully by statisticians, and judgments are made based on these examinations. The most common residual plot shows $\hat{y}$ on the horizontal axis and the residuals on the vertical axis. If the assumptions regarding the error term, $\varepsilon$, are satisfied, then the residual plot will consist of a horizontal band of points. If the residual analysis does not indicate that the model assumptions are satisfied, then it often suggests ways in which the model can be modified to obtain better results.

## Model Building

In regression analysis, model building is the process of developing a probabilistic model that best describes the relationship between the dependent and independent variables. The major issues are finding the proper form (linear or curvilinear) of the relationship and selecting which independent variables to include. In building models it is often desirable to use qualitative as well as quantitative variables.

As previously noted, quantitative variables measure how much or how many, whereas qualitative variables represent types or categories. For example, suppose it is of interest to predict sales of an iced tea that is available in either bottles or cans. Clearly, the independent variable "container type" could influence the dependent variable "sales." Container type is a qualitative variable, however, and must be assigned numerical values if it is to be used in a regression study. So-called dummy variables are used to represent qualitative variables in regression analysis. For example, the dummy variable $x$ could be used to represent container type by setting $x = 0$ if the iced tea is packaged in a bottle and $x = 1$ if the iced tea is in a can. If the beverage could be placed in glass bottles, plastic bottles, or cans, then it would require two dummy variables to properly represent the qualitative variable container type. In general, $k - 1$ dummy variables are needed to model the effect of a qualitative variable that may assume $k$ values.

The general linear model $y = \beta_0 + \beta_1 x_1 + \beta_2 x_2 + \ldots + \beta p x p + \varepsilon$ can be used to model a wide variety of curvilinear relationships between dependent and independent variables. For instance, each of the independent variables could be a nonlinear function of other variables. Also, statisticians sometimes find it necessary to transform the dependent variable in order to build a satisfactory model. A logarithmic transformation is one of the more common types.

## CORRELATION

Correlation and regression analysis are related in the sense that both deal with relationships among variables. The correlation coefficient is a measure of linear association between two variables. Values of the correlation coefficient are always between -1 and +1. A correlation coefficient of +1 indicates that two variables are perfectly related in a positive linear sense, a correlation coefficient of -1 indicates that two variables are perfectly related in a negative linear sense, and a correlation coefficient of 0 indicates that there is no linear relationship between the two variables. For simple linear regression, the sample correlation

coefficient is the square root of the coefficient of determination, with the sign of the correlation coefficient being the same as the sign of $b_1$, the coefficient of $x_1$ in the estimated regression equation.

Neither regression nor correlation analyses can be interpreted as establishing cause-and-effect relationships. They can indicate only how or to what extent variables are associated with each other. The correlation coefficient measures only the degree of linear association between two variables. Any conclusions about a cause-and-effect relationship must be based on the judgment of the analyst.

# TIME SERIES AND FORECASTING

A time series is a set of data collected at successive points in time or over successive periods of time. A sequence of monthly data on new housing starts and a sequence of weekly data on product sales are examples of time series. Usually, the data in a time series are collected at equally spaced periods of time, such as hour, day, week, month, or year.

A primary concern of time series analysis is the development of forecasts for future values of the series. For instance, the federal government develops forecasts of many economic time series such as the gross domestic product, exports, and so on. Most companies develop forecasts of product sales.

Although in practice both qualitative and quantitative forecasting methods are used, statistical approaches to forecasting employ quantitative methods. The two most widely used methods of forecasting are the Box-Jenkins autoregressive integrated moving average (ARIMA) and econometric models.

ARIMA methods are based on the assumption that a probability model generates the time series data. Future values of the time series are assumed to be related to past values as well as to past errors. A time series must be stationary (i.e., one that has a constant mean, variance, and autocorrelation function) for an ARIMA model to be applicable. For nonstationary series, sometimes differences between successive values can be taken and used as a stationary series to which the ARIMA model can be applied.

Econometric models develop forecasts of a time series using one or more related time series and possibly past values of the time series. This approach involves developing a regression model in which the time series is forecast as the dependent variable. The related time series as well as the past values of the time series are the independent or predictor variables.

## NONPARAMETRIC METHODS

The statistical methods discussed earlier generally focus on the parameters of populations or probability distributions and are referred to as parametric methods. Nonparametric methods are statistical methods that require fewer assumptions about a population or probability distribution and are applicable in a wider range of situations. For a statistical method to be classified as a nonparametric method, it must satisfy one of the following conditions: (1) the method is used with qualitative data, or (2) the method is used with quantitative data when no assumption can be made about the population probability distribution. In cases where both parametric and nonparametric methods are applicable, statisticians usually recommend using parametric methods because they tend to provide better precision. Nonparametric methods are useful, however, in situations where the assumptions required by parametric methods appear questionable. A few of the more commonly used nonparametric methods are described below.

Assume that individuals in a sample are asked to state a preference for one of two similar and competing products. A plus (+) sign can be recorded if an individual prefers one product and a minus (-) sign if the individual prefers the other product. With qualitative data in this form, the nonparametric sign test can be used to statistically determine whether a difference in preference for the two products exists for the population. The sign test also can be used to test hypotheses about the value of a population median.

The Wilcoxon signed-rank test can be used to test hypotheses about two populations. In collecting data for this test, each element or experimental unit in the sample must generate two paired or matched data values, one from population 1 and one from population 2. Differences between the paired or matched data values are used to test for a difference between the two populations. The Wilcoxon signed-rank test is applicable when no assumption can be made about the form of the probability distributions for the populations. Another nonparametric test for detecting differences between two populations is the Mann-Whitney-Wilcoxon test. This method is based on data from two independent random samples, one from population 1 and another from population 2. There is no matching or pairing as required for the Wilcoxon signed-rank test.

Nonparametric methods for correlation analysis are also available. The Spearman rank correlation coefficient is a measure of the relationship between two variables when data in the form of rank orders are available. For instance, the Spearman rank correlation coefficient could be used to determine the degree of agreement between men and women concerning their preference ranking of 10 different television shows. A Spearman rank correlation coefficient of 1 would indicate complete agreement, a coefficient of -1 would indicate complete disagreement, and a coefficient of 0 would indicate that the rankings were unrelated.

# STATISTICAL QUALITY CONTROL

Statistical quality control refers to the use of statistical methods in the monitoring and maintaining of the quality of products and services. One method, referred to as acceptance sampling, can be used when a decision must be made to accept or reject a group of parts or items based on the quality found in a sample. A second method, referred to as statistical process control, uses graphical displays known as control charts to determine whether a process should be continued or should be adjusted to achieve the desired quality.

## ACCEPTANCE SAMPLING

Assume that a consumer receives a shipment of parts, or lot, from a producer. A sample of parts will be taken and the number of defective items counted. If the number of defective items is low, then the entire lot will be accepted. If the number of defective items is high, then the entire lot will be rejected. Correct decisions correspond to accepting a good-quality lot and rejecting a poor-quality lot. Because sampling is being used, the probabilities of erroneous decisions need to be considered. The error of rejecting a good-quality lot creates a problem for the producer, but the probability of this error is called the producer's risk. Conversely, the error of accepting a poor-quality lot creates a problem for the purchaser or consumer, and the probability of this error is called the consumer's risk.

The design of an acceptance sampling plan consists of determining a sample size $n$ and an acceptance criterion $c$, where $c$ is the maximum number of defective items that can be found in the sample and the lot still be accepted. The key to understanding both the producer's risk and the consumer's risk is to assume that a lot has some known percentage of defective items and compute the probability of accepting the lot for a given sampling plan. By varying the assumed percentage of defective items in a lot, several different sampling plans can be evaluated and a sampling plan selected such that both the producer's and consumer's risks are reasonably low.

## STATISTICAL PROCESS CONTROL

Statistical process control uses sampling and statistical methods to monitor the quality of an ongoing process such as a production operation. A graphical display referred to as a control chart provides a basis for deciding whether the variation in the output of a process is the result of common causes (randomly occurring variations) or to out-of-the-ordinary assignable causes. Whenever assignable causes are identified, a decision can be made to adjust the process to bring the output back to acceptable quality levels.

Control charts can be classified by the type of data they contain. For instance, an $\bar{x}$-chart is employed in situations where a sample mean is used to measure the quality of the output. Quantitative data such as length, weight, and temperature can be monitored with an $\bar{x}$-chart. Process variability can be monitored using a range or $R$-chart. In cases in which the quality of output is measured in terms of the number of defectives or the proportion of defectives in the sample, an $np$-chart or a $p$-chart can be used.

All control charts are constructed in a similar fashion. For example, the centre line of an $x^-$-chart corresponds to the mean of the process when the process is in control and producing output of acceptable quality. The vertical axis of the control chart identifies the scale of measurement for the variable of interest. The upper horizontal line of the control chart, referred to as the upper control limit, and the lower horizontal line, referred to as the lower control limit, are chosen so that when the process is in control there will be a high probability that the value of a sample mean will fall between the two control limits. Standard practice is to set the control limits at three standard deviations above and below the process mean. The process can be sampled periodically. As each sample is selected, the value of the sample mean is plotted on the control chart. If the value of a sample mean is within the control limits, the process can be continued under the assumption that the quality standards are being maintained. If the value of the sample mean is outside the control limits, an out-of-control conclusion points to the need for corrective action in order to return the process to acceptable quality levels.

## SAMPLE SURVEY METHODS

Statistical inference is the process of using data from a sample to make estimates or test hypotheses about a population. The field of sample survey methods is concerned with effective ways of obtaining sample data. The three most common types of sample surveys are mail surveys, telephone surveys, and personal interview surveys. All involve the use of a questionnaire, for which a large body of knowledge exists concerning the phrasing, sequencing, and grouping of questions. There are other types of sample surveys that do not involve a questionnaire. For example, the sampling of accounting records for audits and the use of a computer to sample a large database are sample surveys that use direct observation of the sampled units to collect the data.

A goal in the design of sample surveys is to obtain a sample that is representative of the population so that precise inferences can be made. Sampling error is the difference between a population parameter and a sample statistic used to estimate it. For example, the difference between a population mean and a sample mean is sampling error. Sampling error occurs because a portion, and not the entire population, is surveyed. Probability sampling methods, where the probability of each unit appearing in the sample is known, enable statisticians to make probability statements about the size of the sampling error. Nonprobability sampling methods, which are based on convenience or judgment rather than on probability, are frequently used for cost and time advantages. However, one should be extremely careful in making inferences from a nonprobability sample. Whether or not the sample is representative is dependent on the judgment of the individuals designing and conducting the survey and not on sound statistical principles. In addition, there is no objective basis for establishing bounds on the sampling error when a nonprobability sample has been used.

Most governmental and professional polling surveys employ probability sampling. It can generally be assumed that any survey that reports a plus or minus margin of error has been conducted using probability sampling. Statisticians prefer probability sampling methods and recommend that they be used whenever possible. A variety of probability sampling methods are available. A few of the more common ones are reviewed here.

Simple random sampling provides the basis for many probability sampling methods. With simple random sampling, every possible sample of size $n$ has the same probability of being selected.

Stratified simple random sampling is a variation of simple random sampling in which the population is partitioned into relatively homogeneous groups called strata and a simple random sample is selected from each stratum. The results from the strata are then aggregated to make inferences about the population. A side benefit of this method is that inferences about the subpopulation represented by each stratum can also be made.

Cluster sampling involves partitioning the population into separate groups called clusters. Unlike in the case of stratified simple random sampling, it is desirable for the clusters to be composed of heterogeneous units. In single-stage cluster sampling, a simple random sample of clusters is selected, and data are collected from every unit in the sampled clusters. In two-stage cluster sampling, a simple random sample of clusters is selected and then a simple random sample is selected from the units in each sampled cluster. One of the primary applications of cluster sampling is called area sampling, where the clusters are counties, townships, city blocks, or other well-defined geographic sections of the population.

## DECISION ANALYSIS

Decision analysis, also called statistical decision theory, involves procedures for choosing optimal decisions in the face of uncertainty. In the simplest situation, a decision maker must choose the best decision from a finite set of alternatives when there are two or more possible future events, called states of nature, that might occur. The list of possible states of nature includes everything that can happen, and the states of nature are defined so that only one of the states will occur. The outcome resulting from the combination of a decision alternative and a particular state of nature is referred to as the payoff.

When probabilities for the states of nature are available, probabilistic criteria may be used to choose the best decision alternative. The most common approach is to use the probabilities to compute the expected value of each decision alternative. The expected value of a decision alternative is the sum of weighted payoffs for the decision. The weight for a payoff is the probability of the associated state of nature and therefore the probability that the payoff occurs. For a maximization problem, the decision alternative with the largest expected value will be chosen. For a minimization problem, the decision alternative with the smallest expected value will be chosen.

Decision analysis can be extremely helpful in sequential decision-making situations—that is, situations in which a decision is made, an event occurs, another decision is made, another event occurs, and so on. For instance, a company trying to decide whether or not to market a new product might first decide to test the acceptance of the product using a consumer panel. Based on the results of the consumer panel, the company then decides whether or not to proceed with further test marketing. After analyzing the results of the test marketing, company executives decide whether or not to produce the new product. A decision tree is a graphical device that helps in structuring and analyzing such problems. With the aid of decision trees, an optimal decision strategy can be developed. A decision strategy is a contingency plan that recommends the best decision alternative depending on what has happened earlier in the sequential process.

# CHAPTER 4
## GAME THEORY

G ame theory is the branch of applied mathematics that provides tools for analyzing situations in which parties, called players, make decisions that are interdependent. This interdependence causes each player to consider the other player's possible decisions, or strategies, in formulating his own strategy. A solution to a game describes the optimal decisions of the players, who may have similar, opposed, or mixed interests, and the outcomes that may result from these decisions.

Although game theory can be and has been used to analyze parlour games, its applications are much broader. In fact, game theory was originally developed by the Hungarian-born American mathematician John von Neumann and his Princeton University colleague Oskar Morgenstern, a German-born American economist, to solve problems in economics. In their book *The Theory of Games and Economic Behavior* (1944), von Neumann and Morgenstern asserted that the mathematics developed for the physical sciences, which describes the workings of a disinterested nature, was a poor model for economics. They observed that economics is much like a game, wherein players anticipate each other's moves, and therefore requires a new kind of mathematics, which they called game theory. (The name may be somewhat of a misnomer, because game theory generally does not share the fun or frivolity associated with games.)

Game theory has been applied to a wide variety of situations in which the choices of players interact to affect the outcome. In stressing the strategic aspects of decision making, or aspects controlled by the players rather than

*Oskar Morgenstern coauthored* Theory of Games and Economic Behavior, *applying Neumann's theory of games of strategy to competitive business.* Ralph Morse/Time & Life Pictures/Getty Images

by pure chance, the theory both supplements and goes beyond the classical theory of probability. It has been used, for example, to determine what political coalitions or business conglomerates are likely to form, the optimal price at which to sell products or services in the face of competition, the power of a voter or a bloc of voters, whom to select for a jury, the best site for a manufacturing plant, and the behaviour of certain animals and plants in their struggle for survival. It has even been used to challenge the legality of certain voting systems.

It would be surprising if any one theory could address such an enormous range of "games," and in fact there is no single game theory. Many theories have been proposed, each applicable to different situations and each with its own concepts of what constitutes a solution. This chapter describes some simple games, discusses different theories, and outlines principles underlying game theory.

## CLASSIFICATION OF GAMES

Games can be classified according to certain significant features, the most obvious of which is the number of players. Thus, a game can be designated as being a one-person, two-person, or n-person (with n greater than two) game, with games in each category having their own distinctive features. In addition, a player need not be an individual. It may be a nation, corporation, or team comprising many people with shared interests.

In games of perfect information, such as chess, each player knows everything about the game at all times. Poker is an example of a game of imperfect information, however, because players do not know all of their opponents' cards.

The extent to which the goals of the players coincide or conflict is another basis for classifying games.

Constant-sum games are games of total conflict, which are also called games of pure competition. For example, poker is a constant-sum game because the combined wealth of the players remains constant, but its distribution shifts in the course of play.

Players in constant-sum games have completely opposed interests, whereas in variable-sum games they may all be winners or losers. In a labour-management dispute, for example, the two parties certainly have some conflicting interests, but both benefit if a strike is averted.

Variable-sum games can be further distinguished as being either cooperative or noncooperative. In cooperative games players can communicate and, most important, make binding agreements. In noncooperative games players may communicate, but they cannot make binding agreements, such as an enforceable contract. An automobile salesperson and a potential customer will be engaged in a cooperative game if they agree on a price and sign a contract. However, the dickering that they do to reach this point will be noncooperative. Similarly, when people bid independently at an auction they are playing a noncooperative game, even though the high bidder agrees to complete the purchase.

Finally, a game is said to be finite when each player has a finite number of options, the number of players is finite, and the game cannot go on indefinitely. Chess, checkers, poker, and most parlour games are finite. Infinite games are more subtle and will only be touched upon in this section.

A game can be described as in extensive, normal, or characteristic-function form. (Sometimes these forms are combined.) Most parlour games, which progress step by step, one move at a time, can be modeled as games in extensive form. Extensive-form games can be described by a "game tree," in which each turn is a vertex of the tree, with each branch indicating the players' successive choices.

The normal (strategic) form is primarily used to describe two-person games. In this form a game is represented by a payoff matrix, wherein each row describes the strategy of one player and each column describes the strategy of the other player. The matrix entry at the intersection of each row and column gives the outcome of each player choosing the corresponding strategy. The payoffs to each player associated with this outcome are the basis for determining whether the strategies are "in equilibrium," or stable.

The characteristic-function form is generally used to analyze games with more than two players. It indicates the minimum value that each coalition of players—including single-player coalitions—can guarantee for itself when playing against a coalition made up of all the other players.

## ONE-PERSON GAMES

One-person games are also known as games against nature. With no opponents, the player only needs to list available options and then choose the optimal outcome. When chance is involved the game might seem to be more complicated, but in principle the decision is still relatively simple. For example, a person deciding whether to carry an umbrella weighs the costs and benefits of carrying or not carrying it. Although this person may make the wrong decision, there does not exist a conscious opponent. That is, nature is presumed to be completely indifferent to the player's decision, and the person can base his decision on simple probabilities. One-person games hold little interest for game theorists.

# TWO-PERSON CONSTANT-SUM GAMES

## GAMES OF PERFECT INFORMATION

The simplest game of any real theoretical interest is a two-person constant-sum game of perfect information. Examples of such games include chess, checkers, and the Japanese game of go. In 1912 the German mathematician Ernst Zermelo proved that such games are strictly determined. By making use of all available information, the players can deduce optimal strategies, which makes the outcome preordained (strictly determined). In chess, for example, exactly one of three outcomes must occur if the players make optimal choices: (1) White wins (has a strategy that wins against any strategy of Black), (2) Black wins, or (3) White and Black draw. In principle, a sufficiently

*By using all available information, players of the Japanese game of go can deduce optimal strategies, making the outcome preordained (strictly determined).* Shutterstock.com

powerful supercomputer could determine which of the three outcomes will occur. However, considering that there are some $10^{43}$ distinct 40-move games of chess possible, there seems no possibility that such a computer will be developed now or in the foreseeable future. Therefore, although chess is of only minor interest in game theory, it is likely to remain a game of enduring intellectual interest.

## GAMES OF IMPERFECT INFORMATION

A "saddlepoint" in a two-person constant-sum game is the outcome that rational players would choose. (Its name derives from its being the minimum of a row that is also the maximum of a column in a payoff matrix—to be illustrated shortly—which corresponds to the shape of a saddle.) A saddlepoint always exists in games of perfect information but may or may not exist in games of imperfect information. By choosing a strategy associated with this outcome, each player obtains an amount at least equal to his payoff at that outcome, no matter what the other player does. This payoff is called the value of the game. As in perfect-information games, it is preordained by the players' choices of strategies associated with the saddlepoint, making such games strictly determined.

The normal-form game is used to illustrate the calculation of a saddlepoint. Two political parties, $A$ and $B$, must each decide how to handle a controversial issue in a certain election. Each party can either support the issue, oppose it, or evade it by being ambiguous. The decisions by $A$ and $B$ on this issue determine the percentage of the vote that each party receives. The entries in the payoff matrix represent party $A$'s percentage of the vote (the remaining percentage goes to $B$). When, for example, $A$ supports the issue and $B$ evades it, $A$ gets 80 percent and $B$ 20 percent of the vote.

## Payoff matrix with saddlepoint

| | | party *B* | | |
|---|---|---|---|---|
| | | support | oppose | evade |
| **party *A*** support | | A 60% · B 40% | A 20% · B 80% | A 80% · B 20% |
| oppose | | A 80% · B 20% | A 25% · B 75% | A 75% · B 25% |
| evade | | A 35% · B 65% | A 30% · B 70% | A 40% · B 60% |

saddlepoint

*Table 1: The normal-form table illustrates the concept of a saddlepoint, or entry, in a payoff matrix at which the expected gain of each participant (row or column) has the highest guaranteed payoff.* Encyclopædia Britannica, Inc.

Assume that each party wants to maximize its vote. *A*'s decision seems difficult at first because it depends on *B*'s choice of strategy. *A* does best to support if *B* evades, oppose if *B* supports, and evade if *B* opposes. *A* must therefore consider *B*'s decision before making its own. Note that no matter what *A* does, *B* obtains the largest percentage of the vote (smallest percentage for *A*) by opposing the issue rather than supporting or evading it. Once *A* recognizes this, its strategy obviously should be to evade, settling for 30 percent of the vote. Thus, a 30 to 70 percent division of the vote, to *A* and *B* respectively, is the game's saddlepoint.

A more systematic way of finding a saddlepoint is to determine the so-called maximin and minimax values. *A* first determines the minimum percentage of votes it can obtain for each of its strategies. It then finds the maximum of these three minimum values, giving the maximin. The minimum percentages *A* will get if it supports, opposes, or evades are, respectively, 20, 25, and 30. The largest of these, 30, is the maximin value. Similarly, for each strategy *B* chooses, it determines the maximum percentage of votes *A* will win (and thus the minimum that it can win). In this case, if *B* supports, opposes, or evades, the maximum *A* will get is 80, 30, and 80, respectively. *B* will obtain its largest percentage by minimizing *A*'s maximum percent of the vote, giving the minimax. The smallest of *A*'s maximum values is 30, so 30 is *B*'s minimax value. Because both the minimax and the maximin values coincide, 30 is a saddlepoint. The two parties might as well announce their strategies in advance, because the other party cannot gain from this knowledge.

## Mixed Strategies and the Minimax Theorem

When saddlepoints exist, the optimal strategies and outcomes can be easily determined, as was just illustrated. However, when there is no saddlepoint the calculation is more elaborate.

A guard is hired to protect two safes in separate locations: *S*1 contains $10,000 and *S*2 contains $100,000. The guard can protect only one safe at a time from a safecracker. The safecracker and the guard must decide in advance, without knowing what the other party will do, which safe to try to rob and which safe to protect. When they go to the same safe, the safecracker gets nothing.

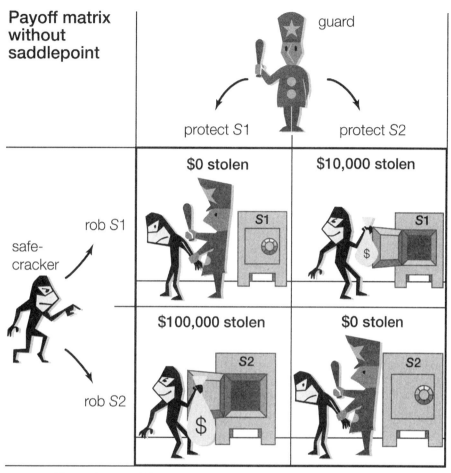

**Payoff matrix without saddlepoint**

guard

protect S1    protect S2

$0 stolen    $10,000 stolen

rob S1

safe-cracker

$100,000 stolen    $0 stolen

rob S2

*Table 2: When a saddlepoint does not exist for a payoff matrix, a probabilistic strategy is optimal. Based on the possible rewards, the participants assign probabilities to each choice so as to maximize their expected (average) rewards. For example, in this example the guard should protect the $100,000 deposit 10 out of 11 times and the $10,000 deposit 1 out of 11 times. Some type of random number generator (such as, here, an 11-sided die) is used to determine the appropriate strategy in order to avoid predictability.* Encyclopædia Britannica, Inc.

When they go to different safes, the safecracker gets the contents of the unprotected safe.

In such a game, game theory does not indicate that any one particular strategy is best. Instead, it prescribes that a strategy be chosen in accordance with a probability distribution, which in this simple example is quite easy to calculate. In larger and more complex games, finding this strategy involves solving a problem in linear programming, which can be considerably more difficult.

To calculate the appropriate probability distribution in this example, each player adopts a strategy that makes him indifferent to what his opponent does. Assume that the guard protects $S_1$ with probability $p$ and $S_2$ with probability $1 - p$. Thus, if the safecracker tries $S_1$, then he will be successful whenever the guard protects $S_2$. In other words, he will get \$10,000 with probability $1 - p$ and \$0 with probability $p$ for an average gain of \$10,000$(1-p)$. Similarly, if the safecracker tries $S_2$, then he will get \$100,000 with probability $p$ and \$0 with probability $1 - p$ for an average gain of \$100,000$p$.

The guard will be indifferent to which safe the safecracker chooses if the average amount stolen is the same in both cases—that is, if \$10,000$(1 - p)$ = \$100,000$p$. Solving for $p$ gives $p = 1/11$. If the guard protects $S_1$ with probability $1/11$ and $S_2$ with probability $10/11$, then he will lose, on average, no more than about \$9,091 whatever the safecracker does.

Using the same kind of argument, it can be shown that the safecracker will get an average of at least \$9,091 if he tries to steal from $S_1$ with probability $10/11$ and from $S_2$ with probability $1/11$. This solution in terms of mixed strategies, which are assumed to be chosen at random with the indicated probabilities, is analogous to the solution of the game with a saddlepoint (in which a pure, or single best, strategy exists for each player).

The safecracker and the guard give away nothing if they announce the probabilities with which they will randomly choose their respective strategies. If they make themselves predictable by exhibiting any kind of pattern in their choices, however, this information can be exploited by the other player.

The minimax theorem, which von Neumann proved in 1928, states that every finite, two-person constant-sum game has a solution in pure or mixed strategies. Specifically, it says that for every such game between players $A$ and $B$, there is a value $v$ and strategies for $A$ and $B$ such that, if $A$ adopts its optimal (maximin) strategy, the outcome will be at least as favourable to $A$ as $v$; if $B$ adopts its optimal (minimax) strategy, the outcome will be no more favourable to $A$ than $v$. Thus, $A$ and $B$ have both the incentive and the ability to enforce an outcome that gives an (expected) payoff of $v$.

## UTILITY THEORY

In the previous example, it was tacitly assumed that the players were maximizing their average profits, but in practice players may consider other factors. For example, few people would risk a sure gain of $1,000,000 for an even chance of winning either $3,000,000 or $0, even though the expected (average) gain from this bet is $1,500,000. In fact, many decisions that people make, such as buying insurance policies, playing lotteries, and gambling at a casino, indicate that they are not maximizing their average profits. Game theory does not attempt to state what a player's goal should be. Instead, it shows how a player can best achieve his or her goal, whatever that goal is.

Von Neumann and Morgenstern understood this distinction, so to accommodate all players, whatever their goals, they constructed a theory of utility. They began by listing certain axioms that they thought all rational decision makers would follow (for example, if a person likes tea better than coffee, and coffee better than milk, then that person should like tea better than milk). They then proved that it was possible to define a utility function for such decision makers that would reflect their preferences. In essence, a utility function assigns a number to each player's alternatives to convey their relative attractiveness. Maximizing someone's expected utility automatically determines a player's most preferred option. In recent years, however, some doubt has been raised about whether people actually behave in accordance with these axioms, and alternative axioms have been proposed.

## TWO-PERSON VARIABLE-SUM GAMES

Much of the early work in game theory was on two-person constant-sum games because they are the easiest to treat mathematically. The players in such games have diametrically opposed interests, and there is a consensus about what constitutes a solution (as given by the minimax theorem). Most games that arise in practice, however, are variable-sum games. The players have both common and opposed interests. For example, a buyer and a seller are engaged in a variable-sum game (the buyer wants a low price and the seller a high one, but both want to make a deal), as are two hostile nations (they may disagree about numerous issues, but both gain if they avoid going to war).

Some "obvious" properties of two-person constant-sum games are invalid in variable-sum games. In constant-sum games, for example, both players cannot gain (they may or may not lose, but they cannot both gain) if they are deprived of some of their strategies. In variable-sum games, however, players may gain if some of their strategies are no longer available. This might not seem possible at first. One would think that if a player benefited from not using certain strategies, then the player would simply avoid those strategies and choose more advantageous ones, but this is not always the case. For example, in a region with high unemployment, a worker may be willing to accept a lower salary to obtain or keep a job, but if a minimum wage law makes that option illegal, then the worker may be "forced" to accept a higher salary.

The effect of communication is particularly revealing of the difference between constant-sum and variable-sum games. In constant-sum games it never helps a player to give an adversary information, and it never hurts a player to learn an opponent's optimal strategy (pure or mixed) in advance. However, these properties do not necessarily hold in variable-sum games. Indeed, a player may want an opponent to be well-informed. In a labour-management dispute, for example, if the labour union is prepared to strike, then it behooves the union to inform management and thereby possibly achieve its goal without a strike. In this example, management is not harmed by the advance information (it, too, benefits by avoiding a costly strike). In other variable-sum games, knowing an opponent's strategy can sometimes be disadvantageous. For example, a blackmailer can only benefit if he first informs his victim that he will harm him—generally by disclosing some sensitive and secret details of the victim's life—if his terms are not met. For such a threat to be credible, the victim must fear the disclosure and believe that the blackmailer is capable of executing the threat. (The credibility of threats is a question that game theory studies.) Although a blackmailer may be able to harm a victim without any communication taking place, a blackmailer cannot extort a victim unless he first adequately informs the victim of his intent and its consequences. Thus, the victim's knowledge of the blackmailer's strategy, including his ability and will to carry out the threat, works to the blackmailer's advantage.

## Cooperative Versus Noncooperative Games

Communication is pointless in constant-sum games because there is no possibility of mutual gain from cooperating. In variable-sum games, however, the ability to communicate, the degree of communication, and even the order in which players communicate can have a profound influence on the outcome.

In the variable-sum game shown, each matrix entry consists of two numbers. (Because the combined wealth of the players is not constant, it is impossible to deduce one player's payoff from the payoff of the other. Consequently, both players' payoffs must be given.) The first number in each entry is the payoff to the row player (player $A$), and the second number is the payoff to the column player (player $B$).

In this example it will be to player $A$'s advantage if the game is cooperative and to player $B$'s advantage if the game is noncooperative. Without communication, assume each

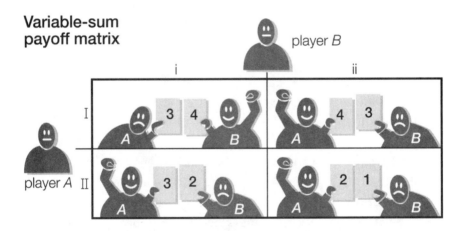

*Table 3: In variable-sum games, each payoff depends on both players' actions. Therefore, each matrix entry lists two payoffs, one for each player.* Encyclopædia Britannica, Inc.

player applies the "sure-thing" principle: It maximizes its minimum payoff by determining the minimum it will receive whatever its opponent does. Thereby, $A$ determines that it will do best to choose strategy I no matter what $B$ does: If $B$ chooses i, $A$ will get 3 regardless of what $A$ does; if $B$ chooses ii, $A$ will get 4 rather than 3. $B$ similarly determines that it will do best to choose i no matter what $A$ does. Selecting these two strategies, $A$ will get 3 and $B$ will get 4 at (3, 4).

In a cooperative game, however, $A$ can threaten to play II unless $B$ agrees to play ii. If $B$ agrees, its payoff will be reduced to 3 while $A$'s payoff will rise to 4 at (4, 3). If $B$ does not agree and $A$ carries out its threat, $A$ will neither gain nor lose at (3, 2) compared to (3, 4), but $B$ will get a payoff of only 2. Clearly, $A$ will be unaffected if $B$ does not agree and thus has a credible threat. $B$ will be affected and obviously will do better at (4, 3) than at (3, 2) and should comply with the threat.

Sometimes both players can gain from the ability to communicate. Two pilots trying to avoid a midair collision clearly will benefit if they can communicate, and the degree of communication allowed between them may even determine whether or not they will crash. Generally, the more two players' interests coincide, the more important and advantageous communication becomes.

The solution to a cooperative game in which players have a common goal involves effectively coordinating the players' decisions. This is relatively straightforward, as is finding the solution to constant-sum games with a saddlepoint. For games in which the players have both common and conflicting interests—in other words, in most variable-sum games, whether cooperative or noncooperative—what constitutes a solution is much harder to define and make persuasive.

## The Nash Solution

Although solutions to variable-sum games have been defined many different ways, they sometimes seem inequitable or are not enforceable. One well-known cooperative solution to two-person variable-sum games was proposed by the American mathematician John F. Nash, who received the Nobel Prize for Economics in 1994 for this and related work he did in game theory.

Given a game with a set of possible outcomes and associated utilities for each player, Nash showed that there is a unique outcome that satisfies four conditions: (1) The outcome is independent of the choice of a utility function (that is, if a player prefers $x$ to $y$, the solution will not change if one function assigns $x$ a utility of 10 and $y$ a utility of 1 or a second function assigns the values of 20 and 2). (2) Both players cannot do better simultaneously (a condition known as Pareto-optimality). (3) The outcome is independent of irrelevant alternatives (in other words, if unattractive options are added to or dropped from the list of alternatives, the solution will not change). (4) The outcome is symmetrical (i.e., if the players reverse their roles, the solution will remain the same, except that the payoffs will be reversed).

In some cases the Nash solution seems inequitable because it is based on a balance of threats (the possibility that no agreement will be reached, so that both players will suffer losses) rather than a "fair" outcome. When, for example, a rich person and a poor person are to receive $10,000 provided they can agree on how to divide the money (if they fail to agree, they receive nothing), most people assume that the fair solution would be for each person to get half, or even that the poor person should get more than half. According to the Nash solution, however, there is a utility for each player associated with all possible outcomes. Moreover, the specific choice of utility functions should not affect the solution (condition 1) as long as they reflect each person's preferences. In this example, assume that the rich person's utility is equal to one-half the money received and that the poor person's utility is equal to the money received. These different functions reflect the fact that additional income is more precious to the poor person. Under the Nash solution, the threat of reaching no agreement induces the poor person to accept one-third of the $10,000, giving the rich person two-thirds. In general, the Nash solution finds an outcome such that each player gains the same amount of utility.

## THE PRISONERS' DILEMMA

To illustrate the kinds of difficulties that arise in two-person noncooperative variable-sum games, consider the celebrated Prisoners' Dilemma (PD), originally formulated by the American mathematician Albert W. Tucker. Two prisoners, $A$ and $B$, suspected of committing a robbery together, are isolated and urged to confess. Each is concerned only with getting the shortest possible prison sentence for himself. Each must decide whether to confess without knowing his partner's decision. Both prisoners, however, know the consequences of their decisions: (1) if both confess, both go to jail for five years; (2) if neither confesses, both go to jail for one year (for carrying concealed weapons); and (3) if one confesses while the other does not, the confessor goes free (for turning state's evidence) and the silent one goes to jail for 20 years.

Superficially, the analysis of PD is simple. Although $A$ cannot be sure what $B$ will do, he knows that he does best to confess when $B$ confesses (he gets five years rather than 20) and also when $B$ remains silent (he serves no time rather than a year). Analogously, $B$ will reach the same conclusion.

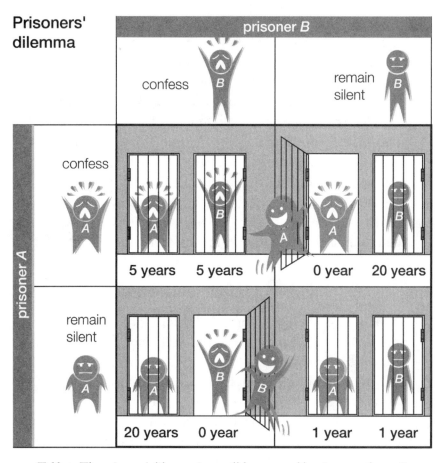

*Table 4: The prisoners' dilemma is a well-known problem in game theory. It demonstrates how communication between the participants can drastically alter their best strategy.* Encyclopædia Britannica, Inc.

So the solution would seem to be that each prisoner does best to confess and go to jail for five years. Paradoxically, however, the two robbers would do better if they both adopted the apparently irrational strategy of remaining silent. Each would then serve only one year in jail. The irony of PD is that when each of two (or more) parties acts selfishly and does not cooperate with the other (i.e., when he confesses), they do worse than when they act unselfishly and cooperate together (i.e., when they remain silent).

PD is not just an intriguing hypothetical problem. Real-life situations with similar characteristics have often been observed. For example, two shopkeepers engaged in a price war may well be caught up in a PD. Each shopkeeper knows that if he has lower prices than his rival, he will attract his rival's customers and thereby increase his own profits. Each therefore decides to lower his prices, with the result that neither gains any customers and both earn smaller profits. Similarly, nations competing in an arms race and farmers increasing crop production can also be seen as manifestations of PD. When two nations keep buying more weapons in an attempt to achieve military superiority, neither gains an advantage and both are poorer than when they started. A single farmer can increase profits by increasing production, but when all farmers increase their output, a market glut ensues, with lower profits for all.

It might seem that the paradox inherent in PD could be resolved if the game were played repeatedly. Players would learn that they do best when both act unselfishly and cooperate. Indeed, if one player failed to cooperate in one game, the other player could retaliate by not cooperating in the next game, and both would lose until they began to "see the light" and cooperated again. When the game is repeated a fixed number of times, however, this argument fails. To see this, suppose two shopkeepers set up their booths at a 10-day county fair. Furthermore, suppose that each maintains full prices, knowing that if he does not, his competitor will retaliate the next day. On the last day, however, each shopkeeper realizes that his competitor can no longer retaliate and so there is little reason not to lower their prices. But if each shopkeeper knows that his rival will lower his prices on the last day, he has no incentive to maintain full prices on the ninth day. Continuing this reasoning, one concludes that rational shopkeepers will have a price war every day. It is only when the game is played repeatedly, and neither player knows when the sequence will end, that the cooperative strategy can succeed.

In 1980 the American political scientist Robert Axelrod engaged a number of game theorists in a round-robin tournament. In each match the strategies of two theorists, incorporated in computer programs, competed against one another in a sequence of PDs with no definite end. A "nice" strategy was defined as one in which a player always cooperates with a cooperative opponent. Also, if a player's opponent did not cooperate during one turn, most strategies prescribed noncooperation on the next turn, but a player with a "forgiving" strategy reverted rapidly to cooperation once its opponent started cooperating again. In this experiment it turned out that every nice strategy outperformed every strategy that was not nice. Furthermore, of the nice strategies, the forgiving ones performed best.

## THEORY OF MOVES

Another approach to inducing cooperation in PD and other variable-sum games is the theory of moves (TOM). Proposed by the American political scientist Steven J. Brams, TOM allows players, starting at any outcome in a payoff matrix, to move and countermove within the matrix, thereby capturing the changing strategic nature of games as they evolve over time. In particular, TOM assumes that players think ahead about the consequences of all of the participants' moves and countermoves when formulating plans. Thereby, TOM embeds extensive-form calculations within the normal form, deriving advantages of both forms: the nonmyopic thinking of the extensive form disciplined by the economy of the normal form.

To illustrate the nonmyopic perspective of TOM, consider what happens in PD as a function of where play starts:

1. When play starts noncooperatively, players are stuck, no matter how far ahead they look, because as soon as one player departs, the other player, enjoying his best outcome, will not move on. Outcome: The players stay at the noncooperative outcome.

2. When play starts cooperatively, neither player will defect, because if he does, the other player will also defect, and they both will end up worse off. Thinking ahead, therefore, neither player will defect. Outcome: The players stay at the cooperative outcome.

3. When play starts at one of the win-lose outcomes (best for one player, worst for the other), the player doing best will know that if he is not magnanimous, and consequently does not move to the cooperative outcome, his opponent will move to the noncooperative outcome, inflicting on the best-off player his next-worst outcome. Therefore, it is in the best-off player's interest, as well as his opponent's, that he act magnanimously, anticipating that if he does not, the noncooperative outcome (next-worst for both), rather than the cooperative outcome (next-best for both), will be chosen. Outcome: The best-off player will move to the cooperative outcome, where play will remain.

Such rational moves are not beyond the pale of most players. Indeed, they are frequently made by those who look beyond the immediate consequences of their own choices. Such far-sighted players can escape the dilemma in PD, as well as poor outcomes in other variable-sum games, provided play does not begin noncooperatively. Hence, TOM does not predict unconditional cooperation in PD but, instead, makes it a function of the starting point of play.

## BIOLOGICAL APPLICATIONS

One fascinating and unexpected application of game theory in general, and PD in particular, occurs in biology. When two males confront each other, whether competing for a mate or for some disputed territory, they can behave either like "hawks"—fighting until one is maimed, killed, or flees—or like "doves"—posturing a bit but leaving before any serious harm is done. (In effect, the doves cooperate while the hawks do not.) Neither type of behaviour, it turns out, is ideal for survival: A species containing only hawks would have a high casualty rate, and a species containing only doves would be vulnerable to an invasion by hawks or a mutation that produces hawks, because the population growth rate of the competitive hawks would be much higher initially than that of the doves.

Thus, a species with males consisting exclusively of either hawks or doves is vulnerable. The English biologist John Maynard Smith showed that a third type of male behaviour, which he called "bourgeois," would be more stable than that of either pure hawks or pure doves. A bourgeois may act like either a hawk or a dove, depending on some external cues. For example, it may fight tenaciously when it meets a rival in its own territory but yield when it meets the same rival elsewhere. In effect, bourgeois animals submit their conflict to external arbitration to avoid a prolonged and mutually destructive struggle.

## Biological competition

| | hawk | | dove | | bourgeois | |
|---|---|---|---|---|---|---|
| **hawk** | lose −5 offspring | lose −5 offspring | gain +10 offspring | gain none, lose none | gain +2.5 offspring | lose −2.5 offspring |
| **dove** | gain none, lose none | gain +10 offspring | gain +2 offspring | gain +2 offspring | gain +1 offspring | gain +6 offspring |
| **bourgeois** | lose −2.5 offspring | gain +2.5 offspring | gain +6 offspring | gain +1 offspring | gain +5 offspring | gain +5 offspring |

*Table 5: Bourgeois, or mixed attack/retreat behaviour, is the most stable strategy for a population. This strategy resists invasion by either hawks (which always attack) or doves (which always retreat). Conversely, an all-hawk or all-dove population can be successfully invaded by bourgeois individuals because their expected payoff is higher (in terms of offspring) than either pure strategy.* Encyclopædia Britannica, Inc.

Smith constructed a payoff matrix in which various possible outcomes (e.g., death, maiming, successful mating), and the costs and benefits associated with them (e.g., cost of lost time), were weighted in terms of the expected number of genes propagated. Smith showed that a bourgeois invasion would be successful against a completely hawk population by observing that when a hawk confronts a hawk it loses 5, whereas a bourgeois loses only 2.5. (Because the population is assumed to be predominantly hawk, the success of the invasion can be predicted by comparing the average number of offspring a hawk will produce when it confronts another hawk with the average number of offspring a bourgeois will produce when confronting a hawk.) Patently, a bourgeois invasion against a completely dove population would be successful as well, gaining the bourgeois 6 offspring. A completely bourgeois population cannot be invaded by either hawks or doves, however, because the bourgeois gets 5 against bourgeois, which is more than either hawks or doves get when confronting bourgeois. Note in this application that the question is not what strategy a rational player will choose—animals are not assumed to make conscious choices, though their types may change through mutation—but what combinations of types are stable and hence likely to evolve.

Smith gave several examples that showed how the bourgeois strategy is used in practice. For example, male speckled wood butterflies seek sunlit spots on the forest floor where females are often found. There is a shortage of such spots, however, and in a confrontation between a stranger and an inhabitant, the stranger yields after a brief duel in which the combatants circle one another. The dueling skills of the adversaries have little effect on the outcome. When one butterfly is forcibly placed on another's territory so that each considers the other the aggressor, the two butterflies duel with righteous indignation for a much longer time.

## N-PERSON GAMES

Theoretically, n-person games in which the players are not allowed to communicate and make binding agreements are not fundamentally different from two-person nonco-operative games. In the two examples that follow, each involving three players, one looks for Nash equilibria—that is, stable outcomes from which no player would normally depart because to do so would be disadvantageous.

## SEQUENTIAL AND SIMULTANEOUS TRUELS

As an example of an $n$-person noncooperative game, imagine three players, $A$, $B$, and $C$, situated at the corners of an equilateral triangle. They engage in a truel, or three-person duel, in which each player has a gun with one bullet. Assume that each player is a perfect shot and can kill one other player at any time. There is no fixed order of play, but any shooting that occurs is sequential: No player fires at the same time as any other. Consequently, if a bullet is fired, the results are known to all players before another bullet is fired.

Suppose that the players order their goals as follows: (1) survive alone; (2) survive with one opponent; (3) survive with both opponents; (4) not survive, with no opponents alive; (5) not survive, with one opponent alive; and (6) not survive, with both opponents alive. Thus, surviving alone is best, dying alone is worst.

If a player can either fire or not fire at another player, who, if anybody, will shoot whom? It is not difficult to see that outcome (3), in which nobody shoots, is the unique Nash equilibrium—any player that departs from not shooting does worse. Suppose, on the contrary, that $A$ shoots $B$, hoping for $A$'s outcome (2), whereby he and $C$ survive. Now, however, $C$ can shoot a disarmed $A$, thereby leaving himself as the sole survivor, or outcome (1). As this is $A$'s penultimate outcome (5), in which $A$ and one opponent ($B$) are killed while the other opponent ($C$) lives, $A$

should not fire the first shot. The same reasoning applies to the other two players. Consequently, nobody will shoot, resulting in outcome (3), in which all three players survive.

Now consider whether any of the players can do better through collusion. Specifically, assume that $A$ and $B$ agree not to shoot each other, and if either shoots another player, they agree it would be $C$. Nevertheless, if $A$ shoots $C$ (for instance), $B$ could now repudiate the agreement with impunity and shoot $A$, thereby becoming the sole survivor.

Thus, thinking ahead about the unpleasant consequences of shooting first or colluding with another player to do so, nobody will shoot or collude. Thereby all players will survive if the players must act in sequence, giving outcome (3). Because no player can do better by shooting, or saying they will do so to another, these strategies yield a Nash equilibrium.

Next, suppose that the players act simultaneously. Hence, they must decide in ignorance of each others' intended actions. This situation is common in life. People often must act before they find out what others are doing. In a simultaneous truel there are three possibilities, depending on the number of rounds and whether or not this number is known:

1. One round. Now everybody will find it rational to shoot an opponent at the start of play. This is because no player can affect his own fate, but each does at least as well, and sometimes better, by shooting another player—whether the shooter lives or dies—because the number of surviving opponents is reduced. Hence, the Nash equilibrium is that everybody will shoot. When each player chooses his target

at random, it is easy to see that each has a 25 percent chance of surviving. Consider player $A$. He will die if $B$, $C$, or both shoot him (three cases), compared with his surviving if $B$ and $C$ shoot each other (one case). Altogether, one of $A$, $B$, or $C$ will survive with probability 75 percent, and nobody will survive with probability 25 percent (when each player shoots a different opponent). Outcome: There will always be shooting, leaving one or no survivors.

2. $N$ rounds ($n \geq 2$ and known). Assume that nobody has shot an opponent up to the penultimate, or ($n$ - 1)st, round. Then, on the penultimate round, either of at least two players will rationally shoot or none will. First, consider the situation in which an opponent shoots $A$. Clearly, $A$ can never do better than shoot, because $A$ is going to be killed anyway. Moreover, $A$ does better to shoot at whichever opponent (there must be at least one) that is not a target of $B$ or $C$. Conversely, suppose that nobody shoots $A$. If $B$ and $C$ shoot each other, $A$ has no reason to shoot (although $A$ cannot be harmed by doing so). However, if one opponent, say $B$, holds his fire, and $C$ shoots $B$, $A$ again cannot do better than hold his fire also, because he can eliminate $C$ on the next round. (Note that $C$, because it has already fired his only bullet, does not threaten $A$.) Finally, suppose that both $B$ and $C$ hold their fire. If $A$ shoots an opponent, say $B$, his other opponent, $C$, will eliminate $A$ on the last, or $n$th, round. But if $A$ holds his fire, the game passes onto the $n$th round and, as previously discussed in (1), $A$

has a 25 percent chance of surviving, assuming random choices. Thus, if nobody else shoots on the $(n - 1)$st round, $A$ again cannot do better than hold his fire during this round. Whether the players refrain from shooting on the $(n - 1)$ st round or not—each strategy may be a best response to what the other players do—shooting will be rational on the $n$th round if there is more than one survivor and at least one player has a bullet remaining. Moreover, the anticipation of shooting on the $(n -1)$st or $n$th round may cause players to fire earlier, perhaps even back to the first and second rounds. Outcome: There will always be shooting, leaving one or no survivors.

3.  $N$ rounds ($n$ unlimited). The new wrinkle here is that it may be rational for no player to shoot on any round, leading to the survival of all three players. How can this happen? The preceding argument in (1) that "if you are shot at, you might as well shoot somebody" still applies. However, even if you are, say, $A$, and $B$ shoots $C$, you cannot do better than shoot $B$, making yourself the sole survivor—outcome (1). As before, you do best—whether you are shot at or not—if you shoot somebody who is not the target of anybody else, beginning on the first round. Suppose, however, that $B$ and $C$ refrain from shooting in the first round, and consider $A$'s situation. Shooting an opponent is not rational for $A$ on the first round because the surviving opponent will then shoot $A$ on the next round (there will always be a next round if $n$ is unlimited). If all the players hold their fire,

and continue to do so in subsequent rounds, however, all three players will remain alive. Although there is no "best" strategy in all situations, the possibilities of survival will increase if $n$ is unlimited. Outcome: There may be zero, one (any of $A$, $B$, or $C$), or three survivors, but never two. To summarize, shooting is never rational in a sequential truel, whereas it is always rational in a simultaneous truel that goes only one round. Thus, "nobody shoots" and "everybody shoots" are the Nash equilibria in these two kinds of truels. In simultaneous truels that go more than one round, by comparison, there are multiple Nash equilibria. If the number of rounds is known, then there is one Nash equilibrium in which a player shoots, and one in which he does not, at the start, but in the end there will be only one or no survivors. When the number of rounds is unlimited, however, a new Nash equilibrium is possible in which nobody shoots on any round. Thus, like PD with an uncertain number of rounds, an unlimited number of rounds in a truel can lead to greater cooperation.

## POWER IN VOTING: THE PARADOX OF THE CHAIR'S POSITION

Many applications of $n$-person game theory are concerned with voting, in which strategic calculations are often rampant. Surprisingly, these calculations can result in the ostensibly most powerful player in a voting body being hurt. For example, assume the chair of a voting body, while not having more votes than other members, can break ties. This would seem to make the chair more powerful, but it turns out that the possession of a tie-breaking vote may backfire, putting the chair at a disadvantage relative to the other members. In this manner the greater resources that a player has may not always translate into greater power, which here will mean the ability of a player to obtain a preferred outcome.

In the three-person noncooperative voting game to be analyzed, players are assumed to rank the possible outcomes that can occur. The problem in finding a solution is not a lack of Nash equilibria, but too many. So the question becomes: Which, if any, are likely to be selected by the players? Specifically, is one more appealing than the others? The answer is "yes," but it requires extending the idea of a sure-thing strategy to its successive application in different stages of play.

To illustrate the chair's problem, suppose there are three voters ($X$, $Y$, and $Z$) and three voting alternatives ($x$, $y$, and $z$). Assume that voter $X$ prefers $x$ to $y$ and $y$ to $z$, indicated by $xyz$. Voter $Y$'s preference is $yzx$, and voter $Z$'s is $zxy$. These preferences give rise to what is known as a Condorcet voting paradox because the social ordering, according to majority rule, is intransitive. Although a majority of voters ($X$ and $Z$) prefers $x$ to $y$, and a majority ($X$ and $Y$) prefers $y$ to $z$, a majority ($Y$ and $Z$) also prefers $z$ to $x$. (The French Enlightenment philosopher Marie-Jean-Antoine-Nicolas Condorcet first examined such voting paradoxes following the French Revolution.) So there is no Condorcet winner—that is, an alternative that would beat every other choice in separate pairwise contests.

Assume that a simple plurality determines the winning alternative. Furthermore, in the event of a three-way tie (there can never be a two-way tie if there are three votes), assume that the chair, $X$, can break the tie, giving the chair what would appear to be an edge over the other two voters, $Y$ and $Z$, who have the same one vote but no tie-breaker.

Under sincere voting, everyone votes for his or her first choice, without taking into account what the other voters might do. In this case, voter $X$ will get his first choice ($x$) by being able to break a three-way tie in favour of $x$. However, $X$'s apparent advantage will disappear if voting is "sophisticated."

To see why, first note that $X$ has a sure-thing, or dominant, strategy of "vote for $x$." It is never worse and sometimes better than any other strategy, whatever the

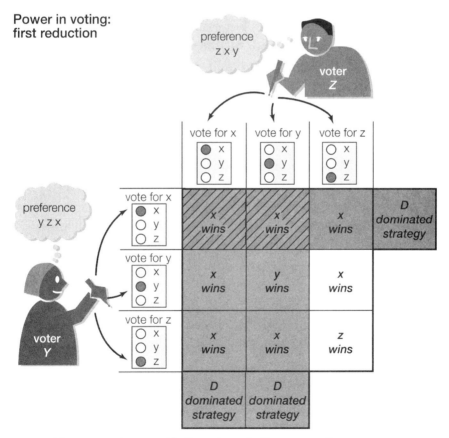

*Table 6: First reduction table.* Encyclopædia Britannica, Inc.

other two voters do. Thus, if the other two voters vote for the same alternative, $x$ will win. $X$ cannot do better than vote sincerely for $x$, so voting sincerely is never worse. If the other two voters disagree, however, $X$'s tie-breaking vote (along with his regular vote) will be decisive in $x$'s selection, which is $X$'s best outcome.

Given the dominant-strategy choice of $x$ on the part of $X$, then $Y$ and $Z$ face reduced strategy choices. (It is a reduction because $X$'s strategy of voting for $x$ is taken as a given.) In this reduction, $Y$ has one, and $Z$ has two, dominated strategies (indicated by $D$), which are never better and sometimes worse than some other strategy, whatever the other two voters do. For example, observe that "vote for $x$" by $Y$ always leads to his worst outcome, $x$. This leaves $Y$ with two undominated strategies, "vote for $y$" and "vote for $z$," which are neither dominant nor dominated strategies: "Vote for $y$" is better than "vote for $z$" if $Z$ chooses $y$ (leading to $y$ rather than $x$), whereas the reverse is the case if $Z$ chooses $z$ (leading to $z$ rather than $x$). By contrast, $Z$ has a dominant strategy of "vote for $z$," which leads to outcomes at least as good as and sometimes better than his other two strategies.

When voters have complete information about each other's preferences, they will eliminate the dominated strategies in the first reduction. The elimination of these strategies gives the second reduction matrix. Then $Y$, choosing between "vote for $y$" and "vote for $z$" in this matrix, would eliminate the now dominated "vote for $y$" because that choice would result in $x$'s winning as a result of the chair's tie-breaking vote. Instead, $Y$ would choose "vote for $z$," ensuring $z$'s election, which is the next-best outcome for $Y$. In this manner $z$, which is not the first choice of a majority and could in fact be beaten by $y$ in a pairwise contest, becomes the sophisticated outcome,

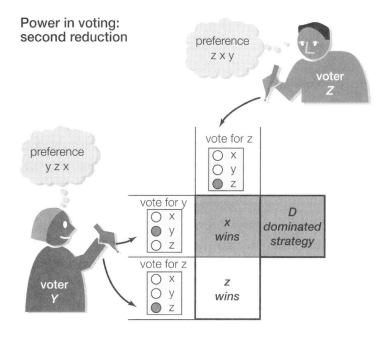

*Table 7: Second reduction table.* Encyclopædia Britannica, Inc.

which is the outcome produced by the successive elimination of dominated strategies by the voters (beginning with *X*'s sincere choice of *x*).

Sophisticated voting results in a Nash equilibrium because none of the players can do better by departing from their sophisticated strategy. This is clearly true for *X*, because *x* is his dominant strategy; given *X*'s choice of *x*, *z* is dominant for *Z*; and given these choices by *X* and *Z*, *z* is dominant for *Y*. These "contingent" dominance relations, in general, make sophisticated strategies a Nash equilibrium.

Observe, however, that there are four other Nash equilibria in this game. First, the choice of each of *x*, *y*, or *z* by all three voters are all Nash equilibria, because no single voter's departure can change the outcome to a different one, much less a better one, for that player. In addition, the choice of $x$ by $X$, $y$ by $Y$, and $x$ by $Z$—resulting in $x$—is also a Nash equilibrium, because no voter's departure would lead to his obtaining a better outcome.

In game-theoretic terms, sophisticated voting produces a different and smaller game in which some formerly undominated strategies in the larger game become dominated in the smaller game. The removal of such strategies—sometimes in several successive stages—can enable each voter to determine what outcomes are likely. In particular, sophisticated voters can foreclose the possibility that their worst outcomes will be chosen by successively removing dominated strategies, given the presumption that other voters will do likewise.

How does sophisticated voting affect the chair's presumed extra voting power? Observe that the chair's tie-breaking vote is not only not helpful but positively harmful: It guarantees that $X$'s worst outcome ($z$) will be chosen if voting is sophisticated. When voters' preferences are not so conflictual (note that the three voters have different first, second, and third choices when, as here, there is a Condorcet voting paradox), the paradox of the chair's position does not occur, making this paradox the exception rather than the rule.

## THE VON NEUMANN–MORGENSTERN THEORY

Von Neumann and Morgenstern were the first to construct a cooperative theory of $n$-person games. They assumed that various groups of players might join together to form coalitions, each of which has an associated value defined as the minimum amount that the coalition can ensure by its own efforts. (In practice, such groups might be blocs in a legislative body or business partners in a conglomerate.) They described these $n$-person games in characteristic-function form—that is, by listing the individual players (one-person coalitions), all possible coalitions of two or more players, and the values that each of these coalitions could ensure if a counter-coalition comprising all other players acted to minimize the amount that the coalition can obtain. They also assumed that the characteristic function is superadditive: The value of a coalition of two formerly separate coalitions is at least as great as the sum of the separate values of the two coalitions.

The sum of payments to the players in each coalition must equal the value of that coalition. Moreover, each player in a coalition must receive no less than what he could obtain playing alone; otherwise, he would not join the coalition. Each set of payments to the players describes one possible outcome of an $n$-person cooperative game and is called an imputation. Within a coalition $S$, an imputation $X$ is said to dominate another imputation $Y$ if each player in $S$ gets more with $X$ than with $Y$ and if the players in $S$ receive a total payment that does not exceed the coalition value of $S$. This means that players in the coalition prefer the payoff $X$ to the payoff $Y$ and have the power to enforce this preference.

Von Neumann and Morgenstern defined the solution to an $n$-person game as a set of imputations satisfying two conditions: (1) No imputation in the solution dominates another imputation in the solution, and (2) any imputation not in the solution is dominated by another one in the solution. A von Neumann–Morgenstern solution is not a single outcome but, rather, a set of outcomes, any one of which may occur. It is stable because, for the members of the coalition, any imputation outside the solution is dominated by (and is therefore less attractive than) an imputation within the solution. The imputations within the solution are viable because they are not dominated by any other imputations in the solution.

In any given cooperative game there are generally many—sometimes infinitely many—solutions. A simple three-person game that illustrates this fact is one in which any two players, as well as all three players, receive one unit, which they can divide between or among themselves in any way that they wish. Individual players receive nothing. In such a case the value of each two-person coalition, and the three-person coalition as well, is 1.

One solution to this game consists of three imputations, in each of which one player receives 0 and the other two players receive 1/2 each. There is no self-domination within the solution, because if one imputation is substituted for another, one player gets more, one gets less, and one gets the same (for domination, each of the players forming a coalition must gain). In addition, any imputation outside the solution is dominated by one in the solution, because the two players with the lowest payoffs must each get less than 1/2. Clearly, this imputation is dominated by an imputation in the solution in which these two players each get 1/2. According to this solution, at any given time one of its three imputations will occur, but von Neumann and Morgenstern do not predict which one.

A second solution to this game consists of all the imputations in which player $A$ receives 1/4 and players $B$ and $C$ share the remaining 3/4. Although this solution gives a different set of outcomes from the first solution, it, too, satisfies von Neumann and Morgenstern's two conditions. For any imputation within the solution, player $A$ always gets 1/4 and therefore cannot gain. In addition, because players $B$ and $C$ share a fixed sum, if one of them gains in a proposed imputation, the other must lose. Thus, no imputation in the solution dominates another imputation in the solution.

For any imputation not in the solution, player $A$ must get either more or less than 1/4. When $A$ gets more than 1/4, players $B$ and $C$ share less than 3/4 and, therefore, can do better with an imputation within the solution. When player $A$ gets less than 1/4, say 1/8, he always does better with an imputation in the solution. Players $B$ and $C$ now have more to share, but no matter how they split the new total of 7/8, there is an imputation in the solution that one of them will prefer. When they share equally, each gets 7/16, but player $B$, for example, can get more in the imputation (1/4, 1/2, 1/4), which is in the solution. When players $B$ and $C$ do not divide the 7/8 equally, the player who gets the smaller amount can always do better with an imputation in the solution. Thus, any imputation outside the solution is dominated by one inside the solution. Similarly, it can be shown that all of the imputations in which player $B$ gets 1/4 and players $A$ and $C$ share 3/4, as well as the set of all imputations in which player $C$ gets 1/4 and players $A$ and $B$ share 3/4, also constitute a solution to the game.

Although there may be many solutions to a game (each representing a different "standard of behaviour"), it was not apparent at first that there would always be at least one in every cooperative game. Von Neumann and Morgenstern found no game without a solution, and they deemed it important that no such game exists. However, in 1967 a fairly complicated 10-person game was discovered by the American mathematician William F. Lucas that did not have a solution. This and later counterexamples indicated that the von Neumann–Morgenstern solution is not universally applicable, but it remains compelling, especially because no definitive theory of $n$-person cooperative games exists.

## THE BANZHAF VALUE IN VOTING GAMES

It was shown that power defined as control over outcomes is not synonymous with control over resources, such as a chair's tie-breaking vote. The strategic situation facing voters intervenes and may cause them to reassess their strategies in light of the additional resources that the chair possesses. In doing so, they may be led to "gang up" against the chair. (Note that $Y$ and $Z$ do this without any explicit communication or binding agreement. The coalition they form against the chair $X$ is an implicit one and the game, therefore, remains noncooperative.) In effect, the chair's resources become a burden to bear, not power to relish.

When players' preferences are unknown beforehand, though, it is useful to define power in terms of their ability to alter the outcome by changing their votes, as governed by a constitution, bylaws, or other rules of the game. Various measures of voting power have been proposed for simple games, in which every coalition has a value of 1 (if it has enough votes to win) or 0 (if it does not). The sum of the powers of all the players is 1. When a player has 0 power, his vote has no influence on the outcome. When a player has a power of 1, the outcome depends only on his vote. The key to calculating voting power is determining the frequency with which a player casts a critical vote.

American attorney John F. Banzhaf III proposed that all combinations in which any player is the critical voter—that is, in which a measure passes only with this voter's support—be considered equally likely. The Banzhaf value for each player is then the number of combinations in which this voter is critical divided by the total number of combinations in which each voter (including this one) is critical.

This view is incompatible with defining the voting power of a player to be proportional to the number of votes he casts, because votes per se may have little or no bearing on the choice of outcomes. For example, in a three-member voting body in which $A$ has 4 votes, $B$ 2 votes, and $C$ 1 vote, members $B$ and $C$ will be powerless if a simple majority wins. The fact that members $B$ and $C$ together control 3/7 of the votes is irrelevant in the selection of outcomes, so these members are called dummies. Member $A$, by contrast, is a dictator by virtue of having enough votes alone to determine the outcome. A voting body can have only one dictator, whose existence renders all other members dummies, but there may be dummies and no dictator (an example is given in the following text).

A minimal winning coalition (MWC) is one in which the subtraction of at least one of its members renders it losing. To illustrate the calculation of Banzhaf values, consider a voting body with two 2-vote members (distinguished as 2a and 2b) and one 3-vote member, in which a simple majority wins. There are three distinct MWCs—(3, 2a), (3, 2b), and (2a, 2b)—or combinations in which some voter is critical. The grand coalition, comprising all three members, (3, 2a, 2b), is not an MWC because no single member's defection would cause it to lose.

Because each member's defection is critical in two MWCs, each member's proportion of voting power is two-sixths, or one-third. Thus, the Banzhaf index, which gives the Banzhaf values for each member in vector form, is (1/3, 1/3, 1/3). Clearly, the voting power of the 3-vote member is the same as that of each of the two 2-vote members, although the 3-vote member has 50 percent greater weight (more votes) than each of the 2-vote members.

The discrepancy between voting weight and voting power is more dramatic in the voting body (50, 49, 1) where, again, a simple majority wins. The 50-vote member is critical in all three MWCs—(50, 1), (50, 49), and (50, 49, 1), giving him a veto because his presence is necessary for a coalition to be winning—whereas the 49-vote member is critical in only (50, 49) and the 1-vote member in only (50, 1). Thus, the Banzhaf index for (50, 49, 1) is (3/5, 1/5, 1/5), making the 49-vote member indistinguishable from the 1-vote member. The 50-vote member, with just one more vote than the 49-vote member, has three times as much voting power.

In 1958 six West European countries formed the European Economic Community (EEC). The three large countries (West Germany, France, and Italy) each had 4 votes on its Council of Ministers, the two medium-size countries (Belgium and The Netherlands) 2 votes each, and the one small country (Luxembourg) 1 vote. The decision rule of the Council was a qualified majority of 12 out of 17 votes, giving the large countries Banzhaf values of 5/21 each, the medium-size countries 1/7 each, and—amazingly—Luxembourg no voting power at all. From 1958 to 1973—when the EEC admitted three additional members—Luxembourg was a dummy. Luxembourg might as well not have gone to Council meetings except to participate in the debate, because its one vote could never change the outcome. To see this without calculating the Banzhaf values of all the members, note that the votes of the five other countries are all even numbers. Therefore, an MWC with exactly 12 votes could never include Luxembourg's (odd) 1 vote. Although a 13-vote MWC that included Luxembourg could form, Luxembourg's defection would never render such an MWC losing. It is worth noting that as the Council kept expanding with the addition of new countries and the formation of the European Union, Luxembourg never reverted to being a dummy, even though its votes became an ever smaller proportion of the total.

The Banzhaf and other power indices, rooted in cooperative game theory, have been applied to many voting bodies, not necessarily weighted, sometimes with surprising results. For example, the Banzhaf index has been used to calculate the power of the 5 permanent and 10 nonpermanent members of the United Nations Security Council. (The permanent members, all with a veto, have 83 percent of the power.) It has also been used to compare the power of representatives, senators, and the president in the U.S. federal system.

Banzhaf himself successfully challenged the constitutionality of the weighted-voting system used in Nassau county, New York, showing that three of the County Board's six members were dummies. Likewise, the former Board of Estimate of New York City, in which three citywide officials (mayor, chair of the city council, and comptroller) had two votes each and the five borough presidents had one vote each, was declared unconstitutional by the U.S. Supreme Court. Brooklyn had approximately six times the population of Staten Island but the same one vote on the Board, in violation of the equal-protection clause of the 14th Amendment of the U.S. Constitution that requires "one person, one vote." Finally, it has been argued that the U.S. Electoral College, which is effectively a weighted voting body because almost all states cast their electoral votes as blocs, violates one person, one vote in presidential elections, because voters from large states have approximately three times as much voting power, on a per-capita basis, as voters from small states.

Game theory is now well established and widely used in a variety of disciplines. The foundations of economics, for example, are increasingly grounded in game theory. Among game theory's many applications in economics is the design of Federal Communications Commission auctions of airwaves, which have netted the U.S. government billions of dollars. Game theory is increasingly used in political science to study strategy in areas as diverse as campaigns and elections, defense policy, and international relations. In biology, business, management science, computer science, and law, game theory has been used to model a variety of strategic situations. Game theory has even penetrated areas of philosophy (e.g., to study the equilibrium properties of ethical rules), religion (e.g., to interpret Bible stories), and pure mathematics (e.g., to analyze how to divide a cake fairly among $n$ people). All in all, game theory holds out great promise not only for advancing the understanding of strategic interaction in very different settings but also for offering prescriptions for the design of better auction, bargaining, voting, and information systems that involve strategic choice.

# CHAPTER 5
## COMBINATORICS

Combinatorics is the field of mathematics concerned with problems of selection, arrangement, and operation within a finite or discrete system. This section also includes the closely related area of combinatorial geometry.

One of the basic problems of combinatorics is to determine the number of possible configurations (e.g., graphs, designs, arrays) of a given type. Even when the rules specifying the configuration are relatively simple, enumeration may sometimes present formidable difficulties. The mathematician may have to be content with finding an approximate answer or at least a good lower and upper bound.

In mathematics, generally, an entity is said to "exist" if a mathematical example satisfies the abstract properties that define the entity. In this sense it may not be apparent that even a single configuration with certain specified properties exists. This situation gives rise to problems of existence and construction. There is again an important class of theorems that guarantee the existence of certain choices under appropriate hypotheses. Besides their intrinsic interest, these theorems may be used as existence theorems in various combinatorial problems.

Finally, there are problems of optimization. As an example, a function $f$, the economic function, assigns the numerical value $f(x)$ to any configuration $x$ with certain specified properties. In this case the problem is to choose a configuration $x_o$ that minimizes $f(x)$ or makes it $\varepsilon$ = minimal—that is, for any number $\varepsilon > 0$, $f(x_o)$ $f(x) + \varepsilon$, for all configurations $x$, with the specified properties.

# HISTORY

Since ancient times in cultures ranging from China to Persia, combinatorial problems have inspired and puzzled mathematicians. Even in our own day, the fiendish game of Sudoku has inspired millions to dabble in combinatorics.

## EARLY DEVELOPMENTS

Certain types of combinatorial problems have attracted the attention of mathematicians since early times. Magic squares, for example, which are square arrays of numbers with the property that the rows, columns, and diagonals add up to the same number, occur in the *I Ching*, a Chinese book dating back to the 12th century BCE. The binomial

*Millions of unwitting Sudoku addicts play at combinatorics every day.* Shutterstock.com

coefficients, or integer coefficients in the expansion of $(a + b)^n$, were known to the 12th-century Indian mathematician Bhāskara, who in his *Līlāvatī* ("The Graceful"), dedicated to a beautiful woman, gave the rules for calculating them together with illustrative examples. "Pascal's triangle," a triangular array of binomial coefficients, had been taught by the 13th-century Persian philosopher Naṣīr ad-Dīn al-Ṭūsī.

In the West, combinatorics may be considered to begin in the 17th century with Blaise Pascal and Pierre de Fermat, both of France, who discovered many classical combinatorial results in connection with the development of the theory of probability. The term *combinatorial* was first used in the modern mathematical sense by the German philosopher and mathematician Gottfried Wilhelm Leibniz in his *Dissertatio de Arte Combinatoria* ("Dissertation Concerning the Combinational Arts"). He foresaw the applications of this new discipline to the whole range of the sciences. The Swiss mathematician Leonhard Euler was finally responsible for the development of a school of authentic combinatorial mathematics beginning in the 18th century. He became the father of graph theory when he settled the Königsberg bridge problem, and his famous conjecture on Latin squares was not resolved until 1959.

In England, Arthur Cayley, near the end of the 19th century, made important contributions to enumerative graph theory, and James Joseph Sylvester discovered many combinatorial results. At about the same time, the British mathematician George Boole used combinatorial methods in connection with the development of symbolic logic, and the combinatorial ideas and methods of Henri Poincaré, which developed in the early part of the 20th century in connection with the problem of *n* bodies, have led to the discipline of topology, which occupies the centre of the stage of mathematics. Many combinatorial problems were posed during the 19th century as purely recreational problems and are identified by such names as "the problem of eight queens" and "the Kirkman school girl problem." Conversely, the study of triple systems begun by Thomas P. Kirkman in 1847 and pursued by Swiss-born German mathematician Jakob Steiner in the 1850s was the beginning of the theory of design. Among the earliest books devoted exclusively to combinatorics are the German mathematician Eugen Netto's *Lehrbuch der Combinatorik* (1901; "Textbook of Combinatorics") and the British mathematician Percy Alexander MacMahon's *Combinatory Analysis* (1915–16), which provide a view of combinatorial theory as it existed before 1920.

## COMBINATORICS DURING THE 20TH CENTURY

Many factors have contributed to the quickening pace of development of combinatorial theory since 1920. One of these was the development of the statistical theory of the design of experiments by the English statisticians Ronald Fisher and Frank Yates, which has given rise to many problems of combinatorial interest. The methods initially developed to solve them have found applications in such fields as coding theory. Information theory, which arose around midcentury, has also become a rich source of combinatorial problems of a quite new type.

Another source of the revival of interest in combinatorics is graph theory, the importance of which lies in the fact that graphs can serve as abstract models for many different kinds of schemes of relations among sets of objects.

Its applications extend to operations research, chemistry, statistical mechanics, theoretical physics, and socioeconomic problems. The theory of transportation networks can be regarded as a chapter of the theory of directed graphs. One of the most challenging theoretical problems, the four-colour problem belongs to the domain of graph theory. It has also applications to such other branches of mathematics as group theory.

The development of computer technology in the second half of the 20th century is a main cause of the interest in finite mathematics in general and combinatorial theory in particular. Combinatorial problems arise in numerical analysis as well as in the design of computer systems and the application of computers to such problems as those of information storage and retrieval.

Statistical mechanics is one of the oldest and most productive sources of combinatorial problems. Much important combinatorial work has been done by applied mathematicians and physicists since the mid-20th century, such as the work on Ising models.

In pure mathematics, combinatorial methods have been used with advantage in such diverse fields as probability, algebra (finite groups and fields, matrix and lattice theory), number theory (difference sets), set theory (Sperner's theorem), and mathematical logic (Ramsey's theorem).

In contrast to the wide range of combinatorial problems and the multiplicity of methods that have been devised to deal with them stands the lack of a central unifying theory. Unifying principles and cross connections, however, have begun to appear in various areas of combinatorial theory. The search for an underlying pattern that may indicate in some way how the diverse parts of combinatorics are interwoven is a challenge that faces mathematicians in the first quarter of the 21st century.

# PROBLEMS OF ENUMERATION

## PERMUTATIONS AND COMBINATIONS

### BINOMIAL COEFFICIENTS

An ordered set $a_1, a_2, \ldots, a_r$ of $r$ distinct objects selected from a set of $n$ objects is called a permutation of $n$ things taken $r$ at a time. The number of permutations is given by $_nP_n = n(n-1)(n-2)\cdots(n-r+1)$. When $r = n$, the number $_nP_r = n(n-1)(n-2)\cdots$ is simply the number of ways of arranging $n$ distinct things in a row. This expression is called factorial $n$ and is denoted by $n!$. It follows that $_nP_r = n!/(n-r)!$. By convention $0! = 1$.

A set of $r$ objects selected from a set of $n$ objects without regard to order is called a combination of $n$ things taken $r$ at a time. Because each combination gives rise to $r!$ permutations, the number of combinations, which is written $\binom{n}{r}$, can be expressed in terms of factorials

$$(1) \qquad \binom{n}{r} = \frac{_nP_r}{r!} = \frac{n!}{r!(n-r)!}.$$

The number $\binom{n}{r}$ is called a binomial coefficient because it occurs as the coefficient of $p^r q^{n-r}$ in the binomial expansion—that is, the re-expression of $(q+p)n$ in a linear combination of products of $p$ and $q$

$$(2) \qquad (q+p)^n = q^n + \binom{n}{1}pq^{n-1} + \cdots + \binom{n}{r}p^r q^{n-r} + \cdots + p^n.$$

If $0 \leqslant p \leqslant 1$, and $q = 1 - p$, then the term $\binom{n}{r} p^r q^{n-r}$

in the binomial expansion is the probability that an event the chance of occurrence of which is $p$ occurs exactly $r$ times in $n$ independent trials.

The answer to many different kinds of enumeration problems can be expressed in terms of binomial coefficients. The number of distinct solutions of the equation $x_1 + x_2 + \cdots + xn = m$, for example, in which $m$ is a non-negative integer $m \geq n$ and in which only non-negative integral values of $xi$ are allowed is expressible this way, as was found by the 17th- and 18th-century French-born British mathematician Abraham De Moivre

$$(3) \qquad N = \binom{m + n - 1}{n - 1} = \frac{(m + n - 1)!}{(n - 1)! \, m!} \ .$$

## MULTINOMIAL COEFFICIENTS

If $S$ is a set of $n$ objects, and $n_1, n_2, \cdots, n_k$ are non-negative integers satisfying $n_1 + n_2 + \cdots + n_k = n$, then the number of ways in which the objects can be distributed into $k$ boxes, $X_1, X_2, \cdots, X_k$, such that the box $X_i$ contains exactly $n_i$ objects is given in terms of a ratio constructed of factorials

$$(4) \qquad \binom{n}{n_1, n_2, \cdots, n_k} = \frac{n!}{n_1! \, n_2! \cdots n_k!} \ .$$

This number, called a multinomial coefficient, is the coefficient in the multinomial expansion of the $n$th power of the sum of the $\{p_i\}$

$$(5) \quad \begin{cases} (p_1 + p_2 + \cdots + p_k)^n \\ = \sum \binom{n}{n_1, n_2, \cdots, n_k} p_1^{n_1} p_2^{n_2} \cdots p_k^{n_k} \\ \text{The summation is over all non-negative } n_1, n_2, \cdots, n_k \\ \text{for which } n_1 + n_2 + \cdots + n_k = n. \end{cases}$$

If all the $\{p_i\}$ are non-negative and sum to 1 and if there are $k$ possible outcomes in a trial in which the chance of the $i$th outcome is $p_i$, then the $i$th summand in the multinomial expansion is the probability that in $n$ independent trials the $i$th outcome will occur exactly $n_i$ times, for each $i$, $1 \leq 1 \leq k$.

## RECURRENCE RELATIONS AND GENERATING FUNCTIONS

If $f_n$ is a function defined on the positive integers, then a relation that expresses $f_{n+k}$ as a linear combination of function values of integer index less than $n + k$, in which a fixed constant in the linear combination is written $a_i$, is called a recurrence relation

$$(6) \quad f_{n+k} = a_1 f_{n+k-1} + a_2 f_{n+k-2} + \cdots + a_k f_n \ .$$

The relation together with the initial values $f_0, f_1, \cdots, f_{k-1}$ determines $f_n$ for all $n$. The function $F(x)$ constructed of a sum of products of the type $f_n x^n$, the convergence of which is assumed in the neighbourhood of the origin, is called the generating function of $f_n$

$$(7) \qquad F(x) = \sum_{n=0}^{\infty} f_n x^n .$$

The set of the first $n$ positive integers will be written $Xn$. It is possible to find the number of subsets of $Xn$ containing no two consecutive integers, with the convention that the null set counts as one set. The required number will be written $fn$. A subset of the required type is either a subset of $Xn_{-1}$ or is obtained by adjoining $n$ to a subset of $Xn_{-2}$. Therefore $fn$ is determined by the recurrence relation $fn = fn_{-1} + fn_{-2}$ with the initial values $f_0 = 1, f_1 = 2$. Thus $f_2 = 3, f_3 = 5, f_4 = 8$, and so on. The generating function $F(x)$ of $f_n$ can be calculated

$$(8) \qquad F(x) = \frac{1 + x}{1 - x(1 + x)} ,$$

and from this a formula for the desired function $f_n$ can be obtained

$$(9) \qquad \begin{cases} f_n = \sum_{k} \binom{n + 1 - k}{k} \\ \text{The summation extends over all values of } k \text{ from 0 to} \\ \text{the largest integer not exceeding } (n + 1)/2. \end{cases}$$

That $f_n = f_{n-1} + f_{n-2}$ can now be directly checked.

## PARTITIONS

A partition of a positive integer $n$ is a representation of $n$ as a sum of positive integers $n = x_1 + x_2 + \cdots + x_k, x_i \geq 1, i = 1,$

2, $\cdots$, $k$. The numbers $x_i$ are called the parts of the partition. The

$$\text{number of ordered partitions into } k \text{ parts is } \binom{n-1}{k-1},$$

for this is the number of ways of putting $k$ - 1 separating marks in the $n$ - 1 spaces between $n$ dots in a row. The theory of unordered partitions is much more difficult and has many interesting features. An unordered partition can be standardized by listing the parts in a decreasing order. Thus $n = x_1 + x_2 + \cdots + x_k, x_1 \geq x_2 \geq \cdots \geq x_k \geq 1$. In what follows partition will mean an unordered partition.

The number of partitions of $n$ into $k$ parts will be denoted by $P_k(n)$, and a recurrence formula for it can be obtained from the definition

$$(10) \quad P_k(n) = P_k(n-k) + P_{k-1}(n-k) + \cdots + P_1(n-k).$$

This recurrence formula, together with the initial conditions $P_k(n) = 0$ if $n < k$, and $P_k(k) = 1$ determines $P_k(n)$. It can be shown that $P_k(n)$ depends on the value of $n$ (mod $k!$), in which the notation $x \equiv a$ (mod $b$) means that $x$ is any number that, if divided by $b$, leaves the same remainder as $a$ does. For example, $P_3(n) = n^2 + c_n$, in which $c_n = 0, -1/12, -1/3, +1/4, -1/3,$ or $-1/12$, according as $n$ is congruent to 0, 1, 2, 3, 4, or 5 (mod 6). $P(n)$, which is a sum over all values of $k$ from 1 to $n$ of $P_k(n)$, denotes the number of partitions of $n$ into $n$ or fewer parts.

## THE FERRERS DIAGRAM

Many results on partitions can be obtained by the use of Ferrers diagram. The diagram of a partition is obtained by

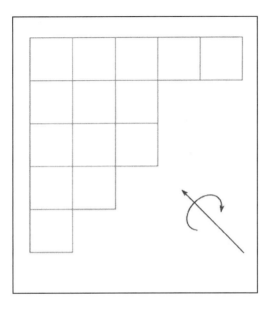

*By using the Ferrers diagram, one can attain many results on partitions.*
Copyright Encyclopaedia Britannica; rendering for this edition by
Rosen Educational Services

putting down a row of squares equal in number to the largest part, then immediately below it a row of squares equal
in number to the next part, and so on.

By rotating the Ferrers diagram of the partition about
the diagonal, it is possible to obtain from the partition $n =$
$x_1 + x_2 + \cdots + x_k$ the conjugate partition $n = x_1^* + x_2^* + \cdots x_n^*$,
in which $x_i^*$ is the number of parts in the original partition
of cardinality $i$ or more. Thus, for example, the conjugate of
the partition of 14 is $14 = 5 + 4 + 3 + 1 + 1$. Hence, the following result is obtained:

> ($F_1$) The number of partitions of $n$ into $k$ parts is
> equal to the number of partitions of $n$ with $k$ as the
> largest part.

Other results obtainable by using Ferrer diagrams are:

(**F$_2$**) The number of self-conjugate partitions of $n$ equals the number of partitions of $n$ with all parts unequal and odd.

(**F$_3$**) the number of partitions of $n$ into unequal parts is equal to the number of partitions of $n$ into odd parts.

Generating functions can be used with advantage to study partitions. For example, it can be proved that:

(**G$_1$**) The generating function $F_1(x)$ of $P(n)$, the number of partitions of the integer $n$, is a product of reciprocals of terms of the type ($1 - xk$), for all positive integers $k$, with the convention that $P(0)=1$:

(11)    $$F_1(x) = (1-x)^{-1}(1-x^2)^{-1}(1-x^3)^{-1}\cdots$$

(**G$_2$**) The generating function $F_2(x)$ of the number of partitions of $n$ into unequal parts is a product of terms like ($1 + x^k$), for all positive integers $k$:

(12)    $$F_2(x) = (1+x)(1+x^2)(1+x^3)\cdots$$

(**G$_3$**) The generating function $F_3(x)$ of the number of partitions of $x$ consisting only of odd parts is a product of reciprocals of terms of the type ($1 - x^k$), for all positive odd integers $k$:

(13)    $$F_3(x) = (1-x)^{-1}(1-x^3)^{-1}(1-x^5)^{-1}\cdots$$

Thus to prove (F$_3$) it is necessary only to show that the generating functions described in (G$_2$) and (G$_3$) are equal. This method was used by Euler.

## The Principle of Inclusion and Exclusion: Derangements

For a case in which there are $N$ objects and $n$ properties $A_1, A_2, \cdots A_n$, the number $N(A_1, A_2)$, for example, will be the number of objects that possess the properties $A_1, A_2$. If $N(\bar{A}_1, \bar{A}_2, \cdots, \bar{A}_n)$ is the number of objects possessing none of the properties $A_1, A_2, \cdots, A_n$, then this number can be computed as an alternating sum of sums involving the numbers of objects that possess the properties

(14)

$$
N(\overline{A_1}, \overline{A_2}, \cdots, \overline{A_n})
$$
$$
= N - \sum N(A_{i_1}) + \sum N(A_{i_1}, A_{i_2}) + \cdots
$$
$$
+ (-1)^k \sum N(A_{i_1}, A_{i_2}, \cdots, A_{i_k}) + \cdots
$$
$$
+ (-1)^n N(A_1, A_2, \cdots, A_n)
$$

In the general term the summation is over all combinations of $k$ properties from the set of $n$ properties $A_1, A_2, \cdots, A_n$.

This is the principle of inclusion and exclusion expressed by Sylvester.

The permutation of $n$ elements that displaces each object is called a derangement. The permutations themselves may be the objects and the property $i$ may be the property that a permutation does not displace the $i$th element. In such a case $N = n!$ and $N(A_1, A_2) = (n - 2)!$, for example. Hence the number $Dn$ of derangements can be shown to be approximated by $n!/e$

(15)

$$
\begin{aligned}
D_n = n! &- \binom{n}{1}(n-1)! + \cdots + (-1)^k \binom{n}{k}(n-k)! \\
&+ \cdots + (-1)^n \binom{n}{n} \\
= n!&\left(1 - \frac{1}{1!} + \frac{1}{2!} + \cdots + (-1)^k \frac{1}{k!}\right. \\
&\left. + \cdots + (-1)^n \frac{1}{n!}\right) \\
= n!/e \ &\text{approximately.}
\end{aligned}
$$

This number was first obtained by Euler. If $n$ persons check their hats in a restaurant, and the waiter loses the checks and returns the hats at random, then the chance that no one receives his own hat is $D_n/n! = e^{-1}$ approximately. It is surprising that the approximate answer is independent of $n$. To six places of decimals $e^{-1} = 0.367879$. When $n = 6$ the error of approximation is less than 0.0002.

If $n$ is expressed as the product of powers of its prime factors $p_1, p_2, \cdots p_k$, if the objects are the integers less than or equal to $n$, and if $A_i$ is the property of being divisible by $p_i$, then Sylvester's formula gives, as the number of integers less than $n$ and prime to it, a function of $n$, written $\phi(n)$, composed of a product of $n$ and $k$ factors of the type $(1 - 1/p_i)$

$$(16) \qquad \varphi(n) = n\left(1 - \frac{1}{p_1}\right)\left(1 - \frac{1}{p_2}\right)\cdots\left(1 - \frac{1}{p_k}\right).$$

The function $\phi(n)$ is the Euler function.

## Polya's Theorem

It is required to make a necklace of $n$ beads out of an infinite supply of beads of $k$ different colours. The number of different necklaces, $c\ (n, k)$, that can be made is given by the reciprocal of $n$ times a sum of terms of the type $\phi(n)$ $k^{n/d}$, in which the summation is over all divisors $d$ of $n$ and $\phi$ is the Euler function

$$(17) \quad c(n,k) = \frac{1}{n} \sum_{d \mid n} \varphi(d) k^{n/d} \quad .$$

Though the problem of the necklaces appears to be frivolous, the formula given above can be used to solve a difficult problem in the theory of Lie algebras, of some importance in modern physics.

The general problem of which the necklace problem is a special case was solved by the Hungarian-born American mathematician George Polya in a famous 1937 memoir in which he established connections between groups, graphs, and chemical bonds. It has been applied to enumeration problems in physics, chemistry, and mathematics.

## The Möbius Inversion Theorem

In 1832 the German astronomer and mathematician August Ferdinand Möbius proved that if $f$ and $g$ are functions defined on the set of positive integers, such that $f$ evaluated at $x$ is a sum of values of $g$ evaluated at divisors of $x$, then inversely $g$ at $x$ can be evaluated as a sum involving $f$ evaluated at divisors of $x$

(18)

$$\text{If} \quad f(x) = \sum_{d \mid x} g(d),$$

in which $d \mid x$ means that $d$ is a divisor of $x$, then

$$g(x) = \sum_{d \mid x} \mu(d, x) f(d),$$

in which

$$\mu(d, n) = \begin{cases} 1 & \text{if } n = d \\ (-1)^k & \text{if } n = p_1 p_2 \cdots p_k d \\ 0 & \text{otherwise.} \end{cases}$$

In 1964 the American mathematician Gian-Carlo Rota obtained a powerful generalization of this theorem, providing a fundamental unifying principle of enumeration. One consequence of Rota's theorem is the following: If $f$ and $g$ are functions defined on subsets of a finite set $A$, such that $f(A)$ is a sum of terms $g(S)$, in which $S$ is a subset of $A$, then $g(A)$ can be expressed in terms of $f$

(19)

$$\text{If} \quad f(A) = \sum_{S \subset A} g(S),$$

$$\text{then} \quad g(A) = \sum_{S \subset A} (-1)^{|A| - |S|} f(S).$$

## SPECIAL PROBLEMS

Despite the general methods of enumeration already described, there are many problems in which they do not apply and therefore require special treatment. Two such problems include the Ising problem and the self-avoiding random walk.

## The Ising Problem

A rectangular $m \times n$ grid is made up of unit squares, each coloured either red or green. How many different colour patterns are there if the number of boundary edges between red squares and green squares is prescribed?

This problem, although easy to state, proved difficult to solve. A complete and rigorous solution was not achieved until the early 1960s. The importance of the problem lies in the fact that it is the simplest model that exhibits the macroscopic behaviour expected from certain natural assumptions made at the microscopic level. Historically, the problem arose from an early attempt, made in 1925, to formulate the statistical mechanics of ferromagnetism. The three-dimensional analogue of the Ising problem remains unsolved in spite of persistent attacks.

## Self-Avoiding Random Walk

A random walk consists of a sequence of $n$ steps of unit length on a flat rectangular grid, taken at random either in the $x$- or the $y$-direction, with equal probability in each of the four directions. What is the number $R_n$ of random walks that do not touch the same vertex twice? This problem has defied solution, except for small values of $n$, though a large amount of numerical data has been amassed.

# PROBLEMS OF CHOICE

## Systems of Distinct Representatives

Subsets $S_1, S_2, \cdots, Sn$ of a finite set $S$ are said to possess a set of distinct representatives if $x_1, x_2, \cdots, x_n$ can be found, such that $x_i \in S_i, i = 1, 2, \cdots, n, x_i \neq x_j$ for $i \neq j$. It is possible that $S_i$ and $S_j, i \neq j$, may have exactly the same elements and are distinguished only by the indices $i, j$. In 1935 American mathematician, M. Hall, Jr., proved that a necessary and sufficient condition for $S_1, S_2, \cdots, S_n$ to possess a system of distinct representatives is that, for every $kn$, any $k$ of the $n$ subsets contain between them at least $k$ distinct elements.

For example, the sets $S_1 = (1, 2, 2)$, $S_2 = (1, 2, 4)$, $S_3 = (1, 2, 5)$, $S_4 = (3, 4, 5, 6)$, $S_5 = (3, 4, 5, 6)$ satisfy the conditions of the theorem, and a set of distinct representatives is $x_1 = 1, x_2 = 2, x_3 = 5, x_4 = 3, x_5 = 4$. Conversely, the sets $T_1 = (1, 2)$, $T_2 = (1, 3)$, $T_3 = (1, 4)$, $T_4 = (2, 3)$, $T_5 = (2, 4)$, $T_6 = (1, 2, 5)$ do not possess a system of distinct representatives because $T_1, T_2, T_3, T_4, T_5$ possess between them only four elements.

The following theorem resulting from König is closely related to Hall's theorem and can be easily deduced from it. Conversely, Hall's theorem can be deduced from König's: If the elements of rectangular matrix are 0s and 1s, then the minimum number of lines that contain all of the 1s is equal to the maximum number of 1s that can be chosen with no two on a line.

## RAMSEY'S NUMBERS

If $X = \{1, 2, \ldots, n\}$, and if $T$, the family of all subsets of $X$ containing exactly $r$ distinct elements, is divided into two mutually exclusive families $\alpha$ and $\beta$, the following conclusion that was originally obtained by the British mathematician Frank Plumpton Ramsey follows. He proved that for $r \geq 1, p \leq r, q \leq r$ there exists a number $N_r(p, q)$ depending solely on $p, q, r$ such that if $n > N_r(p, q)$, there is either a subset $A$ of $p$ elements all of the $r$ subsets of which are in the family $\alpha$ or there is a subset $B$ of $q$ elements all of the $r$ subsets of which are in the family $\beta$.

The set $X$ can be a set of $n$ persons. For $r = 2$, $T$ is the family of all pairs. If two persons have met each other, then the pair can belong to the family $\alpha$. If two persons have not met, then the pair can belong to the family $\beta$. If these things are assumed, then, by Ramsey's theorem, for any given $p \geq 2$, $q \geq 2$ there exists a number $N_2(p, q)$ such that if $n > N_2(p, q)$, then among $n$ persons invited to a party there will be either a set of $p$ persons all of whom have met each other or a set of $q$ persons no two of whom have met.

Although the existence of $N_r(p, q)$ is known, actual values are known only for a few cases. Because $N_r(p, q) = N_r(q, p)$, it is possible to take $p \leq q$. It is known that $N_2(3, 3) = 6$, $N_2(3, 4) = 9$, $N_2(3, 5) = 14$, $N_2(3, 6) = 18$, $N_2(4, 4) = 18$. Some bounds are also known; for example, $35 \leq N_2(4, 6) \leq 41$.

A consequence of Ramsey's theorem is the following result obtained in 1935 by the Hungarian mathematicians Paul Erdös and George Szekeres. For a given integer $n$ there exists an integer $N = N(n)$, such that a set of any $N$ points on a plane, no three on a line, contains $n$ points forming a convex $n$-gon.

## DESIGN THEORY

### BIB (Balanced Incomplete Block) Designs

A design is a set of $T = \{1, 2, \ldots, v\}$ objects called treatments and a family of subsets $B_1, B_2, \ldots, B_b$ of $T$, called blocks, such that the block $B_i$ contains exactly $k_i$ treatments, all distinct. The number $k_i$ is called the size of the block $B_i$, and the $i$th treatment is said to be replicated $r_i$ times if it occurs in exactly $r_i$ blocks. Specific designs are subject to further constraints. The name design comes from statistical theory in which designs are used to estimate effects of treatments applied to experimental units.

A BIB design is a design with $v$ treatments and $b$ blocks in which each block is of size $k$, each treatment is replicated $r$ times, and every pair of distinct treatments occurs together in $\lambda$ blocks. The design is said to have the parameters ($v$, $b$, $r$, $k$, $\lambda$). Some basic relations are easy to establish

(20)     $bk = vr$,     $\lambda(v-1) = r(k-1)$.

These conditions are necessary but not sufficient for the existence of the design. The design is said to be proper if $k < v$—that is, the blocks are incomplete. For a proper BIB design Fisher's inequality $b \geq v$, or equivalently $r \geq k$, holds.

A BIB design is said to be symmetric if $v = b$, and consequently $r = k$. Such a design is called a symmetric ($v$, $k$, $\lambda$) design, and $\lambda(v - 1) = k(k - 1)$. A necessary condition for the existence of a symmetric ($v$, $k$, $\lambda$) design is given by the following:

A. If $v$ is even, $k - \lambda$ is a perfect square.
B. If $v$ is odd, a certain Diophantine equation

(21)     $x^2 = (k - \lambda) y^2 + (-1)^{(v-1)/2} \lambda z^2$

has a solution in integers not all zero.

For example, the designs ($v$, $k$, $\lambda$) = (22, 7, 2) and (46, 10, 2) are ruled out by (A) and the design (29, 8, 2) by (B). Because necessary and sufficient conditions for the existence of a BIB design with given parameters are unknown, it is often a difficult problem to decide whether a design with given parameters (satisfying the known necessary conditions) really exists.

Methods of constructing BIB designs depend on the use of finite fields, finite geometries, and number theory. Some general methods were given in 1939 by the Indian mathematician Raj Chandra Bose, who has since emigrated to the United States.

A finite field is a finite set of marks with two operations, addition and multiplication, subject to the usual nine laws of addition and multiplication obeyed by rational numbers. In particular the marks may be taken to be the set $X$ of non-negative integers less than a prime $p$. If this is so, then addition and multiplication are defined by modified addition and multiplication laws

$$(22) \quad a + b = s \ (\mathrm{mod}\, p), \qquad ab = c \ (\mathrm{mod}\, p)$$

in which $a$, $b$, $r$, and $p$ belong to $X$. For example, if $p = 7$, then $5 + 4 = 2, 5 \cdot 4 = 6$. There exist more general finite fields in which the number of elements is $pn, p$ a prime. There is essentially one field with $pn$ elements, with given $p$ and $n$. It is denoted by $GF(pn)$.

Finite geometries can be obtained from finite fields in which the coordinates of points are now elements of a finite field. A set of $k + 1$ non-negative integers $d_0, d_1, \cdots, d_k$, is said to form a perfect difference set mod $v$, if among the $k(k - 1)$ differences $d_i - d_j, i \neq j, i, j = 0, 1, \cdots, k$, reduced mod $v$, each nonzero positive integer less than $v$ occurs exactly the same number of times $\lambda$. For example, 1, 4, 5, 9, 3 is a difference set mod 11, with $\lambda = 2$. From a perfect difference set can be obtained the symmetric $(v, k, \lambda)$ design using the integers $0, 1, 2, \cdots, v - 1$. The $j$th block contains the treatments obtained by reducing mod $v$ the numbers $d_0 + j, j_1 + j, \cdots, d_i + j, j = 0, 1, \cdots, v - 1$.

It can be shown that any two blocks of a symmetric $(v, k, \lambda)$ design intersect in exactly $k$ treatments. By deleting one block and all the treatments contained in it, it is possible to obtain from the symmetric design its residual, which is a BIB design (unsymmetric) with parameters $v^* = v - k, b^* = v - 1, r^* = k, k^* = k - \lambda, \lambda^* = \lambda$. One may ask whether it is true that a BIB design with the parameters of a residual can be embedded in a symmetric BIB design. The truth of this is rather easy to demonstrate when $\lambda = 1$. Hall and W.S. Connor in 1953 showed that it is also true for $\lambda = 2$. The Indian mathematician K.N. Bhattacharya in 1944, however, gave a counterexample for $\lambda = 3$ by exhibiting a BIB design with parameters $v = 16, b = 24, r = 9, k = 6, \lambda = 3$ for which two particular blocks intersect in four treatments and which for that reason cannot be embedded in a symmetric BIB design.

A BIB design is said to be resolvable if the set of blocks can be partitioned into subsets, such that the blocks in any subset contain every treatment exactly once. For the case $k = 3$, this problem was first posed during the 19th century by the British mathematician T.P. Kirkman as a recreational problem. There are $v$ girls in a class. Their teacher wants to take the class out for a walk for a number of days, the girls marching abreast in triplets. It is required to arrange the walk so that any two girls march abreast in the same triplet exactly once. It is easily shown that this is equivalent to the construction of a resolvable BIB design with $v = 6t + 3, b = (2t + 1)(3t + 1), r = 3t + 1, k = 3, \lambda = 1$. Solutions were known for only a large number of special values of $t$ until a completely general solution was finally given by the Indian and American mathematicians Dwijendra K. Ray-Chaudhuri and R.M. Wilson in 1970.

## PBIB (PARTIALLY BALANCED INCOMPLETE BLOCK) DESIGNS

Given $v$ objects $1, 2, \cdots, v$, a relation satisfying the following conditions is said to be an $m$-class partially balanced association scheme:

A. Any two objects are either 1st, or 2nd, $\cdots$, or $m$th associates, the relation of association being symmetrical.

B. Each object α has *nii*th associates, the number
   *ni* being independent of α.
C. If any two objects α and β are *i*th associates, then
   the number of objects that are *j*th associates of
   α and *k*th associates of β is *pjki* and is independent of the pair of *i*th associates α and β.

The constants $v$, $n_i$, $p_{jk}^i$ are the parameters of the association scheme. A number of identities connecting these
parameters were given by the Indian mathematicians Bose
and K.R. Nair in 1939, but Bose and the American mathematician D.M. Mesner in 1959 discovered new identities
when $m > 2$.

A PBIB design is obtained by identifying the $v$ treatments with the $v$ objects of an association scheme and
arranging them into $b$ blocks satisfying the following
conditions:

A. Each contains $k$ treatments.
B. Each treatment occurs in $r$ blocks.
C. If two treatments are *i*th associates, they occur
   together in λ*i* blocks.

Two-class association schemes and the corresponding
designs are especially important both from the mathematical point of view and because of statistical applications.
For a two-class association scheme the constancy of $v$, *ni*,
$p_{11}^1$, and $p_{11}^2$ ensures the constancy of the other parameters.
Seven relations hold:

$$(23) \quad \begin{cases} p_{12}^1 = n_1 - p_{11}^1 - 1 = p_{21}^1, & p_{22}^1 = n_2 - n_1 + p_{11}^1 + 1 \\ p_{12}^2 = n_1 - p_{11}^2 = p_{21}^2, & p_{22}^2 = n_2 - n_1 + p_{11}^2 \\ v = n_1 + n_2 + 1, & n_1 p_{12}^1 = n_2 p_{11}^2, \quad n_1 p_{22}^1 = n_2 p_{12}^2. \end{cases}$$

Sufficient conditions for the existence of association schemes with given parameters are unknown, but for a two-class association scheme W.S. Connor and the American mathematician Willard H. Clatworthy in 1954 obtained some necessary conditions

$$
(24) \quad
\begin{cases}
\alpha_1, \alpha_2 = \dfrac{n_1 + n_2}{2} \pm \dfrac{(n_1 - n_2) + \gamma(n_1 + n_2)}{2\sqrt{\Delta}} \\[2mm]
\text{These numbers must be non-negative integers, in which} \\[2mm]
\gamma = p_{12}^2 - p_{12}^1, \qquad \Delta = (p_{12}^2 - p_{12}^1)^2 + 2(p_{12}^2 + p_{12}^1) + 1.
\end{cases}
$$

# LATIN SQUARES AND THE PACKING PROBLEM

## ORTHOGONAL LATIN SQUARES

A Latin square of order $k$ is defined as a $k \times k$ square grid, the $k^2$ cells of which are occupied by $k$ distinct symbols of a set $X = 1, 2, \ldots, k$, such that each symbol occurs once in each row and each column. Two Latin squares are said to be orthogonal if, when superposed, any symbol of the first square occurs exactly once with each symbol of the second square.

A set of mutually orthogonal Latin squares is a set of Latin squares any two of which are orthogonal. It is easily shown that there cannot exist more than $k - 1$ mutually orthogonal Latin squares of a given order $k$. When $k - 1$ mutually orthogonal Latin squares of order $k$ exist, the set is complete. A complete set always exists if $k$ is the power of a prime. An unsolved question is whether there can exist a complete set of mutually orthogonal Latin squares of order $k$ if $k$ is not a prime power.

Many types of experimental designs are based on Latin squares. Hence, the construction of mutually orthogonal Latin squares is an important combinatorial problem. Letting the prime power decomposition of an integer $k$ be given, the arithmetic function $n(k)$ is defined by taking the minimum of the factors in such a decomposition

$$(25) \quad \text{If } k = p_1^{n_1} p_2^{n_2} \cdots p_u^{n_u}, \, n(k) = \min(p_1^{n_1}, p_2^{n_2}, \cdots, p_u^{n_u}).$$

Letting $N(k)$ denote the maximum number of mutually orthogonal Latin squares of order $k$, the American mathematician H.F. MacNeish in 1922 showed that there always exist $n(k)$ mutually orthogonal Latin squares of order $k$ and conjectured that this is the maximum number of such squares — that is, $N(k) = n(k)$. There was also the long-standing conjecture of Euler, formulated in 1782, that there cannot exist mutually orthogonal Latin squares of order $4t + 2$, for any integer $t$. MacNeish's conjecture, if true, would imply the truth of Euler's but not conversely. The American mathematician E.T. Parker in 1958 disproved the conjecture of MacNeish. This left open the question of Euler's conjecture. Bose and the Indian mathematician S.S. Shrikhande in 1959–60 obtained the first counterexample to Euler's conjecture by obtaining two mutually orthogonal Latin squares of order 22 and then generalized their method to disprove Euler's conjecture for an infinity of values of $k = 2 \pmod 4$. In 1959 Parker used the method of differences to show the falsity of Euler's conjecture for all $k = (3q + 1)/2$, in which $q$ is a prime power, $q \equiv 3 \pmod 4$. Finally, these three mathematicians in 1960 showed that $N(k) \geq 2$ whenever $k > 6$. It is pertinent to inquire about the behaviour of $N(k)$ for large $k$. The best result in this direction is due to R.M. Wilson in 1971. He shows that $N(k) \geq k^{1/17} - 2$ for large $k$.

## ORTHOGONAL ARRAYS AND THE PACKING PROBLEM

A $k \times N$ matrix $A$ with entries from a set $X$ of $s \geq 2$ symbols is called an orthogonal array of strength $t$, size $N$, $k$ constraints, and $s$ levels if each $t \times N$ submatrix of $A$ contains all possible $t \times 1$ column vectors with the same frequency $\lambda$. The array may be denoted by $(N, k, s, t)$. The number $\lambda$ is called the index of the array, and $N = \lambda s^t$. This concept is due to the Indian mathematician C.R. Rao and was obtained in 1947.

Orthogonal arrays are a generalization of orthogonal Latin squares. Indeed, the existence of an orthogonal array of $k$ constraints, $s$ levels, strength 2, and index unity is combinatorially equivalent to the existence of a set of $k - 2$ mutually orthogonal Latin squares of order $s$. For a given $\lambda$, $s$, and $t$ it is an important combinatorial problem to obtain an orthogonal array $(N, k, s, t)$, $N = s^t$, for which the number of constraints $k$ is maximal.

Orthogonal arrays play an important part in the theory of factorial designs in which each treatment is a combination of factors at different levels. For an orthogonal array $(\lambda s^t, k, s, t)$, $t \geq 2$, the number of constraints $k$ satisfies an inequality

$$(26) \quad \begin{cases} \lambda s^t \geq 1 + \binom{k}{1}(s-1) + \cdots + \binom{k}{u}(s-1)^u, \text{ if } t = 2u \\[2mm] \lambda s^t \geq 1 + \binom{k}{1}(s-1) + \cdots + \binom{k}{u}(s-1)^u \\[2mm] \qquad + \binom{k-1}{u}(s-1)^{u+1}, \text{ if } t = 2u+1. \end{cases}$$

in which $\lambda s^t$ is greater than or equal to a linear expression in powers of $(s - 1)$, with binomial coefficients giving the number of combinations of $k - 1$ or $k$ things taken $i$ at a time $(iu)$.

Letting $GF(q)$ be a finite field with $q = p^h$ elements, an $n \times r$ matrix with elements from the field is said to have the property $P_t$ if any $t$ rows are independent. The problem is to construct for any given $r$ a matrix $H$ with the maximum number of rows possessing the property $P_t$. The maximal number of rows is denoted by $n_t(r, q)$. This packing problem is of great importance in the theory of factorial designs and also in communication theory, because the existence of an $n \times r$ matrix with the property $P_t$ leads to the construction of an orthogonal array $(q^r, n, q, t)$ of index unity.

Again $n \times r$ matrices $H$ with the property $P_t$ may be used in the construction of error-correcting codes. A row vector $c'$ is taken as a code word if and only if $c'H = 0$. The code words then are of length $n$ and differ in at least $t + 1$ places. If $t = 2u$, then $u$ or fewer errors of transmission can be corrected if such a code is used. If $t = 2u + 1$, an additional error can be detected.

A general solution of the packing problem is known only for the case $t = 2$, the corresponding codes being the one-error-correcting codes of the American mathematician Richard W. Hamming. When $t = 3$ the solution is known for general $r$ when $q = 2$ and for general $q$ when $r = 4$. Thus, $n_2(r, 2) = (q^r - 1)/(q - 1)$, $n_3(r, 2) = 2^{r-1}$, $n_3(3, q) = q + 1$ or $q + 2$, according as $q$ is odd or even. If $q > 2$, then $n_3(4, q) = q^2 + 1$. The case $q = 2$ is especially important because in practice most codes use only two symbols, 0 or 1. Only fairly large values of $r$ are useful, say, $r \geq 25$. The optimum value of $n_t(r, 2)$ is not known. The BCH codes obtained by Bose and Ray-Chaudhuri and independently by the French mathematician Alexis Hocquenghem in 1959 and 1960 are based on a construction that yields an $n \times r$ matrix $H$ with the property $P_{2u}$ in which $r$ mu, $n = 2^m - 1$, $q = 2$. They can correct up to $u$ errors.

# GRAPH THEORY

## DEFINITIONS

A graph $G$ consists of a non-empty set of elements $V(G)$ and a subset $E(G)$ of the set of unordered pairs of distinct elements of $V(G)$. The elements of $V(G)$, called vertices of $G$, may be represented by points. If $(x, y) \in E(G)$, then the edge $(x, y)$ may be represented by an arc joining $x$ and $y$. Then $x$ and $y$ are said to be adjacent, and the edge $(x, y)$ is incident with $x$ and $y$. If $(x, y)$ is not an edge, then the vertices $x$ and $y$ are said to be nonadjacent. $G$ is a finite graph if $V(G)$ is finite. A graph $H$ is a subgraph of $G$ if $V(H) \subset V(G)$ and $E(H) \subset E(G)$.

A chain of a graph $G$ is an alternating sequence of vertices and edges $x_0, e_1, x_1, e_2, \cdots e_n, x_n$, beginning and ending with vertices in which each edge is incident with the two vertices immediately preceding and following it. This chain joins $x_0$ and $x_n$ and may also be denoted by $x_0, x_1, \cdots, x_n$, the edges being evident by context. The chain is closed if $x_0 = x_n$ and open otherwise. If the chain is closed, it is called a cycle, provided its vertices (other than $x_0$ and $x_n$) are distinct and $n \geq 3$. The length of a chain is the number of edges in it.

A graph $G$ is labelled when the various $v$ vertices are distinguished by such names as $x_1, x_2, \cdots x_v$. Two graphs $G$ and $H$ are said to be isomorphic (written $G \simeq H$) if there exists a one–one correspondence between their vertex sets that preserves adjacency. Two isomorphic graphs count as the same (unlabelled) graph. A graph is said to be a tree if it contains no cycle.

## ENUMERATION OF GRAPHS

The number of labelled graphs with $v$ vertices is $2^{v(v-1)/2}$ because $v(v-1)/2$ is the number of pairs of vertices, and each pair is either an edge or not an edge. Cayley in 1889 showed that the number of labelled trees with $v$ vertices is $v^{v-2}$.

The number of unlabelled graphs with $v$ vertices can be obtained by using Polya's theorem. The first few terms of the generating function $F(x)$, in which the coefficient of $x^v$ gives the number of (unlabelled) graphs with $v$ vertices, can be given

$$(27) \quad \begin{cases} F(x) = 1 + x + 2x^2 + 4x^3 + 11x^4 + 34x^5 + 156x^6 \\ \qquad\quad + 1{,}044x^7 + 12{,}346x^8 + 308{,}708\,x^9 + \cdots. \end{cases}$$

A rooted tree has one point, its root, distinguished from others. If $T_v$ is the number of rooted trees with $v$ vertices, the generating function for $T_v$ can also be given

$$(28) \quad T(x) = \sum_{v=1}^{\infty} T_v\, x^v = x \prod_{r=1}^{\infty} (1 - x^r)^{-T_r}.$$

Polya in 1937 showed in his memoir already referred to that the generating function for rooted trees satisfies a functional equation

$$(29) \quad T(x) = x \exp \sum_{r=1}^{\infty} \frac{1}{r} T(x^r).$$

Letting $t_v$ be the number of (unlabelled) trees with $v$ vertices, the generating function $t(x)$ for $t_v$ can be obtained in terms of $T(x)$

$$(30) \quad t(x) = T(x) - \tfrac{1}{2}\left[T^2(x) - T(x^2)\right].$$

This result was obtained in 1948 by the American mathematician Richard R. Otter.

Many enumeration problems on graphs with specified properties can be solved by the application of Polya's theorem and a generalization of it made by a Dutch mathematician, N.G. de Bruijn, in 1959.

## CHARACTERIZATION PROBLEMS OF GRAPH THEORY

If there is a class $C$ of graphs each of which possesses a certain set of properties $P$, then the set of properties $P$ is said to characterize the class $C$, provided every graph $G$ possessing the properties $P$ belongs to the class $C$. Sometimes it happens that there are some exceptional graphs that possess the properties $P$. Many such characterizations are known. Consider a typical example.

A complete graph $K_m$ is a graph with $m$ vertices, any two of which are adjacent. The line graph $H$ of a graph $G$ is a graph the vertices of which correspond to the edges of $G$, any two vertices of $H$ being adjacent if and only if the corresponding edges of $G$ are incident with the same vertex of $G$.

A graph $G$ is said to be regular of degree $n_I$ if each vertex is adjacent to exactly $n_I$ other vertices. A regular graph of degree $n_I$ with $v$ vertices is said to be strongly regular with parameters $(v, n_I, p_{II}{}^1, p_{II}{}^2)$ if any two adjacent vertices are both adjacent to exactly $p_{II}{}^1$ other vertices and any two nonadjacent vertices are both adjacent to exactly $p_{II}{}^2$ other

vertices. A strongly regular graph and a two-class association are isomorphic concepts. The treatments of the
scheme correspond to the vertices of the graph, two treatments being either first associates or second associates
according as the corresponding vertices are either adjacent or nonadjacent.

It is easily proved that the line graph $T_2(m)$ of a complete graph $K_m$, $m \geq 4$ is strongly regular with parameters
$v = m(m - 1)/2, n_1 = 2(m - 2), p_{11}^1 = m - 2, p_{11}^2 = 4$.

It is surprising that these properties characterize $T_2(m)$
except for $m = 8$, in which case there exist three other
strongly regular graphs with the same parameters noniso-
morphic to each other and to $T_2(m)$.

A partial geometry $(r, k, t)$ is a system of two kinds of
objects, points, and lines, with an incidence relation obey-
ing the following axioms:

1. Any two points are incident with not more
   than one line.
2. Each point is incident with $r$ lines.
3. Each line is incident with $k$ points.
4. Given a point $P$ not incident with a line l, there
   are exactly $t$ lines incident with $P$ and also with
   some point of l.

A graph $G$ is obtained from a partial geometry by taking the points of the geometry as vertices of $G$, two vertices
of $G$ being adjacent if and only if the corresponding points
are incident with the same line of the geometry. It is
strongly regular with parameters

$$v = k[(r - 1)(k - 1) + t]/t, \quad n_1 = r(k - 1),$$

$$p_{11}^1 = (r - 1)(t - 1) + (k - 2), \quad p_{11}^2 = rt.$$

The question of whether a strongly regular graph with the previous parameters is the graph of some partial geometry is of interest. It was shown by Bose in 1963 that the answer is in the affirmative if a certain condition holds

$$(31) \quad k > \tfrac{1}{2}\left[r(r-1) + t(r+1)(r^2 - 2r + 2)\right].$$

Not much is known about the case if this condition is not satisfied, except for certain values of $r$ and $t$. For example, $T_2(m)$ is isomorphic with the graph of a partial geometry $(2, m - 1, 2)$. Hence, for $m > 8$ its characterization is a consequence of the above theorem. Another consequence is the following:

Given a set of $k$-1-$d$ mutually orthogonal Latin squares of order $k$, the set can be extended to a complete set of $k$-1 mutually orthogonal squares if a condition holds

$$(32) \quad k > \tfrac{1}{2}(d-1)(d^3 - d^2 + d + 2).$$

The case $d = 2$ is due to Shrikhande in 1961 and the general result to the American mathematician Richard H. Bruck in 1963.

## APPLICATIONS OF GRAPH THEORY

### PLANAR GRAPHS

A graph $G$ is said to be planar if it can be represented on a plane in such a fashion that the vertices are all distinct points, the edges are simple curves, and no two edges meet one another except at their terminals. Two graphs are said to be homeomorphic if both can be obtained from the same graph by subdivisions of edges.

The $Km\,n$ graph is a graph for which the vertex set can be divided into two subsets, one with $m$ vertices and the other with $n$ vertices. Any two vertices of the same subset are nonadjacent, whereas any two vertices of different subsets are adjacent. The Polish mathematician Kazimierz Kuratowski in 1930 proved the following famous theorem:

> *A necessary and sufficient condition for a graph G to be planar is that it does not contain a subgraph homeomorphic to either $K_5$ or $K_{3,3}$.*

An elementary contraction of a graph $G$ is a transformation of $G$ to a new graph $G_1$, such that two adjacent vertices $u$ and $v$ of $G$ are replaced by a new vertex $w$ in $G_1$ and $w$ is adjacent in $G_1$ to all vertices to which either $u$ or $v$ is adjacent in $G$. A graph $G^*$ is said to be a contraction of $G$ if $G^*$ can be obtained from $G$ by a sequence of elementary contractions.

The following is another characterization of a planar graph due to the German mathematician K. Wagner in 1937. A graph is planar if and only if it is not contractible to $K_5$ or $K_{3,3}$.

## THE FOUR-COLOUR MAP PROBLEM

For more than a century the solution of the four-colour map problem eluded every analyst who attempted it. The problem may have attracted the attention of Möbius, but the first written reference to it seems to be a letter from one Francis Guthrie to his brother, a student of Augustus De Morgan, in 1852.

The problem concerns planar maps—that is, subdivisions of the plane into nonoverlapping regions bounded by simple closed curves. In geographical maps it has been observed empirically, in as many special cases as have been tried, that, at most, four colours are needed to colour the

THE BRITANNICA GUIDE TO STATISTICS AND PROBABILITY

regions so that two regions that share a common boundary are always coloured differently, and in certain cases that at least four colours are necessary. (Regions that meet only at a point, such as the states of Colorado and Arizona in the United States, are not considered to have a common boundary.) A formalization of this empirical observation constitutes what is called "the four-colour theorem." The problem is to prove or disprove the assertion that this is the case for every planar map. That three colours will not suffice is easily demonstrated, whereas the sufficiency of five colours was proved in 1890 by the British mathematician P.J. Heawood.

In 1879 A.B. Kempe, an Englishman, proposed a solution of the four-colour problem. Although Heawood showed that Kempe's argument was flawed, two of its concepts proved fruitful in later investigation. One of these, called unavoidability, correctly states the impossibility of constructing a map in which every one of four configurations is absent (these configurations consist of a region with two neighbours, one with three, one with four, and one with five). The second concept, that of reducibility, takes its name from Kempe's valid proof that if there is a map that requires at least five colours and that contains a region with four (or three or two) neighbours, there must be a map requiring five colours for a smaller number of regions. Kempe's attempt to prove the reducibility of a map containing a region with five neighbours was erroneous, but it was rectified in a proof published in 1976 by Kenneth Appel and Wolfgang Haken of the United States. Their proof attracted some criticism because it necessitated the evaluation of 1,936 distinct cases, each involving as many as 500,000 logical operations. Appel, Haken, and their collaborators devised programs that made it possible for a large digital computer to handle these details. The computer required more than

1,000 hours to perform the task, and the resulting formal proof is several hundred pages long.

## Eulerian Cycles and the Königsberg Bridge Problem

A multigraph $G$ consists of a non-empty set $V(G)$ of vertices and a subset $E(G)$ of the set of unordered pairs of distinct elements of $V(G)$ with a frequency $f \geq 1$ attached to each pair. If the pair $(x_1, x_2)$ with frequency $f$ belongs to $E(G)$, then vertices $x_1$ and $x_2$ are joined by $f$ edges.

An Eulerian cycle of a multigraph $G$ is a closed chain in which each edge appears exactly once. Euler showed that a multigraph possesses an Eulerian cycle if and only if it is connected (apart from isolated points) and the number of vertices of odd degree is either zero or two.

This problem first arose in the following manner. The Pregel River, formed by the confluence of its two branches, runs through the town of Königsberg and flows on either

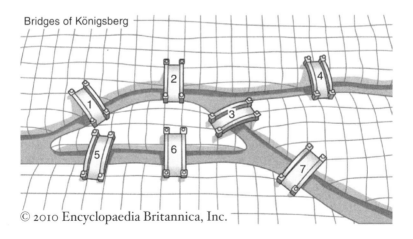

Bridges of Königsberg

© 2010 Encyclopaedia Britannica, Inc.

*With the Königsberg bridge problem, Euler showed it to be impossible to go for a walk and cross each bridge once and once only.*

side of the island of Kneiphof. There were seven bridges. The townspeople wondered whether it was possible to go for a walk and cross each bridge once and once only. This is equivalent to finding an Eulerian cycle for a specific multigraph. Euler showed it to be impossible because there are four vertices of odd order.

## DIRECTED GRAPHS

A directed graph $G$ consists of a non-empty set of elements $V(G)$, called vertices, and a subset $E(G)$ of ordered pairs of distinct elements of $V(G)$. Elements $(x, y)$ of $E(G)$ may be called edges, the direction of the edge being from $x$ to $y$. Both $(x, y)$ and $(y, x)$ may be edges.

A closed path in a directed graph is a sequence of vertices $x_0 x_1 x_2 \cdots x_n = x_0$, such that $(x_i, x_{i+1})$ is a directed edge for $i = 0, 1, \cdots, n - 1$. To each edge $(x, y)$ of a directed graph $G$ there can be assigned a non-negative weight function $f(x, y)$. The problem then is to find a closed path in $G$ traversing all vertices so that the sum of the weights of all edges in the path is a minimum. This is a typical optimization problem. If the vertices are certain cities, the edges are routes joining cities, and the weights are the lengths of the routes, then this becomes the travelling salesman problem: Can the salesman visit each city without retracing his steps? This problem still remains unsolved except for certain special cases.

## COMBINATORIAL GEOMETRY

The name combinatorial geometry, first used by Swiss mathematician Hugo Hadwiger, is not quite accurately descriptive of the nature of the subject. Combinatorial geometry does touch on those aspects of geometry that deal with arrangements, combinations, and enumerations of geometric objects, but it takes in much more. The field is so new that there has scarcely been time for it to acquire a well-defined position in the mathematical world. Rather it tends to overlap parts of topology (especially algebraic topology), number theory, analysis, and, of course, geometry. The subject concerns itself with relations among members of finite systems of geometric figures subject to various conditions and restrictions. More specifically, it includes problems of covering, packing, symmetry, extrema (maxima and minima), continuity, tangency, equalities, and inequalities, many of these with special emphasis on their application to the theory of convex bodies. A few of the fundamental problems of combinatorial geometry originated with Newton and Euler. Most significant advances in the field, however, have been made since the 1940s.

The unifying aspect of these disparate topics is the quality or style or spirit of the questions and the methods of attacking these questions. Among those branches of mathematics that interest serious working mathematicians, combinatorial geometry is one of the few branches that can be presented on an intuitive basis, without recourse by the investigator to any advanced theoretical considerations or abstractions.

Yet the problems are far from trivial, and many remain unsolved. They can be handled only with the aid of the most careful and often delicate reasoning that displays the variety and vitality of geometric methods in a modern setting. A few answers are natural and are intuitively suggested by the questions. Many others, however, require proofs of unusual ingenuity and depth even in the two-dimensional case. Sometimes a plane solution may be readily extendible to higher dimensions, but sometimes just the opposite is true, and a three-dimensional or $n$-dimensional problem may be entirely different from its two-dimensional counterpart. Each new problem must be attacked individually.

The continuing charm and challenge of the subject are at least in part a result of the relative simplicity of the statements coupled with the elusive nature of their solutions.

## SOME HISTORICALLY IMPORTANT TOPICS OF COMBINATORIAL GEOMETRY

### PACKING AND COVERING

It is easily seen that six equal circular disks may be placed around another disk of the same size so that the central one is touched by all the others but no two overlap and that it is not possible to place seven disks in such a way. In the analogous three-dimensional situation, around a given ball (solid sphere) it is possible to place 12 balls of equal size, all touching the first one but not overlapping it or each other. One such arrangement may be obtained by placing the 12 surrounding balls at the midpoints of edges of a suitable cube that encloses the central ball. Each of the 12 balls touching four other balls in addition to the central one. But if the 12 balls are centred at the 12 vertices of a suitable regular icosahedron surrounding the given ball, there is an appreciable amount of free space between each of the surrounding balls and its neighbours. (If the spheres have radius 1, the distances between the centres of the surrounding spheres are at least $2/\cos 18° = 2.1029 \cdots$.) It appears, therefore, that by judicious positioning it might be possible to have 13 equal non-overlapping spheres touch another of the same size. This dilemma between 12 and 13, one of the first nontrivial problems of combinatorial geometry, was the object of discussion between Isaac Newton and David Gregory in 1694. Newton believed 12 to be the correct number, but this claim was not proved until 1953. The analogous problem in four-dimensional space was solved in 2003, the answer being 24.

The problem of the 13 balls is a typical example of the branch of combinatorial geometry that deals with packings and coverings. In packing problems, the aim is to place figures of a given shape or size without overlap as economically as possibly, either inside another given figure or subject to some other restriction.

Problems of packing and covering have been the objects of much study, and some striking conclusions have been obtained. For each plane convex set $K$, for example, it is possible to arrange nonoverlapping translates of $K$ so as to cover at least two-thirds of the plane. If $K$ is a triangle (and only in that case), no arrangement of nonoverlapping translates covers more than two-thirds of the plane. Another famous problem was Kepler's conjecture, which concerns the densest packing of spheres. If the spheres are packed in cannonball fashion—that is, in the way cannonballs are stacked to form a triangular pyramid, indefinitely extended—then they fill $\pi/\sqrt{18}$, or about 0.74, of the space. In 1611 the German astronomer Johannes Kepler conjectured that this is the greatest density possible, but it was only proved in 1998 by the American mathematician Thomas Hales.

Covering problems deal in an analogous manner with economical ways of placing given figures so as to cover (that is, contain in their union) another given figure. One famous covering problem, posed by the French mathematician Henri Lebesgue in 1914, is still unsolved: What is the size and shape of the universal cover of least area? Here a convex set $C$ is called universal cover if for each set $A$ in the plane such that diam $A = 1$ it is possible to move $C$ to a suitable position in which it covers $A$. The diameter diam $A$ of a set $A$ is defined as the least upper bound of the mutual distances of points of the set $A$. If $A$ is a compact set, then diam $A$ is simply the greatest distance between any two points of $A$. Thus, if $A$ is an equilateral triangle of

*Johannes Kepler conjectured that spheres stacked to form a triangular pyramid demonstrate the greatest density possible.* Shutterstock.com

side 1, then diam $A$ = 1; and if $B$ is a cube of edge length 1, then diam $B$ = $\sqrt{3}$.

## POLYTOPES

A (convex) polytope is the convex hull of some finite set of points. Each polytope of dimensions $d$ has as faces finitely many polytopes of dimensions 0 (vertices), 1 (edge), 2 (2-faces), $\cdots$, $d$-1 (facets). Two-dimensional polytopes are usually called polygons, three-dimensional ones polyhedra. Two polytopes are said to be isomorphic, or of the same combinatorial type, provided there exists a one-to-one correspondence between their faces, such that two faces of the first polytope meet if and only if the corresponding faces of the second meet. The prism and the truncated pyramid are isomorphic. To classify the convex polygons by their combinatorial types, it is sufficient to determine the number of vertices $v$. For each $v \geq 3$, all polygons with $v$ vertices ($v$-gons) are of the same combinatorial type, whereas a $v$-gon and a $v'$-gon are not isomorphic if $v \neq v'$. Euler was the first to investigate in 1752 the analogous question concerning polyhedra. He found that $v - e + f = 2$ for every convex polyhedron, where $v, e,$ and $f$ are the numbers of vertices, edges, and faces of the polyhedron. Though this formula became one of the starting points of topology, Euler was unsuccessful in his attempts to find a classification scheme for convex polytopes or to determine the number of different types for each $v$. Despite efforts of many famous mathematicians since Euler (Steiner, Kirkman, Cayley, Hermes, and Brückner, to mention only a few from the 19th century), the problem is still open for polyhedra with more than 19 vertices. The numbers of different types with four, five, six, seven, or eight vertices are 1, 2, 7, 34, and 257, respectively. It was established by American mathematician P.J. Federico in 1969 that there are 2,606 different combinatorial types of convex polyhedra with nine vertices. The number of different types for 18 vertices is more than 107 trillion.

The theory of convex polytopes has been successful in developments in other directions. The regular polytopes have been under investigation since 1880 in dimensions higher than three, together with extensions of Euler's relation to the higher dimensions. (The Swiss geometer Ludwig Schläfli made many of these discoveries some 30 years earlier, but his work was published only posthumously in 1901.) The interest in regular polyhedra and other special polyhedra goes back to ancient Greece, as indicated by the names Platonic solids and Archimedean solids.

Since 1950 there has been considerable interest, in part created by practical problems related to computer techniques such as linear programming, in questions of the following type: For polytopes of a given dimension $d$ and having a given number $v$ of vertices, how large and how small can the number of facets be? Such problems have provided great impetus to the development of the theory. The American mathematician Victor L. Klee solved the maximum problem in 1963 in most cases (that is, for all but a finite number of $v$'s for each $d$), but the remaining cases were disposed of only in 1970 by P. McMullen, in the United States, who used a completely new method.

## INCIDENCE PROBLEMS

In 1893 the British mathematician J.J. Sylvester posed the question: If a finite set $S$ of points in a plane has the property that each line determined by two points of $S$ meets at least one other point of $S$, must all points of $S$ be on one line? Sylvester never found a satisfactory solution to the problem, and the first (affirmative) solutions were published a half century later. Since then, Sylvester's problem has inspired many investigations and led to many other questions, both in the plane and in higher dimensions.

## HELLY'S THEOREM

In 1912 Austrian mathematician Eduard Helly proved the following theorem, which has since found applications in many areas of geometry and analysis and has led to numerous generalizations, extensions, and analogues known as Helly-type theorems. If $K_1, K_2, \cdots, Kn$ are convex sets in $d$-dimensional Euclidean space $Ed$, in which $n \geq d + 1$, and if for every choice of $d + 1$ of the sets $Ki$ there exists a point that belongs to all the chosen sets, then there exists a point that belongs to all the sets $K_1, K_2, \cdots Kn$. The theorem stated in two dimensions is easier to visualize and yet is not shorn of its strength: If every three of a set of $n$ convex figures in the plane have a common point (not necessarily the same point for all trios), then all $n$ figures have a point in common. If, for example, convex sets $A$, $B$, and $C$ have the point $p$ in common, and convex sets $A$, $B$, and $D$ have the point $q$ in common, and sets $A$, $C$, and $D$ have the point $r$ in common, and sets $B$, $C$, and $D$ have the point $s$ in common, then some point $x$ is a member of $A$, $B$, $C$, and $D$.

Although the connection is often far from obvious, many consequences may be derived from Helly's theorem. Among them are the following, stated for $d = 2$ with some higher dimensional analogues indicated in square brackets:

A. Two finite subsets $X$ and $Y$ of the plane [$d$-space] may be strictly separated by a suitable straight line [hyperplane] if and only if, for every set $Z$ consisting of at most 4 [$d + 2$] points taken from $X \cup Y$, the points of $X \cap Z$ may be strictly separated from those of $Y \cap Z$. (A line [hyperplane] $L$ strictly separates $X$ and $Y$ if $X$ is contained in one of the open half planes [half spaces] determined by $L$ and if $Y$ is contained in the other.)

B. Each compact convex set $K$ in the plane [$d$-space] contains a point $P$ with the following property: Each chord of $K$ that contains $P$ is divided by $P$ into a number of segments so the ratio of their lengths is at most $2d$.

C. If $G$ is an open subset of the plane [$d$-space] with finite area [$d$-dimensional content], then there exists a point $P$, such that each open half plane [half space] that contains $P$ contains also at least 1/3 [1/($d$ + 1)] of the area [$d$-content] of $G$.D. If $I_1, \cdots, In$ are segments parallel to the $y$-axis in a plane with a coordinate system $(x, y)$, and if for every choice of three of the segments there exists a straight line intersecting each of the three segments, then there exists a straight line that intersects all the segments $I_1, \cdots, In$.

Theorem D has generalizations in which $k$th degree polynomial curves $y = akxk + \cdots + a_1x + a_0$ take the place of the straight lines and $k + 2$ replaces 3 in the assumptions. These are important in the theory of best approximation of functions by polynomials.

## METHODS OF COMBINATORIAL GEOMETRY

Many other branches of combinatorial geometry are as important and interesting as those previously mentioned, but rather than list them here it is more instructive to provide a few typical examples of frequently used methods of reasoning. Because the emphasis is on illustrating the methods rather than on obtaining the most general results, the examples will deal with problems in two and three dimensions.

### EXHAUSTING THE POSSIBILITIES

Using the data available concerning the problem under investigation, it is often possible to obtain a list of all potential, a priori possible, solutions. The final step then consists in eliminating the possibilities that are not actual solutions or that duplicate previously found solutions. An example is the proof that there are only five regular convex polyhedra (the Platonic solids) and the determination of what these five are.

From the definition of regularity it is easy to deduce that all the faces of a Platonic solid must be congruent regular $k$-gons for a suitable $k$, and that all the vertices must belong to the same number $j$ of $k$-gons. Because the sum of the face angles at a vertex of a convex polyhedron is less than $2\pi$, and because each angle of the $k$-gon is $(k - 2)\pi/k$, it follows that $j(k - 2)\pi/k < 2\pi$, or $(j - 2)(k - 2) < 4$. Therefore, the only possibilities for the pair $(j, k)$ are $(3, 3)$, $(3, 4)$, $(3, 5)$, $(4, 3)$, and $(5, 3)$. It may be verified that each pair actually corresponds to a Platonic solid, namely, to the tetrahedron, the cube, the dodecahedron, the octahedron, and the icosahedron, respectively. Very similar arguments may be used in the determination of Archimedean solids and in other instances.

The most serious drawback of the method is that in many instances the number of potential (and perhaps actual) solutions is so large as to render the method unfeasible. Therefore, sometimes the exact determination of these numbers by the method just discussed is out of the question, certainly if attempted by hand and probably even with the aid of a computer.

## USE OF EXTREMAL PROPERTIES

In many cases the existence of a figure or an arrangement with certain desired properties may be established by considering a more general problem (or a completely different problem) and by showing that a solution of the general problem that is extremal in some sense provides also a solution to the original problem. Frequently there seems to be little connection between the initial question and the extremal problem. As an illustration the following theorem will be proved: If $K$ is a two-dimensional compact convex set with a centre of symmetry, there exists a parallelogram $P$ containing $K$, such that the midpoints of the sides of $P$ belong to $K$. The proof proceeds as follows: Of all the parallelograms that contain $K$, the one with least possible area is labeled $P_0$. The existence of such a $P_0$ is a consequence of the compactness of $K$ and may be established by standard arguments. It is also easily seen that the centres of $K$ and $P_0$ coincide. The interesting aspect of the situation is that $P_0$ may be taken as the $P$ required for the theorem. In fact, if the midpoints $A'$ and $A$ of a pair of sides of $P_0$ do not belong to $K$, it is possible to strictly separate them from $K$ by parallel lines $L'$ and $L$ that, together with the other pair of sides of $P_0$, determine a new parallelogram containing $K$ but with area smaller than that of $P_0$. The preceding theorem and its proof generalize immediately to higher dimensions and lead to results that are important in functional analysis.

Sometimes this type of argument is used in reverse to establish the existence of certain objects by disproving the possibility of existence of some extremal figures. As an example the following solution of the previously discused problem of Sylvester can be mentioned. By a standard argument of projective geometry (duality), it is evident that Sylvester's problem is equivalent to the question: If through the point of intersection of any two of $n$ coplanar lines, no two of which are parallel, there passes a third, are the $n$ lines necessarily concurrent? To show that they must be concurrent, contradiction can be derived from the assumption that they are not concurrent. If $L$ is one of the lines, then not all the intersection points lie on $L$. Among the intersection points not on $L$, there must be one nearest to $L$, which can be called $A$. Through $A$ pass at least three lines, which meet $L$ in points $B$, $C$, $D$, so that $C$ is between $B$ and $D$. Through $C$ passes a line $L^*$ different from $L$ and from the line through $A$. Because $L^*$ enters the triangle $ABD$, it intersects either the segment $AB$ or the segment $AD$, yielding an intersection point nearer to $L$ than the supposedly nearest intersection point $A$, thus providing the contradiction.

The difficulties in applying this method are caused in part by the absence of any systematic procedure for devising an extremal problem that leads to the solution of the original question.

### Use of Transformations Between Different Spaces and Applications of Helly's Theorem

The methods of proof in combinatorial geometry may be illustrated in one example: the proof of a theorem concerning parallel segments. Let the segment $I_i$ have end-points $(x_i, y_i)$ and $(x_i, \leq y'_i)$, where $y_i y'_i$ and $i = 1, 2, \cdots, n$. The case that two segments are on one line is easily dismissed, so it may be assumed that $x_1, x_2, \cdots, x_n$ are all different. With each straight line $y = ax + b$ in the $(x, y)$-plane can be associated a point $(a, b)$ in another plane, the $(a, b)$-plane. Now, for $i = 1, 2, \cdots, n$, the set consisting of all those points $(a, b)$ for which the corresponding line $y = ax + b$ in the $(x, y)$ plane meets the segment $I_i$ can be denoted by $K_i$. This condition means that $y_i ax_i + by'_i$ so that each set $K_i$ is convex. The existence of a line intersecting three of the segments $I_i$ means that the corresponding sets $K_i$ have a common point. Then Helly's theorem for the $(a, b)$-plane implies the existence of a point $(a^*, b^*)$ common to all sets $K_i$. This in turn means that the line $y = a^*x + b^*$ meets all the segments $I_1, I_2, \cdots, I_n$, and the proof of theorem D is complete.

In addition to the methods illustrated earlier, many other techniques of proof are used in combinatorial geometry, ranging from simple mathematical induction to sophisticated decidability theorems of formal logic. The variety of methods available and the likelihood that there are many more not yet invented continue to stimulate research in this rapidly developing branch of mathematics.

# CHAPTER 6
## BIOGRAPHIES

In this chapter, we encounter the fascinating personalities that have advanced our understanding of probability and statistics. In the 12th century, Bhāskara II named one of his greatest mathematical works after his daughter. In the 20th century, John von Neumann applied his mathematical knowledge to the greatest military problem, the atomic bomb.

## JEAN LE ROND D'ALEMBERT
(b. Nov. 17, 1717, Paris, France—d. Oct. 29, 1783, Paris)

The French mathematician, philosopher, and writer Jean Le Rond d'Alembert achieved fame as a mathematician and scientist before acquiring a considerable reputation as a contributor to and editor of the famous *Encyclopédie*.

The illegitimate son of a famous hostess, Mme. de Tencin, and one of her lovers, the chevalier Destouches-Canon, d'Alembert was abandoned on the steps of the Parisian church of Saint-Jean-le-Rond, from which he derived his Christian name. Through his father's influence, he was admitted to a prestigious Jansenist school, enrolling first as Jean-Baptiste Daremberg and subsequently changing his name, perhaps for reasons of euphony, to d'Alembert. Although Destouches never disclosed his identity as father of the child, he left his son an annuity of 1,200 livres. D'Alembert's teachers at first hoped to train him for theology, being perhaps encouraged by a commentary he wrote on St. Paul's Letter to the Romans, but they inspired in him only a lifelong aversion to the subject. After taking up medicine for a year, he finally devoted himself to mathematics—"the only occupation," he said later, "which really interested me." Apart from some private lessons, d'Alembert was almost entirely self-taught.

In 1739 he read his first paper to the Academy of Sciences, of which he became a member in 1741. In 1743, at the age of 26, he published his important *Traité de dynamique,* a fundamental treatise on dynamics containing the famous "d'Alembert's principle," which states that Newton's third law of motion (for every action there is an equal and opposite reaction) is true for bodies that are free to move as well as for bodies rigidly fixed. Other mathematical works rapidly followed. In 1744 he applied his principle to the theory of equilibrium and motion of fluids, in his *Traité de l'équilibre et du mouvement des fluides.* This discovery was followed by the development of partial differential equations, a branch of the theory of calculus, the first papers on which were published in his *Réflexions sur la cause générale des vents* (1747). It won him a prize at the Berlin Academy, to which he was elected the same year. In 1747 he applied his new calculus to the problem of vibrating strings, in his *Recherches sur les cordes vibrantes.* In 1749 he furnished a method of applying his principles to the motion of any body of a given shape. That same year he found an explanation of the precession of the equinoxes (a gradual change in the position of the Earth's orbit), determined its characteristics, and explained the phenomenon of the nutation (nodding) of the Earth's axis, in *Recherches sur la précession des équinoxes et sur la nutation de l'axe de la terre.* In the *Memoirs* of the Berlin Academy he published findings of his research on integral calculus, which devises relationships of variables by means of rates of change of their numerical value, a branch of mathematical science that is greatly indebted to him. In his *Recherches sur différents points importants du système du monde* (1754–56), he perfected the solution of the problem of the perturbations (variations of orbit) of the planets that he had presented to the academy some years before. From 1761 to 1780 he published eight volumes of his *Opuscules mathématiques*.

Meanwhile, d'Alembert began an active social life and frequented well-known salons, where he acquired a considerable reputation as a witty conversationalist and mimic. Like his fellow Philosophes—those thinkers, writers, and scientists who believed in the sovereignty of reason and nature (as opposed to authority and revelation) and rebelled against old dogmas and institutions—he turned to the improvement of society. Believing in man's need to rely on his own powers, they promulgated a new social morality to replace Christian ethics. Science, the only real source of knowledge, had to be popularized for the benefit of the people, and it was in this tradition that he became associated with the *Encyclopédie* about 1746. When the original idea of a translation into French of Ephraim Chambers' English *Cyclopædia* was replaced by that of a new work under the general editorship of the Philosophe Denis Diderot, d'Alembert was appointed editor of the mathematical and scientific articles. In fact, he not only helped with the general editorship and contributed articles on other subjects but also tried to secure support for the enterprise in influential circles. He wrote the *Discours préliminaire* that introduced the first volume of the work in 1751. This was a remarkable attempt to present a unified view of contemporary knowledge, tracing the development and interrelationship of its various branches and showing how they formed coherent parts of a single structure. The second section of the *Discours* was devoted to the intellectual history of Europe from the time of the Renaissance. In 1752 d'Alembert wrote a preface to Volume III, which was a vigorous rejoinder to the

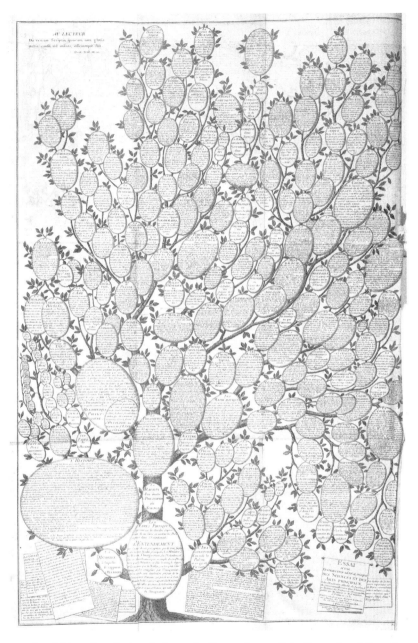

*This foldout frontispiece is from the first volume of the* Encyclopédie, *of which Jean Le Rond d'Alembert was editor and contributor.* SSPL via Getty Images

*Encyclopédie*'s critics. Gradually discouraged by the growing difficulties of the enterprise, d'Alembert gave up his share of the editorship at the beginning of 1758, thereafter limiting his commitment to the production of mathematical and scientific articles.

His earlier literary and philosophical activity, however, led to the publication of his *Mélanges de littérature, d'histoire et de philosophie* (1753). This work contained the impressive *Essai sur les gens de lettres*, which exhorted writers to pursue "liberty, truth and poverty" and also urged aristocratic patrons to respect the talents and independence of such writers. Largely as a result of the persistent campaigning of Mme du Deffand, a prominent hostess to writers and scientists, d'Alembert was elected to the French Academy in 1754, proving to be a zealous member, working hard to enhance the dignity of the institution in the eyes of the public and striving steadfastly for the election of members sympathetic to the cause of the Philosophes. His personal position became even more influential in 1772 when he was made permanent secretary. In 1776 he transferred his home to an apartment at the Louvre—to which he was entitled as secretary to the Academy—where he lived for the rest of his life.

## THOMAS BAYES

(b. 1702, London, Eng.—d. April 17, 1761, Tunbridge Wells, Kent)

Thomas Bayes was an English Nonconformist theologian and mathematician who was the first to use probability inductively and who established a mathematical basis for probability inference (a means of calculating, from the frequency with which an event has occurred in prior trials, the probability that it will occur in future trials.

Bayes set down his findings on probability in "Essay Towards Solving a Problem in the Doctrine of Chances"

(1763), posthumously published in the *Philosophical Transactions* of the Royal Society. That work became the basis of a statistical technique, now called Bayesian estimation, for calculating the probability of the validity of a proposition on the basis of a prior estimate of its probability and new relevant evidence. Disadvantages of the method—pointed out by later statisticians—include the different ways of assigning prior distributions of parameters and the possible sensitivity of conclusions to the choice of distributions.

The only works that Bayes is known to have published in his lifetime are *Divine Benevolence; or, An Attempt to Prove That the Principal End of the Divine Providence and Government Is the Happiness of His Creatures* (1731) and *An Introduction to the Doctrine of Fluxions, and a Defence of the Mathematicians Against the Objections of the Author of The Analyst* (1736), which was published anonymously and countered the attacks by Bishop George Berkeley on the logical foundations of Sir Isaac Newton's calculus.

Bayes was elected a fellow of the Royal Society in 1742.

## DANIEL BERNOULLI

(b. Feb. 8 [Jan. 29, Old Style], 1700, Groningen, Neth.—d. March 17, 1782, Basel, Switz.)

Daniel Bernoulli was the most distinguished of the second generation of the Bernoulli family of Swiss mathematicians. He investigated not only mathematics but also such fields as medicine, biology, physiology, mechanics, physics, astronomy, and oceanography. Bernoulli's theorem (*q.v.*), which he derived, is named after him.

Daniel Bernoulli was the second son of Johann Bernoulli, who first taught him mathematics. After studying philosophy, logic, and medicine at the universities of Heidelberg, Strasbourg, and Basel, he received an M.D.

degree (1721). In 1723–24 he wrote *Exercitationes quaedam Mathematicae* on differential equations and the physics of flowing water, which won him a position at the influential Academy of Sciences in St. Petersburg, Russia. Bernoulli lectured there until 1732 in medicine, mechanics, and physics, and he researched the properties of vibrating and rotating bodies and contributed to probability theory. In that same year he returned to the University of Basel to accept the post in anatomy and botany. By then he was widely esteemed by scholars and also admired by the public throughout Europe.

Daniel's reputation was established in 1738 with *Hydrodynamica,* in which he considered the properties of basic importance in fluid flow, particularly pressure, density, and velocity, and set forth their fundamental relationship. He put forward what is called Bernoulli's principle, which states that the pressure in a fluid decreases as its velocity increases. He also established the basis for the kinetic theory of gases and heat by demonstrating that the impact of molecules on a surface would explain pressure and that, assuming the constant, random motion of molecules, pressure and motion increase with temperature. About 1738 his father published *Hydraulica.* An aparent attempt to obtain priority for himself, this was yet another instance of his antagonism toward his son.

Between 1725 and 1749 Daniel won 10 prizes from the Paris Academy of Sciences for work on astronomy, gravity, tides, magnetism, ocean currents, and the behaviour of ships at sea. He also made substantial contributions in probability. He shared the 1735 prize for work on planetary orbits with his father, who, it is said, threw him out of the house for thus obtaining a prize he felt should be his alone. Daniel's prizewinning papers reflected his success on the research frontiers of science and his ability to set forth clearly before an interested public the scientific problems of the day. In 1732 he accepted a post in botany and anatomy at Basel; in 1743, one in physiology; and in 1750, one in physics.

## JAKOB BERNOULLI

(b. Jan. 6, 1655 [Dec. 27, 1654, Old Style], Basel, Switz.—d. Aug. 16, 1705, Basel)

The first of the Bernoulli family of Swiss mathematicians was Jakob Bernoulli. He introduced the first principles of the calculus of variation. Bernoulli numbers, a concept that he developed, were named for him.

The scion of a family of drug merchants, Jakob Bernoulli was compelled to study theology but became interested in mathematics despite his father's opposition. His travels led to a wide correspondence with mathematicians. Refusing a church appointment, he accepted a professorial chair of mathematics at the University of Basel in 1687. Following his mastery of the mathematical works of John Wallis, Isaac Barrow (both English), René Descartes (French), and G. W. Leibniz, who first drew his attention to calculus, he embarked on original contributions. In 1690 Bernoulli became the first to use the term "integral" in analyzing a curve of descent. His 1691 study of the catenary, or the curve formed by a chain suspended between its two extremities, was soon applied in building suspension bridges. In 1695 he also applied calculus to the design of bridges. During these years, he often engaged in disputes with his brother Johann Bernoulli over mathematical issues.

Jakob Bernoulli's pioneering work *Ars Conjectandi* (published posthumously, 1713; "The Art of Conjecturing") contained many of his finest concepts: his theory of permutations and combinations; the so-called Bernoulli

JACQ. BERNOULLI
Professeur de Mathematique a Basle,
de la Societe Royale de Londes et des Academies
des Sciences de Paris et de Berlin.

*Among other things, Jakob (known also as Jacques) Bernoulli is renowned for the Bernoulli numbers and the Bernoulli law of large numbers.* SSPL via Getty Images

numbers, by which he derived the exponential series; his treatment of mathematical and moral predictability; and the subject of probability—containing what is now called the Bernoulli law of large numbers, basic to all modern sampling theory. His works were published as *Opera Jacobi Bernoullii*, 2 vol. (1744).

## BHĀSKARA II

(b. 1114, Biddur, India—d. *c.* 1185, probably Ujjain)

Bhāskara II was the leading mathematician of the 12th century and wrote the first work with full and systematic use of the decimal number system.

Bhāskara II was the lineal successor of the noted Indian mathematician Brahmagupta (598–*c.* 665) as head of an astronomical observatory at Ujjain, the leading mathematical centre of ancient India.

In his mathematical works, particularly *Līlāvatī* ("The Beautiful") and *Bījaganita* ("Seed Counting"), he not only used the decimal system but also compiled problems from Brahmagupta and others. He filled many gaps in Brahmagupta's work, especially in obtaining a general solution to the Pell equation ($x^2 = 1 + py^2$) and in giving many particular solutions. Bhāskara II anticipated the modern convention of signs (minus by minus makes plus, minus by plus makes minus) and evidently was the first to gain some understanding of the meaning of division by zero. He specifically stated that the value of $3/_0$ is an infinite quantity, but his understanding seems to have been limited, for he also wrongly stated that $a/_0 \times 0 = a$. Bhāskara II used letters to represent unknown quantities, much as in modern algebra, and solved indeterminate equations of 1st and 2nd degrees. He reduced quadratic equations to a single type and solved them and investigated regular polygons up to those having 384 sides, thus obtaining a good approximate value of $\pi = 3.141666$.

In other of his works, notably *Siddhāntaśiromaṇi* ("Head Jewel of Accuracy") and *Karan ̦akutūhala* ("Calculation of Astronomical Wonders"), he wrote on his astronomical observations of planetary positions, conjunctions, eclipses, cosmography, geography, and the mathematical techniques and astronomical equipment used in these studies. Bhāskara II was also a noted astrologer, and tradition has it that he named his first work, *Līlāvatī,* after his daughter to console her when his astrological meddling, coupled with an unfortunate twist of fate, is said to have deprived her of her only chance for marriage and happiness.

## LUDWIG EDUARD BOLTZMANN

(b. Feb. 20, 1844, Vienna, Austria—d. Sept. 5, 1906, Duino, Italy)

The physicist Ludwig Eduard Boltzmann had his greatest achievement in the development of statistical mechanics, which explains and predicts how the properties of atoms (such as mass, charge, and structure) determine the visible properties of matter (such as viscosity, thermal conductivity, and diffusion).

After receiving his doctorate from the University of Vienna in 1866, Boltzmann held professorships in mathematics and physics at Vienna, Graz, Munich, and Leipzig.

In the 1870s Boltzmann published a series of papers in which he showed that the second law of thermodynamics, which concerns energy exchange, could be explained by applying the laws of mechanics and the theory of probability to the motions of the atoms. In so doing, he made clear that the second law is essentially statistical and that a system approaches a state of thermodynamic equilibrium (uniform energy distribution throughout) because equilibrium is overwhelmingly the most probable state of a material system. During these investigations Boltzmann worked out the general law for the distribution of energy among the various parts of a system at a specific temperature and derived the theorem of equipartition of energy (Maxwell-Boltzmann distribution law). This law states that the average amount of energy involved in each different direction of motion of an atom is the same. He derived an equation for the change of the distribution of energy among atoms resulting from atomic collisions and laid the foundations of statistical mechanics.

Boltzmann was also one of the first continental scientists to recognize the importance of the electromagnetic theory proposed by James Clerk Maxwell of England. Though his work on statistical mechanics was strongly attacked and long misunderstood, his conclusions were finally supported by the discoveries in atomic physics that began shortly before 1900 and by recognition that fluctuation phenomena, such as Brownian motion (random movement of microscopic particles suspended in a fluid), could be explained only by statistical mechanics.

## GEORGE BOOLE

(b. Nov. 2, 1815, Lincoln, Lincolnshire, Eng. — d. Dec. 8, 1864, Ballintemple, County Cork, Ire.)

The English mathematician George Boole helped establish modern symbolic logic and whose algebra of logic, now called Boolean algebra, is basic to the design of digital computer circuits.

Boole was given his first lessons in mathematics by his father, a tradesman, who also taught him to make optical instruments. Aside from his father's help and a few years at local schools, however, Boole was self-taught in mathematics. When his father's business declined, George had to work to support the family. From the age of 16 he taught in village schools in the West Riding of Yorkshire, opening his own school in Lincoln when he was 20. During scant leisure time he read mathematics journals in the Lincoln's Mechanics Institute. There he also read Isaac Newton's *Principia*, Pierre-Simon Laplace's *Traité de mécanique céleste*, and Joseph-Louis Lagrange's *Mécanique analytique* and began to solve advanced algebra problems.

Boole submitted a stream of original papers to the new *Cambridge Mathematical Journal*, beginning in 1839 with his "Researches on the Theory of Analytical Transformations." These papers were on differential equations and the algebraic problem of linear transformation, emphasizing the concept of invariance. In 1844, in an important paper in the *Philosophical Transactions of the Royal Society* for which he was awarded the Royal Society's first gold medal for mathematics, he discussed how methods of algebra and calculus might be combined. Boole soon saw that his algebra could also be applied in logic.

Developing novel ideas on logical method and confident in the symbolic reasoning he had derived from his mathematical investigations, he published in 1847 a pamphlet, "Mathematical Analysis of Logic," in which he argued persuasively that logic should be allied with mathematics, not philosophy. He won the admiration of the English logician Augustus De Morgan, who published *Formal Logic* the same year. On the basis of his publications, Boole in 1849 was appointed professor of mathematics at Queen's College, County Cork, even though he lacked a university degree. In 1854 he published *An Investigation into the Laws of Thought, on Which Are Founded the Mathematical Theories of Logic and Probabilities*, which he regarded as a mature statement of his ideas. The next year he married Mary Everest, niece of Sir George

Everest, for whom the mountain is named. The Booles had five daughters.

One of the first Englishmen to write about logic, Boole pointed out the analogy between algebraic symbols and those that can represent logical forms and syllogisms, showing how the symbols of quantity can be separated from those of operation. With Boole in 1847 and 1854 began the algebra of logic, or what is now called Boolean algebra. Boole's original and remarkable general symbolic method of logical inference, fully stated in *Laws of Thought* (1854), enables one, given any propositions involving any number of terms, to draw conclusions that are logically contained in the premises. He also attempted a general method in probabilities, which would make it possible from the given probabilities of any system of events to determine the consequent probability of any other event logically connected with the given events.

In 1857 Boole was elected a fellow of the Royal Society. The influential *Treatise on Differential Equations* appeared in 1859 and was followed the next year by its sequel, *Treatise on the Calculus of Finite Differences*. Used as textbooks for many years, these works embody an elaboration of Boole's more important discoveries. Boole's abstruse reasoning has led to applications of which he never dreamed. For example, telephone switching and electronic computers use binary digits and logical elements that rely on Boolean logic for their design and operation.

## GIROLAMO CARDANO

(b. Sept. 24, 1501, Pavia, duchy of Milan [Italy]—d. Sept. 21, 1576, Rome)

The Italian physician, mathematician, and astrologer Girolamo Cardano wrote a book, *Ars magna* (*The Great*

*Art; or, The Rules of Algebra*), that is one of the cornerstones in the history of algebra.

Educated at the universities of Pavia and Padua, Cardano received his medical degree in 1526. In 1534 he moved to Milan, where he lived in great poverty until he became a lecturer in mathematics. Admitted to the college of physicians in 1539, he soon became rector. Although his fame as a physician rapidly grew, and many of Europe's crowned heads solicited his services, he valued his independence too much to become a court physician. In 1543 he accepted a professorship in medicine in Pavia.

Cardano was the most outstanding mathematician of his time. In 1539 he published two books on arithmetic embodying his popular lectures, the more important being *Practica arithmetica et mensurandi singularis* ("Practice of Mathematics and Individual Measurements"). His *Ars magna* (1545) contained the solution of the cubic equation, for which he was indebted to the Venetian mathematician Niccolò Tartaglia, and also the solution of the quartic equation found by Cardano's former servant, Lodovico Ferrari. His *Liber de ludo aleae* (*The Book on Games of Chance*) presents the first systematic computations of probabilities, a century before Blaise Pascal and Pierre de Fermat. Cardano's popular fame was based largely on books dealing with scientific and philosophical questions, especially *De subtilitate rerum* ("The Subtlety of Things"), a collection of physical experiments and inventions, interspersed with anecdotes.

Cardano's favourite son, having married a disreputable girl, poisoned her and was executed in 1560. Cardano never recovered from the blow. From 1562 he was a professor in Bologna, but in 1570 he was suddenly arrested on the accusation of heresy. After several months in jail, he was permitted to abjure privately, but he lost his position and the right to publish books. Before his death he completed his autobiography, *De propria vita* (*The Book of My Life*).

## ARTHUR CAYLEY

(b. Aug. 16, 1821, Richmond, Surrey, Eng.—d. Jan. 26, 1895, Cambridge, Cambridgeshire)

The English mathematician Arthur Cayley was the leader of the British school of pure mathematics that emerged in the 19th century.

Although Cayley was born in England, his first seven years were spent in St. Petersburg, Russia, where his parents lived in a trading community affiliated with the Muscovy Company. On the family's permanent return to England in 1828 he was educated at a small private school in Blackheath, followed by the three-year course at King's College, London. Cayley entered Trinity College, Cambridge, in 1838 and emerged as the champion student of 1842, the "Senior Wrangler" of his year. A fellowship enabled him to stay on at Cambridge, but in 1846 he left the university to study the law at Lincoln's Inn in London. Cayley practised law in London from 1849 until 1863, while writing more than 300 mathematical papers in his spare time. In recognition of his mathematical work, he was elected to the Royal Society in 1852 and presented with its Royal Medal seven years later. In 1863 he accepted the Sadleirian professorship in mathematics at Cambridge—sacrificing his legal career to devote himself full-time to mathematical research. In that same year he married Susan Moline, the daughter of a country banker.

Cayley's manner was diffident but decisive. He was a capable administrator who quietly and effectively discharged his academic duties. He was an early supporter of women's higher education and steered Newnham

College, Cambridge (founded in 1871), during the 1880s. Despite aiding the careers of a few students who naturally took to pure mathematics, Cayley never established a full-fledged research school of mathematics at Cambridge.

In mathematics Cayley was an individualist. He handled calculations and symbolic manipulations with formidable skill, guided by a deep intuitive understanding of mathematical theories and their interconnections. His ability to keep abreast of current work while seeing the wider view enabled him to perceive important trends and to make valuable suggestions for further investigation.

Cayley made important contributions to the algebraic theory of curves and surfaces, group theory, linear algebra, graph theory, combinatorics, and elliptic functions. He formalized the theory of matrices. Among Cayley's most important papers were his series of 10 "Memoirs on Quantics" (1854–78). A quantic, known today as an algebraic form, is a polynomial with the same total degree for each term. For example, every term in the following polynomial has a total degree of 3:

$$x^3 + 7x^2y - 5xy^2 + y^3.$$

Alongside work produced by his friend James Joseph Sylvester, Cayley's study of various properties of forms that are unchanged (invariant) under some transformation, such as rotating or translating the coordinate axes, established a branch of algebra known as invariant theory.

In geometry Cayley concentrated his attention on analytic geometry, for which he naturally employed invariant theory. For example, he showed that the order of points formed by intersecting lines is always invariant, regardless of any spatial transformation. In 1859 Cayley outlined a notion of distance in projective geometry (a projective metric), and he was one of the first to realize that Euclidean geometry is a special case of projective geometry—an insight that reversed current thinking. Ten years later, Cayley's projective metric provided a key for understanding the relationship between the various types of non-Euclidean geometries.

Cayley was essentially a pure mathematician, but he also pursued mechanics and astronomy. He was active in lunar studies and produced two widely praised reports on dynamics (1857, 1862). Cayley had an extraordinarily prolific career, producing almost a thousand mathematical papers. His habit was to embark on long studies punctuated by rapidly written "bulletins from the front." Cayley effortlessly wrote French and often published in Continental journals. As a young graduate at Cambridge, he was inspired by the work of the mathematician Karl Jacobi (1804–51). In 1876 Cayley published his only book, *An Elementary Treatise on Elliptic Functions*, which drew out this widely studied subject from Jacobi's point of view.

Cayley was awarded numerous honours, including the Copley Medal in 1882 by the Royal Society. At various times he was president of the Cambridge Philosophical Society, the London Mathematical Society, the British Association for the Advancement of Science, and the Royal Astronomical Society.

## FRANCIS YSIDRO EDGEWORTH

(b. Feb. 8, 1845, Edgeworthstown, County Longford, Ire.—d. Feb. 13, 1926, Oxford, Oxfordshire, Eng.)

Francis Ysidro Edgeworth was an Irish economist and statistician who innovatively applied mathematics to the fields of economics and statistics.

Edgeworth was educated at Trinity College in Dublin and Balliol College, Oxford, graduating in 1869. In 1877 he qualified as a barrister. He lectured at King's College in London from 1880, becoming professor of political economy in 1888. From 1891 to 1922 he was Drummond Professor of Economics at Oxford. He also played an important role as editor of the *Economic Journal* (1891–1926).

Although Edgeworth was strong in mathematics, he was weak at prose, and his publications failed to reach a popular audience. He had hoped to use mathematics to illuminate ethical questions, but his first work, *New and Old Methods of Ethics* (1877), depended so heavily on mathematical techniques—especially the calculus of variations—that the book may have deterred otherwise interested readers. His most famous work, *Mathematical Psychics* (1881), presented his new ideas on the generalized utility function, the indifference curve, and the contract curve, all of which have become standard devices of economic theory.

Edgeworth contributed to the pure theory of international trade and to taxation and monopoly theory. He also made important contributions to the theory of index numbers and to statistical theory, in particular to probability, advocating the use of data from past experience as the basis for estimating future probabilities. John Kenneth Galbraith once remarked that "all races have produced notable economists, except the Irish." Edgeworth is a strong counterexample to Galbraith's claim.

## PIERRE DE FERMAT

(b. Aug. 17, 1601, Beaumont-de-Lomagne, France—d. Jan. 12, 1665, Castres)

The French mathematician Pierre de Fermat is often called the founder of the modern theory of numbers.

*Co-founder of the theory of probability, Pierre de Fermat was the most productive mathematician of his day.* Photos.com

Together with René Descartes, Fermat was one of the two leading mathematicians of the first half of the 17th century. Through his correspondence with Blaise Pascal, he was a co-founder of the theory of probability.

In 1631 Fermat received the baccalaureate in law from the University of Orléans. He served in the local parliament at Toulouse, becoming councillor in 1634. Sometime before 1638 he became known as Pierre de Fermat, but the authority for this designation is uncertain. In 1638 he was named to the Criminal Court.

Through the mathematician and theologian Marin Mersenne, who, as a friend of Descartes, often acted as an intermediary with other scholars, Fermat in 1638 maintained a controversy with Descartes on the validity of their respective methods for tangents to curves. Fermat's views were fully justified some 30 years later in the calculus of Sir Isaac Newton. Recognition of the significance of Fermat's work in analysis was tardy, in part because he adhered to the system of mathematical symbols devised by François Viète, notations that Descartes's *Géométrie* had rendered largely obsolete. The handicap imposed by the awkward notations operated less severely in Fermat's favourite field of study, the theory of numbers, but, unfortunately, he found no correspondent to share his enthusiasm. In 1654 he had enjoyed an exchange of letters with his fellow mathematician Blaise Pascal on problems in probability concerning games of chance, the results of which were extended and published by Huygens in his *De Ratiociniis in Ludo Aleae* (1657).

Fermat vainly sought to persuade Pascal to join him in research in number theory. Inspired by an edition in 1621 of the *Arithmetic* of Diophantus, the Greek mathematician of the 3rd century CE, Fermat had discovered new results in the so-called higher arithmetic, many of which concerned properties of prime numbers (those positive integers that have no factors other than 1 and themselves). One of the most elegant of these had been the theorem that every prime of the form $4n + 1$ is uniquely expressible as the sum of two squares. A more important result, now known as Fermat's lesser theorem, asserts that if $p$ is a prime number and if $a$ is any positive integer, $a^p - a$ is divisible by $p$. For occasional demonstrations of his theorems Fermat used a device that he called his method of "infinite descent," an inverted form of reasoning by recurrence or mathematical induction. By far the best known of Fermat's many theorems is a problem known as his "great," or "last," theorem. This appeared in the margin of his copy of Diophantus' *Arithmetica* and states that the equation $x^n + y^n = z^n$, where $x, y, z$, and $n$ are positive integers, has no solution if $n$ is greater than 2. This theorem remained unsolved until the late 20th century.

Fermat was the most productive mathematician of his day. But his influence was circumscribed by his reluctance to publish.

## SIR RONALD AYLMER FISHER

(b. Feb. 17, 1890, London, Eng.—d. July 29, 1962, Adelaide, Austl.)

The British statistician and geneticist Sir Ronald Aylmer Fisher pioneered the application of statistical procedures to the design of scientific experiments.

In 1909 Fisher was awarded a scholarship to study mathematics at the University of Cambridge, from which he graduated in 1912 with a B.A. in astronomy. He remained at Cambridge for another year to continue course work in astronomy and physics and to study the theory of errors. (The connection between astronomy and statistics dates back to Carl Friedrich Gauss, who formulated the law of observational error and the normal distribution based on his analysis of astronomical observations.)

Fisher taught high school mathematics and physics from 1914 until 1919 while continuing his research in statistics and genetics. Fisher had evidenced a keen interest in evolutionary theory during his student days—he was a

founder of the Cambridge University Eugenics Society—
and he combined his training in statistics with his
avocation for genetics. In particular, he published an
important paper in 1918 in which he used powerful statistical tools to reconcile what had been apparent
inconsistencies between Charles Darwin's ideas of natural
selection and the recently rediscovered experiments of
the Austrian botanist Gregor Mendel.

In 1919 Fisher became the statistician for the
Rothamsted Experimental Station near Harpenden,
Hertfordshire, and did statistical work associated with
the plant-breeding experiments conducted there. His
*Statistical Methods for Research Workers* (1925) remained in
print for more than 50 years. His breeding experiments
led to theories about gene dominance and fitness, published in *The Genetical Theory of Natural Selection* (1930).
In 1933 Fisher became Galton Professor of Eugenics at
University College, London. From 1943 to 1957 he was
Balfour Professor of Genetics at Cambridge. He investigated the linkage of genes for different traits and
developed methods of multivariate analysis to deal with
such questions.

At Rothamsted Fisher designed plant-breeding
experiments that provided greater information with less
investments of time, effort, and money. One major problem he encountered was avoiding biased selection of
experimental materials, which results in inaccurate or
misleading experimental data. To avoid such bias, Fisher
introduced the principle of randomization. This principle states that before an effect in an experiment can be
ascribed to a given cause or treatment independently of
other causes or treatments, the experiment must be
repeated on a number of control units of the material
and that all units of material used in the experiments must
be randomly selected samples from the whole population

they are intended to represent. In this way, random selection is used to diminish the effects of variability in experimental materials.

An even more important achievement was Fisher's origination of the concept of analysis of variance, or ANOVA. This statistical procedure enabled experiments to answer several questions at once. Fisher's principal idea was to arrange an experiment as a set of partitioned subexperiments that differ from each other in one or more of the factors or treatments applied in them. By permitting differences in their outcome to be attributed to the different factors or combinations of factors by means of statistical analysis, these subexperiments constituted a notable advance over the prevailing procedure of varying only one factor at a time in an experiment. It was later found that the problems of bias and multivariate analysis that Fisher had solved in his plant-breeding research are encountered in many other scientific fields as well.

Fisher summed up his statistical work in *Statistical Methods and Scientific Inference* (1956). He was knighted in 1952 and spent the last years of his life conducting research in Australia.

## JOHN GRAUNT

(b. April 24, 1620, London, Eng.—d. April 18, 1674, London)

John Graunt was an English statistician who is generally deemed the founder of the science of demography, the statistical study of human populations. His analysis of the vital statistics of the London populace influenced the pioneer demographic work of his friend Sir William Petty and, even more importantly, that of Edmond Halley, the astronomer royal.

A prosperous haberdasher until his business was destroyed in the London fire of 1666, Graunt held municipal offices and a militia command. While still active as a merchant, he began to study the death records that had been kept by the London parishes since 1532. Noticing that certain phenomena of death statistics appeared regularly, he was inspired to write *Natural and Political Observations . . . Made upon the Bills of Mortality* (1662). He produced four editions of this work. The third (1665) was published by the Royal Society, of which Graunt was a charter member.

Graunt classified death rates according to the causes of death, among which he included overpopulation, observing that the urban death rate exceeded the rural. He also found that although the male birth rate was higher than the female, it was offset by a greater mortality rate for males, so that the population was divided almost evenly between the sexes. Perhaps his most important innovation was the life table, which presented mortality in terms of survivorship. Using only two rates of survivorship (to ages 6 and 76), derived from actual observations, he predicted the percentage of persons that will live to each successive age and their life expectancy year by year. Petty was able to extrapolate from mortality rates an estimate of community economic loss caused by deaths.

# PIERRE-SIMON, MARQUIS DE LAPLACE

(b. March 23, 1749, Beaumount-en-Auge, Normandy, France—d. March 5, 1827, Paris)

The French mathematician, astronomer, and physicist Pierre-Simon, marquis de Laplace is best known for his investigations into the stability of the solar system. He also demonstrated the usefulness of probability for interpreting scientific data.

Laplace was the son of a peasant farmer. Little is known of his early life except that he quickly showed his mathematical ability at the military academy at Beaumont. In 1767 he arrived in Paris with a letter of recommendation to the mathematician Jean d'Alembert, who helped him secure a professorship at the École Militaire, where he taught from 1769 to 1776.

In 1773 he began his major lifework—applying Newtonian gravitation to the entire solar system—by taking up a particularly troublesome problem: why Jupiter's orbit appeared to be continuously shrinking while Saturn's continually expanded. The mutual gravitational interactions within the solar system were so complex that mathematical solution seemed impossible. Indeed, Newton had concluded that divine intervention was periodically required to preserve the system in equilibrium. Laplace announced the invariability of planetary mean motions (average angular velocity). This discovery in 1773 was the first and most important step in establishing the stability of the solar system and the most important advance in physical astronomy since Newton. He removed the last apparent anomaly from the theoretical description of the solar system in 1787 with the announcement that lunar acceleration depends on the eccentricity of the Earth's orbit.

In 1796 Laplace published *Exposition du système du monde* (*The System of the World*), a semipopular treatment of his work in celestial mechanics and a model of French prose. The book included his "nebular hypothesis"—attributing the origin of the solar system to cooling and contracting of a gaseous nebula—which strongly influenced future thought on planetary origin. His *Traité de mécanique céleste* (*Celestial Mechanics*), appearing in five volumes between 1798 and 1827, summarized the results

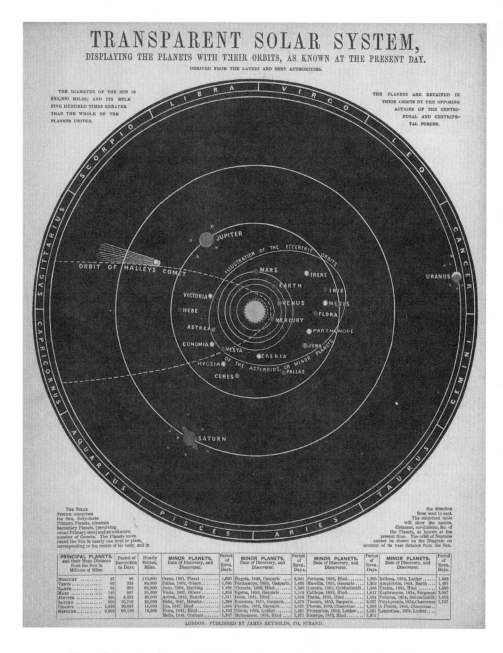

*Pierre-Simon Laplace applied Newtonian gravitation to the entire solar system, particularly investigating why Jupiter's orbit appeared to be continuously shrinking while Saturn's continually expanded. SSPL via Getty Images*

obtained by his mathematical development and application of the law of gravitation. He offered a complete mechanical interpretation of the solar system by devising methods for calculating the motions of the planets and their satellites and their perturbations, including the resolution of tidal problems. The book made him a celebrity.

In 1814 Laplace published a popular work for the general reader, *Essai philosophique sur les probabilités* (*A Philosophical Essay on Probability*). This work was the introduction to the second edition of his comprehensive and important *Théorie analytique des probabilités* (*Analytic Theory of Probability*), first published in 1812, in which he described many of the tools he invented for mathematically predicting the probabilities that particular events will occur in nature. He applied his theory not only to the ordinary problems of chance but also to the inquiry into the causes of phenomena, vital statistics, and future events, while emphasizing its importance for physics and astronomy. The book is notable also for including a special case of what became known as the central limit theorem. Laplace proved that the distribution of errors in large data samples from astronomical observations can be approximated by a Gaussian or normal distribution.

## ADRIEN-MARIE LEGENDRE

(b. Sept. 18, 1752, Paris, France—d. Jan. 10, 1833, Paris)

The distinguished work of the French mathematician Adrien-Marie Legendre on elliptic integrals provided basic analytic tools for mathematical physics.

Little is known about Legendre's early life except that his family wealth allowed him to study physics and mathematics, beginning in 1770, at the Collège Mazarin (Collège des Quatre-Nations) in Paris and that, at least until the French Revolution, he did not have to work. Nevertheless, Legendre taught mathematics at the École Militaire in Paris from 1775 to 1780. In 1782 he won a prize offered by the Berlin Academy of Sciences for his effort to "determine the curve described by cannonballs and bombs, taking into consideration the resistance of air[, and] give rules for obtaining the ranges corresponding to different initial velocities and to different angles of projection." The next year he presented research on celestial mechanics to the French Academy of Sciences, and he was soon rewarded with membership. In 1787 he joined the French team, led by Jacques-Dominique Cassini and Pierre Mechain, in the geodetic measurements jointly conducted with the Royal Greenwich Observatory in London. At this time he also became a member of the British Royal Society. In 1791 he was named along with Cassini and Mechain to a special committee to develop the metric system and, in particular, to conduct the necessary measurements to determine the standard metre. He also worked on projects to produce logarithmic and trigonometric tables.

The Academy of Sciences was forced to close in 1793 during the French Revolution, and Legendre lost his family wealth during the upheaval. Nevertheless, he married at this time. The following year he published *Éléments de géométrie* (*Elements of Geometry*), a reorganization and simplification of the propositions from Euclid's *Elements* that was widely adopted in Europe, even though it is full of fallacious attempts to defend the parallel postulate. Legendre also gave a simple proof that $\pi$ is irrational, as well as the first proof that $\pi^2$ is irrational, and he conjectured that $\pi$ is not the root of any algebraic equation of finite degree with rational coefficients (i.e., $\pi$ is a transcendental number). His *Éléments* was even more pedagogically influential in the United States, undergoing numerous translations starting in 1819. One such translation went through some 33 editions. The French Academy of Sciences was reopened in 1795 as the Institut Nationale des Sciences et des Arts, and Legendre was installed in the mathematics section. When Napoleon reorganized the institute in 1803, Legendre was retained in the new geometry section. In 1824 he refused to endorse the government's candidate for the Institut and lost his pension from the École Militaire, where he had served from 1799 to 1815 as the mathematics examiner for graduating artillery students.

Legendre's *Nouvelles méthodes pour la détermination des orbites des comètes* (1806; "New Methods for the Determination of Comet Orbits") contains the first comprehensive treatment of the method of least squares, but priority for its discovery is shared with his German rival Carl Friedrich Gauss.

In 1786 Legendre took up research on elliptic integrals. In his most important work, *Traité des fonctions elliptiques* (1825–37; "Treatise on Elliptic Functions"), he reduced elliptic integrals to three standard forms now known by his name. He also compiled tables of the values of his elliptic integrals and showed how they can be used to solve important problems in mechanics and dynamics. Shortly after his work appeared, the independent discoveries of Niels Henrik Abel and Carl Jacobi completely revolutionized the subject of elliptic integrals.

Legendre published his own researches in number theory and those of his predecessors in a systematic form under the title *Théorie des nombres*, 2 vol. (1830). This work included his flawed proof of the law of quadratic reciprocity. The law was regarded by Gauss, the greatest mathematician of the day, as the most important general result in number theory since the work of Pierre de Fermat in the 17th century. Gauss also gave the first rigorous proof of the law.

## ABRAHAM DE MOIVRE

(b. May 26, 1667, Vitry, France—d. Nov. 27, 1754, London, Eng.)

French mathematician Abraham de Moivre was a pioneer in the development of analytic trigonometry and in the theory of probability.

A French Huguenot, de Moivre was jailed as a Protestant upon the revocation of the Edict of Nantes in 1685. When he was released shortly thereafter, he fled to England where, once in London, he became a close friend of Sir Isaac Newton and the astronomer Edmond Halley. De Moivre was elected to the Royal Society of London in 1697 and later to the Berlin and Paris academies. Despite his distinction as a mathematician, he never succeeded in securing a permanent position but eked out a precarious living by working as a tutor and a consultant on gambling and insurance.

De Moivre expanded his paper "De mensura sortis" (written in 1711), which appeared in *Philosophical Transactions,* into *The Doctrine of Chances* (1718). Although the modern theory of probability had begun with the unpublished correspondence (1654) between Blaise Pascal and Pierre de Fermat and the treatise *De Ratiociniis in Ludo Aleae* (1657; "On Ratiocination in Dice Games") by Christiaan Huygens of Holland, de Moivre's book greatly advanced probability study. The definition of statistical independence—namely, that the probability of a compound event composed of the intersection of statistically independent events is the product of the probabilities of its components—was first stated in de Moivre's *Doctrine.* Many problems in dice and other games were included, some of which appeared in the Swiss mathematician Jakob (Jacques) Bernoulli's *Ars conjectandi* (1713; "The Conjectural Arts"), which was published before de Moivre's *Doctrine* but after his "De mensura." He derived the principles of probability from the mathematical expectation of events, just the reverse of present-day practice.

De Moivre's second important work on probability was *Miscellanea Analytica* (1730; "Analytical Miscellany"). He was the first to use the probability integral in which the integrand is the exponential of a negative quadratic,

$$\int_0^\infty e^{-x^2} dx = \frac{\sqrt{\pi}}{2}.$$

He originated Stirling's formula, incorrectly attributed to James Stirling (1692–1770) of England, which states that for a large number $n$, $n!$ equals approximately $(2\pi n)^{1/2} e^{-n} n^n$; that is, $n$ factorial (a product of integers with values descending from $n$ to 1) approximates the square root of $2\pi n$, times the exponential of $-n$, times $n$ to the $n$th power. In 1733 he used Stirling's formula to derive the normal frequency curve as an approximation of the binomial law.

De Moivre was one of the first mathematicians to use complex numbers in trigonometry. The formula known by his name, $(\cos x + i \sin x)^n = \cos nx + i \sin nx$, was instrumental in bringing trigonometry out of the realm of geometry and into that of analysis.

## JOHN F. NASH, JR.

(b. June 13, 1928, Bluefield, W.Va., U.S.)

The American mathematician John Forbes Nash, Jr., was awarded the 1994 Nobel Prize for Economics for his landmark work, first begun in the 1950s, on the mathematics of game theory. He shared the Nobel Prize with the Hungarian American economist John C. Harsanyi and German mathematician Reinhard Selten.

In 1948 Nash received bachelor's and master's degrees in mathematics from the Carnegie Institute of Technology (now Carnegie-Mellon University) in Pittsburgh, Pennsylvania. Two years later, at age 22, he completed his doctorate at Princeton University, publishing his influential thesis "Non-cooperative Games" in the journal *Annals of Mathematics*. He joined the faculty of the Massachusetts Institute of Technology in 1951 but resigned in the late 1950s after bouts of mental illness. He then began an informal association with Princeton.

Nash established the mathematical principles of game theory, a branch of mathematics that examines the rivalries among competitors with mixed interests. Known as the Nash solution or the Nash equilibrium, his theory attempted to explain the dynamics of threat and action among competitors. Despite its practical limitations, the Nash solution was widely applied by business strategists.

A film version of Nash's life, *A Beautiful Mind* (2001), based on Sylvia Nasar's 1998 biography of the same name, won an Academy Award for best picture. It portrays Nash's long struggle with schizophrenia.

## JERZY NEYMAN

(b. April 16, 1894, Bendery, Bessarabia, Russia [now Tighina, Moldova] — d. Aug. 5, 1981, Oakland, Calif., U.S.)

Jerzy Neyman was a Polish mathematician and statistician who, working in Russian, Polish, and then English, helped to establish the statistical theory of hypothesis testing. Neyman was a principal founder of modern theoretical statistics.

Neyman was born into a Polish-speaking family and was raised in Bessarabia, the Crimea, and Ukraine under the Russian Empire. After serving as a lecturer at the Institute of Technology, Kharkov, in Ukraine, from 1917 to 1921, Neyman was appointed statistician of the Institute of Agriculture at Bydgoszcz, Pol. In 1923 he became a lecturer at the College of Agriculture, Warsaw, and he joined the faculty of the University of Warsaw in 1928. He served on the staff of University College, London, from 1934 to 1938, and then immigrated to the United States, where he joined the faculty of the University of California, Berkeley, becoming chairman of a new department of statistics in 1955 and residing as a U.S. citizen for the rest of his life. At Berkeley he built, with the help of a growing number of statisticians and mathematicians who studied under him, what became known as a leading world centre for mathematical statistics. A highly successful series of symposia on probability and statistics were carried out under his guidance.

Neyman's work in mathematical statistics, which includes theories of estimation and of testing hypotheses, has found wide application in genetics, medical diagnosis, astronomy, meteorology, and agricultural experimentation. He was noted especially for combining theory and its applications in his thinking. In 1969 he was awarded the prestigious National Medal of Science by U.S. President Lyndon Johnson.

## KARL PEARSON

(b. March 27, 1857, London, Eng.—d. April 27, 1936, Coldharbour, Surrey)

British statistician Karl Pearson was a leading founder of the modern field of statistics, prominent proponent of eugenics, and influential interpreter of the philosophy and social role of science.

In 1875 Pearson won a scholarship to King's College, University of Cambridge, where he achieved the rank of third wrangler in the highly competitive Mathematical Tripos of 1879. In 1884 Pearson was appointed professor of applied mathematics and mechanics at University College, London. He taught graphical methods, and this work formed the basis for his original interest in statistics. In 1892 he published *The Grammar of Science*, in which he argued that the scientific method is essentially descriptive rather than explanatory. Soon he was making the same argument about statistics, emphasizing especially the importance of quantification for biology, medicine, and social science. It was the problem of measuring the effects of natural selection, brought to him by his colleague Walter F.R. Weldon, that captivated Pearson and turned statistics into his personal scientific mission. Their work owed much to Francis Galton, who especially sought to apply statistical reasoning to the study of biological evolution and eugenics. Pearson, likewise, was intensely devoted to the development of a mathematical theory of evolution, and he became an acerbic advocate for eugenics.

Through his mathematical work and his institution building, Pearson played a leading role in the creation of modern statistics. The basis for his statistical mathematics came from a long tradition of work on the method of least squares approximation. Pearson drew from these studies in creating a new field whose task it was to manage and make inferences from data in almost every field. His positivistic philosophy of science provided a persuasive justification for statistical reasoning and inspired many champions of the quantification of the biological and social sciences during the early decades of the 20th century.

As statistician, Pearson emphasized measuring correlations and fitting curves to the data, and for the latter purpose he developed the new chi-square distribution. Rather than just dealing with mathematical theory, Pearson's papers most often applied the tools of statistics to scientific problems. With the help of his first assistant, George Udny Yule, Pearson built up a biometric laboratory on the model of the engineering laboratory at University College. As his resources expanded, he was able to recruit a devoted group of female assistants. They measured skulls, gathered medical and educational data, calculated tables, and derived and applied new ideas in statistics. In 1901, assisted by Weldon and Galton, Pearson founded the journal *Biometrika*, the first journal of modern statistics.

Pearson's grand claims for statistics led him into a series of bitter controversies. Pearson battled with doctors and economists who used statistics without mastering the mathematics or who emphasized environmental over hereditary causation. And he fought with a long line of fellow statisticians, including many of his own students. The bitterest of these disputes was with Ronald Aylmer Fisher. In the 1920s and '30s, as Fisher's reputation grew, Pearson's dimmed. Upon his retirement in 1933, Pearson's position at University College was divided between Fisher and Pearson's son Egon.

## SIR WILLIAM PETTY

(b. May 26, 1623, Romsey, Hampshire, Eng.—d. Dec. 16, 1687, London)

Sir William Petty was an English political economist and statistician whose main contribution to political economy, *Treatise of Taxes and Contributions* (1662), examined the role of the state in the economy and touched on the labour theory of value.

Petty studied medicine at the Universities of Leiden, Paris, and Oxford. He was successively a physician; professor of anatomy at Oxford; professor of music in London; inventor, surveyor, and landowner in Ireland; and a member of Parliament. As a proponent of the empirical scientific doctrines of the newly established Royal Society, of which he was a founder, Petty was one of the originators of political arithmetic, which he defined as the art of reasoning by figures upon things relating to government. His *Essays in Political Arithmetick and Political Survey or Anatomy of Ireland* (1672) presented rough but ingeniously calculated estimates of population and of social income. His ideas on monetary theory and policy were developed in *Verbum Sapienti* (1665) and in *Quantulumcunque Concerning Money, 1682* (1695).

Petty originated many of the concepts that are still used in economics today. He coined the term *full employment*, for example, and stated that the price of land equals the discounted present value of expected future rent on the land.

## SIMÉON-DENIS POISSON

(b. June 21, 1781, Pithiviers, France—d. April 25, 1840, Sceaux)

The French mathematician Siméon-Denis Poisson was known for his work on definite integrals, electromagnetic theory, and probability.

Poisson's family had intended him for a medical career, but he showed little interest or aptitude and in 1798 began studying mathematics at the École Polytechnique in Paris under the mathematicians Pierre-Simon Laplace and Joseph-Louis Lagrange, who became his lifelong friends.

He became a professor at the École Polytechnique in 1802. In 1808 he was made an astronomer at the Bureau of Longitudes, and, when the Faculty of Sciences was instituted in 1809, he was appointed a professor of pure mathematics.

Poisson's most important work concerned the application of mathematics to electricity and magnetism, mechanics, and other areas of physics. His *Traité de mécanique* (1811 and 1833; "Treatise on Mechanics") was the standard work in mechanics for many years. In 1812 he provided an extensive treatment of electrostatics, based on Laplace's methods from planetary theory, by postulating that electricity is made up of two fluids in which like particles are repelled and unlike particles are attracted with a force that is inversely proportional to the square of the distance between them.

Poisson contributed to celestial mechanics by extending the work of Lagrange and Laplace on the stability of planetary orbits and by calculating the gravitational attraction exerted by spheroidal and ellipsoidal bodies. His expression for the force of gravity in terms of the distribution of mass within a planet was used in the late 20th century for deducing details of the shape of the Earth from accurate measurements of the paths of orbiting satellites.

Poisson's other publications include *Théorie nouvelle de l'action capillaire* (1831; "A New Theory of Capillary Action") and *Théorie mathématique de la chaleur* (1835; "Mathematical Theory of Heat"). In *Recherches sur la probabilité des jugements en matière criminelle et en matière civile* (1837; "Research on the Probability of Criminal and Civil Verdicts"), an important investigation of probability, the Poisson distribution appears for the first and only time in his work. Poisson's contributions to the law of large numbers (for independent random variables with a common distribution, the average value for a sample tends to the mean as sample size increases) also appeared therein. Although originally derived as merely an approximation to the binomial distribution (obtained by repeated, independent trials that have only one of two possible outcomes), the Poisson distribution is now fundamental in the analysis of problems concerning radioactivity, traffic, and the random occurrence of events in time or space.

In pure mathematics his most important works were a series of papers on definite integrals and his advances in Fourier analysis. These papers paved the way for the research of the German mathematicians Peter Dirichlet and Bernhard Riemann.

## ADOLPHE QUETELET
(b. Feb. 22, 1796, Ghent, Belg.—d. Feb. 17, 1874, Brussels)

The Belgian mathematician, astronomer, statistician, and sociologist Lambert Adolphe Jacques Quetelet was known for his application of statistics and probability theory to social phenomena.

From 1819 Quetelet lectured at the Brussels Athenaeum, military college, and museum. In 1823 he went to Paris to study astronomy, meteorology, and the management of an astronomical observatory. While there he learned probability from Joseph Fourier and, conceivably, from Pierre-Simon Laplace. Quetelet founded (1828) and directed the Royal Observatory in Brussels, served as perpetual secretary of the Belgian Royal Academy (1834–74), and organized the first International Statistical Congress (1853). For the Dutch and Belgian governments, he collected and analyzed statistics on crime, mortality, and other subjects and devised improvements in census taking. He also developed methods for simultaneous observations of astronomical, meteorological, and geodetic phenomena from scattered points throughout Europe.

In *Sur l'homme et le développement de ses facultés, ou essai de physique sociale* (1835; *A Treatise on Man and the Development of His Faculties*), he presented his conception of the *homme moyen* ("average man") as the central value about which measurements of a human trait are grouped according to the normal distribution. His studies of the numerical constancy of such presumably voluntary acts as crimes stimulated extensive studies in "moral statistics" and wide discussion of free will versus social determinism. In trying to discover through statistics the causes of antisocial acts, Quetelet conceived of the idea of relative propensity to crime of specific age groups. Like his *homme moyen* idea, this evoked great controversy among social scientists in the 19th century.

## JAKOB STEINER

(b. March 18, 1796, Utzenstorf, Switz.—d. April 1, 1863, Bern)

The Swiss mathematician Jakob Steiner was one of the founders of modern synthetic and projective geometry.

As the son of a small farmer, Steiner had no early schooling and did not learn to write until he was 14. Against the wishes of his parents, at 18 he entered the Pestalozzi School at Yverdon, Switzerland, where his extraordinary geometric intuition was discovered. Later, he went to the University of Heidelberg and the University of Berlin to study, supporting himself precariously as a tutor. By 1824 he had studied the geometric transformations that led him to the theory of inversive geometry, but he did not publish this work. In 1826 the first regular publication devoted to mathematics, *Crelle's Journal*, was founded, giving Steiner an opportunity to publish some of his other original geometric discoveries. In 1832 he received an honorary doctorate from the University of Königsberg, and two years later he occupied the chair of geometry established for him at Berlin, a post he held until his death.

During his lifetime some considered Steiner the greatest geometer since Apollonius of Perga (c. 262–190 BCE), and his works on synthetic geometry were considered authoritative. He had an extreme dislike for the use of algebra and analysis, and he often expressed the opinion that calculation hampered thinking, whereas pure geometry stimulated creative thought. By the end of the century, however, it was generally recognized that Karl von Staudt (1798–1867), who worked in relative isolation at the University of Erlangen, had made far deeper contributions to a systematic theory of pure geometry. Nevertheless, Steiner contributed many basic concepts and results in projective geometry. For example, he discovered a transformation of the real projective plane (the set of lines through the origin in ordinary three-dimensional space) that maps each line of the projective plane to one point on the Steiner surface (also known as the Roman surface). His other work was primarily on the properties of algebraic curves and surfaces and on the solution of isoperimetric problems. His collected writings were published posthumously as *Gesammelte Werke*, 2 vol. (1881–82; "Collected Works").

## JAMES JOSEPH SYLVESTER

(b. Sept. 3, 1814, London, Eng. — d. March 15, 1897, London)

British mathematician James Joseph Sylvester, with Arthur Cayley, was a cofounder of invariant theory, the study of properties that are unchanged (invariant) under some transformation, such as rotating or translating the coordinate axes. He also made significant contributions to number theory and elliptic functions.

In 1837 Sylvester came second in the mathematical tripos at the University of Cambridge but, as a Jew, was prevented from taking his degree or securing an appointment there. The following year he became a professor of natural philosophy at University College, London (the only nonsectarian British university). In 1841 he accepted a professorship of mathematics at the University of Virginia, Charlottesville, U.S., but resigned after only three months following an altercation with a student for which the school's administration did not take his side. He returned to England in 1843. The following year he went to London, where he became an actuary for an insurance company, retaining his interest in mathematics only through tutoring (his students included Florence Nightingale). In 1846 he became a law student at the Inner Temple, and in 1850 he was admitted to the bar. While working as a lawyer, Sylvester began an enthusiastic and profitable collaboration with Cayley.

From 1855 to 1870 Sylvester was a professor of mathematics at the Royal Military Academy in Woolwich. He went to the United States once again in 1876 to become a professor of mathematics at Johns Hopkins University in Baltimore, Maryland. While there he founded (1878) and became the first editor of the *American Journal of Mathematics*, introduced graduate work in mathematics into American universities, and greatly stimulated the American mathematical scene. In 1883 he returned to England to become the Savilian Professor of Geometry at the University of Oxford.

Sylvester was primarily an algebraist. He did brilliant work in the theory of numbers, particularly in partitions (the possible ways a number can be expressed as a sum of positive integers) and Diophantine analysis (a means for finding whole-number solutions to certain algebraic equations). He worked by inspiration, and frequently it is difficult to detect a proof in his confident assertions. His work is characterized by powerful imagination and inventiveness. He was proud of his mathematical vocabulary and coined many new terms, but few have survived. In 1839 he was elected a fellow of the Royal Society, and he was the second president of the London Mathematical Society (1866–68). His mathematical output includes several hundred papers and one book, *Treatise on Elliptic Functions* (1876). He also wrote poetry, although not to critical acclaim, and published *Laws of Verse* (1870).

## JOHN VON NEUMANN

(b. Dec. 28, 1903, Budapest, Hung.—d. Feb. 8, 1957, Washington, D.C., U.S.)

Hungarian-born American mathematician John von Neumann grew from a child prodigy to one of the world's foremost mathematicians by his mid-twenties. He pioneered game theory and, along with Alan Turing and Claude Shannon, was one of the conceptual inventors of the stored-program digital computer.

Von Neumann showed signs of genius in early childhood: He could joke in Classical Greek and, for a family stunt, he could quickly memorize a page from a telephone book and recite its numbers and addresses. Upon completion of von Neumann's secondary schooling in 1921, his father discouraged him from pursuing a career in mathematics, fearing that there was not enough money in the field. As a compromise, von Neumann simultaneously studied chemistry and mathematics. He earned a degree in chemical engineering (1925) from the Swiss Federal Institute in Zürich and a doctorate in mathematics (1926) from the University of Budapest.

Von Neumann commenced his intellectual career when the influence of David Hilbert and his program of establishing axiomatic foundations for mathematics was at a peak, working under Hilbert from 1926 to 1927 at the University of Göttingen. The goal of axiomatizing mathematics was defeated by Kurt Gödel's incompleteness theorems, a barrier that Hilbert and von Neumann immediately understood. The work with Hilbert culminated in von Neumann's book *The Mathematical Foundations of Quantum Mechanics* (1932), in which quantum states are treated as vectors in a Hilbert space. This mathematical synthesis reconciled the seemingly contradictory quantum mechanical formulations of Erwin Schrödinger and Werner Heisenberg.

In 1928 von Neumann published "Theory of Parlor Games," a key paper in the field of game theory. The nominal inspiration was the game of poker. Game theory focuses on the element of bluffing, a feature distinct from the pure logic of chess or the probability theory of roulette. Though von Neumann knew of the earlier work of the French mathematician Émile Borel, he gave the subject mathematical substance by proving the mini-max theorem. This asserts that for every finite, two-person zero-sum game, there is a rational outcome in the sense that two perfectly logical adversaries can arrive at a mutual choice of game strategies, confident that they could not expect to do better by choosing another strategy. In games like poker, the optimal strategy incorporates a chance element. Poker players must bluff occasionally—and unpredictably—to avoid exploitation by a savvier player.

In 1933 von Neumann became one of the first professors at the Institute for Advanced Study (IAS), Princeton, N.J. The same year, Adolf Hitler came to power in Germany, and von Neumann relinquished his German academic posts.

Although Von Neumann once said he felt he had not lived up to all that had been expected of him, he became a Princeton legend. It was said that he played practical jokes on Einstein and could recite verbatim books that he had read years earlier. Von Neumann's natural diplomacy helped him move easily among Princeton's intelligentsia, where he often adopted a tactful modesty. Never much like the stereotypical mathematician, he was known as a wit, bon vivant, and aggressive driver—his frequent auto accidents led to one Princeton intersection being dubbed "von Neumann corner."

In late 1943 von Neumann began work on the Manhattan Project, working on Seth Neddermeyer's implosion design for an atomic bomb at Los Alamos, N.M. This called for a hollow sphere containing fissionable plutonium to be symmetrically imploded to drive the plutonium into a critical mass at the centre. The implosion had to be so symmetrical that it was compared to crushing a beer can without splattering any beer. Adapting an idea proposed by James Tuck, von Neumann calculated that a "lens" of faster- and slower-burning chemical explosives could achieve the needed degree of symmetry. The *Fat Man* atomic bomb dropped on Nagasaki used this design.

Overlapping with this work was von Neumann's magnum opus of applied math, *Theory of Games and Economic Behavior* (1944), cowritten with Princeton economist Oskar Morgenstern. Game theory had been orphaned since the 1928 publication of "Theory of Parlor Games," with neither von Neumann nor anyone else significantly developing it. The collaboration with Morgernstern

*John von Neumann pioneered game theory, contributed to the infamous Manhattan Project, and was one of the conceptual inventors of the stored-program digital computer.* Alfred Eisenstaedt/Time & Life Pictures/ Getty Images

burgeoned to 641 pages, the authors arguing for game theory as the "Newtonian science" underlying economic decisions. The book invigorated a vogue for game theory among economists that has partly subsided. The theory has also had broad influence in fields ranging from evolutionary biology to defense planning.

Starting in 1944, he contributed important ideas to the U.S. Army's hard-wired Electronic Numerical Integrator and Computer (ENIAC) computer. Most important, von Neumann modified the ENIAC to run as a stored-program machine. He then lobbied to build an improved computer at the Institute for Advanced Studies (IAS). The IAS machine, which began operating in 1951, used binary arithmetic (the ENIAC had used decimal numbers) and shared the same memory for code and data, a design that greatly facilitated the "conditional loops" at the heart of all subsequent coding.

Another important consultancy was at the RAND Corporation, a think tank charged with planning nuclear strategy for the U.S. Air Force. Von Neumann insisted on the value of game-theoretic thinking in defense policy. He supported development of the hydrogen bomb and was reported to have advocated a preventive nuclear strike to destroy the Soviet Union's nascent nuclear capability circa 1950.

Von Neumann's shift to applied mathematics after the midpoint of his career mystified colleagues, who felt that a genius of his calibre should concern himself with "pure" mathematics. In an essay written in 1956, von Neumann made an eloquent defense of applied mathematics. He praised the invigorating influence of "some underlying empirical, worldly motif" in mathematics, warning that "at a great distance from its empirical source, or after much abstract inbreeding, a mathematical subject is in danger of degeneration." With his pivotal work on game theory, quantum theory, the atomic bomb, and the computer, von Neumann likely exerted a greater influence on the modern world than any other mathematician of the 20th century.

# CHAPTER 7
## SPECIAL TOPICS

S ome topics discussed earlier are treated here in greater detail. For example, you will learn how Sir Ronald Fisher used Bayes's theorem to throw suspicion on a famous scientist. You may also be amazed at how statistics was used to settle a controversy about Earth's shape.

## BAYES'S THEOREM

Bayes's theorem is a means for revising predictions in light of relevant evidence, also known as conditional probability or inverse probability. The theorem was discovered among the papers of the English Presbyterian minister and mathematician Thomas Bayes and posthumously published in 1763. Related to the theorem is Bayesian inference, or Bayesianism, based on the assignment of some a priori distribution of a parameter under investigation. In 1854 the English logician George Boole criticized the subjective character of such assignments, and Bayesianism declined in favour of "confidence intervals" and "hypothesis tests"—now basic research methods.

As a simple application of Bayes's theorem, consider the results of a screening test for infection with the human immunodeficiency virus (HIV). Suppose an intravenous drug user undergoes testing where experience has indicated a 25 percent chance that the person has HIV. A quick test for HIV can be conducted, but it is not infallible: Almost all individuals who have been infected long enough to produce an immune system response can be detected, but very recent infections may go undetected.

In addition, "false positive" test results (i.e., a false indication of infection) occur in 0.4 percent of people who are not infected. Hence, positive test results do not prove that the person is infected. Nevertheless, infection seems more likely for those who test positive, and Bayes's theorem provides a formula for evaluating the probability.

The logic of this formula is explained as follows: Suppose that there are 10,000 intravenous drug users in the population, of which 2,500 are infected with HIV. Suppose further that if all 2,500 people are tested, 95 percent (2,375 people) will produce a positive test result. The other 5 percent are known as "false negatives." In addition, of the remaining 7,500 people who are not infected, about 0.4 percent, or 30 people, will test positive ("false positives"). Because there are 2,405 positive tests in all, the probability that a person testing positive is actually infected can be calculated as 2,375/2,405, or about 98.8 percent.

Applications of Bayes's theorem used to be limited mostly to such straightforward problems, even though the original version was more complex. There are two key difficulties in extending these sorts of calculations, however. First, the starting probabilities are rarely so easily quantified. They are often highly subjective. To return to the HIV screening previously described, a patient might appear to be an intravenous drug user but might be unwilling to admit it. Subjective judgment would then enter into the probability that the person indeed fell into this high-risk category. Hence, the initial probability of HIV infection would in turn depend on subjective judgment. Second, the evidence is not often so simple as a positive or negative test result. If the evidence takes the form of a numerical score, the sum used in the denominator of the above calculation must be replaced by an integral. More complex evidence can easily lead to multiple integrals that, until recently, could not be readily evaluated.

Nevertheless, advanced computing power, along with improved integration algorithms, has overcome most calculation obstacles. In addition, theoreticians have developed rules for delineating starting probabilities that correspond roughly to the beliefs of a "sensible person" with no background knowledge. These rules can often be used to reduce undesirable subjectivity. These advances have led to a recent surge of applications of Bayes's theorem, more than two centuries since it was first put forth. It is now applied to such diverse areas as the productivity assessment for a fish population and the study of racial discrimination.

## BINOMIAL DISTRIBUTION

The binomial distribution is a common distribution function for discrete processes in which a fixed probability prevails for each independently generated value. First studied in connection with games of pure chance, the binomial distribution is now widely used to analyze data in virtually every field of human inquiry. It applies to any fixed number ($n$) of repetitions of an independent process that produces a certain outcome with the same probability ($p$) on each repetition. For example, it provides a formula for the probability of obtaining 10 sixes in 50 rolls of a die. Swiss mathematician Jakob Bernoulli, in a proof posthumously published in 1713, determined that the probability of $k$ such outcomes in $n$ repetitions is equal to the $k$th term (where $k$ starts with 0) in the expansion of the binomial expression $(p + q)n$, where $q = 1 - p$. (Hence the name *binomial distribution*.) In the example of the die, the probability of turning up any number on each roll is 1 out

*Binomial distribution provides a formula for the probability of obtaining 10 sixes in 50 rolls of a die.* Shutterstock.com

of 6 (the number of faces on the die). The probability of turning up 10 sixes in 50 rolls, then, is equal to the 10th term (starting with the 0th term) in the expansion of $(5/6 + 1/6)^{50}$, or 0.115586.

In 1936 the British statistician Ronald Fisher used the binomial distribution to publish evidence of possible scientific chicanery in the famous experiments on pea genetics reported by the Austrian botanist Gregor Mendel in 1866. Fisher observed that Mendel's laws of inheritance would dictate that the number of yellow peas in one of Mendel's experiments would have a binomial distribution with $n = 8,023$ and $p = \frac{3}{4}$, for an average of $np \cong 6,017$ yellow peas. Fisher found remarkable agreement between this number and Mendel's data, which showed 6,022 yellow peas out of 8,023. One would expect the number to be close, but a figure that close should occur only 1 in 10 times. Fisher found, moreover, that all seven results in

Mendel's pea experiments were extremely close to the expected values—even in one instance where Mendel's calculations contained a minor error. Fisher's analysis sparked a lengthy controversy that remains unresolved to this day.

## CENTRAL LIMIT THEOREM

The central limit theorem establishes the normal distribution as the distribution to which the mean (average) of almost any set of independent and randomly generated variables rapidly converges. The central limit theorem explains why the normal distribution arises so commonly and why it is generally an excellent approximation for the mean of a collection of data (often with as few as 10 variables).

The standard version of the central limit theorem, first proved by the French mathematician Pierre-Simon Laplace in 1810, states that the sum or average of an infinite sequence of independent and identically distributed random variables, when suitably rescaled, tends to a normal distribution. Fourteen years later the French mathematician Siméon-Denis Poisson began a continuing process of improvement and generalization. Laplace and his contemporaries were interested in the theorem primarily because of its importance in repeated measurements of the same quantity. If the individual measurements could be viewed as approximately independent and identically distributed, their mean could be approximated by a normal distribution.

The Belgian mathematician Adolphe Quetelet (1796–1874), famous today as the originator of the concept of the *homme moyen* ("average man"), was the first to use the normal distribution for something other than analyzing error. For example, he collected data on soldiers' chest girths and showed that the distribution of recorded values corresponded approximately to the normal distribution. Such examples are now viewed as consequences of the central limit theorem.

The central limit theorem also plays an important role in modern industrial quality control. The first step in improving the quality of a product is often to identify the major factors that contribute to unwanted variations. Efforts are then made to control these factors. If these efforts succeed, any residual variation will typically be caused by a large number of factors, acting roughly independently. In other words, the remaining small amounts of variation can be described by the central limit theorem, and the remaining variation will typically approximate a normal distribution. For this reason, the normal distribution is the basis for many key procedures in statistical quality control.

## CHEBYSHEV'S INEQUALITY

Chebyshev's inequality (also called the Bienaymé-Chebyshev inequality) characterizes the dispersion of data away from its mean (average). Although the general theorem is attributed to the 19th-century Russian mathematician Pafnuty Chebyshev, credit for it should be shared with the French mathematician Irénée-Jules Bienaymé, whose (less general) 1853 proof predated Chebyshev's by 14 years.

Chebyshev's inequality puts an upper bound on the probability that an observation should be far from its mean. It requires only two minimal conditions: (1) that the underlying distribution have a mean and (2) that the average size of the deviations away from this mean (as gauged by the standard deviation) not be infinite. Chebyshev's inequality then states that the probability that an observation will be more than $k$ standard deviations from the mean is at most $1/k^2$. Chebyshev used the inequality to prove his version of the law of large numbers.

Unfortunately, with virtually no restriction on the shape of an underlying distribution, the inequality is so weak as to be virtually useless to anyone looking for a precise statement on the probability of a large deviation. To achieve this goal, people usually try to justify a specific error distribution, such as the normal distribution as proposed by the German mathematician Carl Friedrich Gauss. Gauss also developed a tighter bound, $4/9k^2$ (for $k > 2/\sqrt{3}$), on the probability of a large deviation by imposing the natural restriction that the error distribution decline symmetrically from a maximum at 0.

The difference between these values is substantial. According to Chebyshev's inequality, the probability that a value will be more than two standard deviations from the mean ($k = 2$) cannot exceed 25 percent. Gauss's bound is 11 percent, and the value for the normal distribution is just less than 5 percent. Thus, it is apparent that Chebyshev's inequality is useful only as a theoretical tool for proving generally applicable theorems, not for generating tight probability bounds.

## DECISION THEORY

In statistics, decision theory is a set of quantitative methods for reaching optimal decisions. A solvable decision problem must be capable of being tightly formulated in terms of initial conditions and choices or courses of action, with their consequences. In general, such consequences are not known with certainty but are expressed as a set of probabilistic outcomes. Each outcome is assigned a "utility" value based on the preferences of the decision maker.

An optimal decision, following the logic of the theory, is one that maximizes the expected utility. Thus, the ideal of decision theory is to make choices rational by reducing them to a kind of routine calculation.

## DISTRIBUTION FUNCTION

The mathematical expression that describes the probability that a system will take on a specific value or set of values is called a distribution function. The classic examples are associated with games of chance. The binomial distribution gives the probabilities that heads will come up $a$ times and tails $n - a$ times (for $0 \le a \le n$), when a fair coin is tossed $n$ times. Many phenomena, such as the distribution of IQs, approximate the classic bell-shaped, or normal, curve. The highest point on the curve indicates the most common or modal value, which in most cases will be close to the average (mean) for the population. A well-known example from physics is the Maxwell-Boltzmann distribution law, which specifies the probability that a molecule of gas will be found with velocity components $u$, $v$, and $w$ in the $x$, $y$, and $z$ directions. A distribution function may take into account as many variables as one chooses to include.

## ERROR

In applied mathematics, the error is the difference between a true value and an estimate, or approximation, of that value. In statistics, a common example is the difference between the mean of an entire population and the mean of a sample drawn from that population. In numerical analysis, round-off error is exemplified by the difference between the true value of the irrational number $\pi$ and the value of rational expressions such as 22/7, 355/113, 3.14, or 3.14159. Truncation error results from ignoring all but a finite number of terms of an infinite series. For example, the exponential function $e^x$ may be expressed as the sum of the infinite series

$$1 + x + x^2/2 + x^3/6 + \cdots + x^n/n! + \cdots$$

Stopping the calculation after any finite value of $n$ will give an approximation to the value of $ex$ that will be in error, but this error can be made as small as desired by making $n$ large enough.

The relative error is the numerical difference divided by the true value, and the percentage error is this ratio expressed as a percent. The term *random error* is sometimes used to distinguish the effects of inherent imprecision from so-called systematic error, which may originate in faulty assumptions or procedures. The methods of mathematical statistics are particularly suited to the estimation and management of random errors.

## ESTIMATION

In statistics, any procedure used to calculate the value of some property of a population from observations of a sample drawn from the population is called an estimation. A point estimate, for example, is the single number most likely to express the value of the property. An interval estimate defines a range within which the value of the property can be expected (with a specified degree of confidence) to fall. The 18th-century English theologian and mathematician Thomas Bayes was instrumental in the development of Bayesian estimation to facilitate revision of estimates on the basis of further information.

*Estimation calculates the value of some property of a population from observations of a sample drawn from the population.* Roslan Rahman/AFP/ Getty Images

In sequential estimation, a parameter is estimated by analyzing a sample just large enough to ensure a previously chosen degree of precision. The fundamental technique is to take a sequence of samples, the outcome of each sampling determining the need for another sampling. The procedure is terminated when the desired degree of precision is achieved. On average, fewer total observations will be needed using this procedure than with any procedure using a fixed number of observations.

## INDIFFERENCE

Indifference is a classical principle in the mathematical theory of probability stated by the Swiss mathematician Jakob Bernoulli and formulated (and named) by the English economist John Maynard Keynes in *A Treatise on Probability*

(1921): Two cases are equally likely if no reason is known why either case should be the preferable one. The assumption of indifference was frequently used by the French mathematician Pierre-Simon Laplace beginning in the 1780s to calculate "inverse," now known as Bayesian probabilities. Such assumptions became controversial in the 19th century. Keynes and his followers worked to define the conditions under which they are justified.

## INFERENCE

Inference is the process of drawing conclusions about a parameter one is seeking to measure or estimate. Often scientists have many measurements of an object—say, the mass of an electron—and wish to choose the best measure. One principal approach of statistical inference is Bayesian estimation, which incorporates reasonable expectations or prior judgments (perhaps based on previous studies), as well as new observations or experimental results. Another method is the likelihood approach, in which "prior probabilities" are eschewed in favour of calculating a value of the parameter that would be most "likely" to produce the observed distribution of experimental outcomes.

In parametric inference, a particular mathematical form of the distribution function is assumed. Nonparametric inference avoids this assumption and is used to estimate parameter values of an unknown distribution having an unknown functional form.

## INTERVAL ESTIMATION

Interval estimation is the evaluation of a parameter (i.e., the mean or average) of a population by computing an interval, or range of values, within which the parameter is most likely to be located. Intervals are commonly chosen such that the parameter falls within with a 95 or 99 percent probability, called the confidence coefficient. Hence, the intervals are called confidence intervals, and the end points of such an interval are called upper and lower confidence limits. The interval containing a population parameter is established by calculating that statistic from values measured on a random sample taken from the population and applying the knowledge (derived from probability theory) of the fidelity with which the properties of a sample represent those of the entire population. The probability tells what percentage of the time the assignment of the interval will be correct but not what the chances are that it is true for any given sample. Of the intervals computed from many samples, a certain percentage will contain the true value of the parameter being sought.

## LAW OF LARGE NUMBERS

In statistics, the law of large numbers is the theorem that, as the number of identically distributed, randomly generated variables increases, their sample mean (average) approaches their theoretical mean. The law of large numbers was first proved by the Swiss mathematician Jakob Bernoulli in 1713. He and his contemporaries were developing a formal probability theory with a view toward analyzing games of chance. Bernoulli envisaged an endless sequence of repetitions of a game of pure chance with only two outcomes, a win or a loss. Labeling the probability of a win $p$, Bernoulli considered the fraction of times that such a game would be won in a large number of repetitions. It was commonly believed that this fraction should eventually be close to $p$. This is what Bernoulli proved in a precise manner by showing that as the number of repetitions increases indefinitely, the probability of this fraction being within any prespecified distance from $p$ approaches 1.

There is also a more general version of the law of large numbers for averages, Chebyshev's inequality, proved more than a century later by the Russian mathematician Pafnuty Chebyshev. The law of large numbers is closely related to what is commonly called the law of averages. In coin tossing, the law of large numbers stipulates that the fraction of heads will eventually be close to ½. Hence, if the first 10 tosses produce only 3 heads, it seems that some mystical force must somehow increase the probability of a head, producing a return of the fraction of heads to its ultimate limit of ½. Yet the law of large numbers requires no such mystical force. Indeed, the fraction of heads can take a long time to approach ½. For example, to obtain a 95 percent probability that the fraction of heads falls between 0.47 and 0.53, the number of tosses must exceed 1,000. In other words, after 1,000 tosses, an initial shortfall of only 3 heads out of 10 tosses is swamped by results of the remaining 990 tosses.

## LEAST SQUARES APPROXIMATION

The least squares approximation is a method for estimating the true value of some quantity based on a consideration of errors in observations or measurements. In particular, the line (function) that minimizes the sum of the squared distances (deviations) from the line to each observation is used to approximate a relationship that is assumed to be linear. The method has also been generalized for use with nonlinear relationships.

One of the first applications of the method of least squares was to settle a controversy involving the shape of the Earth. The English mathematician Isaac Newton asserted in the *Principia* (1687) that the Earth has an oblate (grapefruit) shape as a result of its spin, causing the equatorial diameter to exceed the polar diameter by about 1 part in 230. In 1718 the director of the Paris Observatory, Jacques Cassini, asserted on the basis of his own measurements that the Earth has a prolate (lemon) shape.

To settle the dispute, in 1736 the French Academy of Sciences sent surveying expeditions to Ecuador and Lapland. However, distances cannot be measured perfectly, and the measurement errors at the time were large enough to create substantial uncertainty. Several methods were proposed for fitting a line through this data—that is, to obtain the function (line) that best fit the data relating the measured arc length to the latitude. It was generally agreed that the method ought to minimize deviations in the y-direction (the arc length), but many options were available, including minimizing the largest such deviation and minimizing the sum of their absolute sizes. The measurements seemed to support Newton's theory, but the relatively large error estimates for the measurements left too much uncertainty for a definitive conclusion (but this was not immediately recognized). In fact, although Newton was essentially right, later observations showed that his prediction for excess equatorial diameter was about 30 percent too large.

In 1805 the French mathematician Adrien-Marie Legendre published the first known recommendation to use the line that minimizes the sum of the squares of these deviations (i.e., the modern least squares approximation). The German mathematician Carl Friedrich Gauss, who may have used the same method previously, contributed important computational and theoretical advances. The method of least squares is now widely used for fitting lines and curves to scatterplots (discrete sets of data).

# MARKOV PROCESS

A Markov process is a sequence of possibly dependent random variables $(x_1, x_2, x_3, ...)$—identified by increasing values of a parameter, commonly time—with the property that any prediction of the next value of the sequence $(xn)$, knowing the preceding states $(x_1, x_2, ..., xn_{-1})$, may be based on the last state $(xn_{-1})$ alone. That is, the future value of such a variable is independent of its past history.

These sequences are named for the Russian mathematician Andrey Andreyevich Markov (1856–1922), who was the first to study them systematically. Sometimes the term Markov process is restricted to sequences in which the random variables can assume continuous values, and analogous sequences of discrete-valued variables are called Markov chains.

# MEAN

In mathematics, the mean is a quantity that has a value intermediate between those of the extreme members of some set. Several kinds of mean exist, and the method of calculating a mean depends on the relationship known or assumed to govern the other members. The arithmetic mean, denoted $x$, of a set of $n$ numbers $x_1, x_2, ..., x_n$ is defined as the sum of the numbers divided by $n$:

$$\overline{x} = \frac{x_1 + x_2 + \cdots + x_n}{n}.$$

The arithmetic mean (usually synonymous with average) represents a point about which the numbers balance. For example, if unit masses are placed on a line at points with coordinates $x_1, x_2, ..., x_n$, then the arithmetic mean is the coordinate of the centre of gravity of the system. In statistics, the arithmetic mean is commonly used as the single value typical of a set of data. For a system of particles having unequal masses, the centre of gravity is determined by a more general average, the weighted arithmetic mean. If each number (x) is assigned a corresponding positive weight (w), the weighted arithmetic mean is defined as the sum of their products (wx) divided by the sum of their weights. In this case,

$$\bar{x} = \frac{w_1 x_1 + w_2 x_2 + \cdots + w_n x_n}{w_1 + w_2 + \cdots + w_n}.$$

The weighted arithmetic mean also is used in statistical analysis of grouped data: Each number $x_i$ is the midpoint of an interval, and each corresponding value of $w_i$ is the number of data points within that interval.

For a given set of data, many possible means can be defined, depending on which features of the data are of interest. For example, suppose five squares are given, with sides 1, 1, 2, 5, and 7 cm. Their average area is $(1^2 + 1^2 + 2^2 + 5^2 + 7^2)/5$, or 16 square cm, the area of a square of side 4 cm. The number 4 is the quadratic mean (or root mean square) of the numbers 1, 1, 2, 5, and 7 and differs from their arithmetic mean, which is $3\,^1/_5$. In general, the quadratic mean of $n$ numbers $x_1, x_2, ..., x_n$ is the square root of the arithmetic mean of their squares,

$$\sqrt{(x_1^2 + x_2^2 + \cdots + x_n^2)/n}.$$

The arithmetic mean gives no indication of how widely the data are spread or dispersed about the mean. Measures of the dispersion are provided by the arithmetic and quadratic means of the $n$ differences $x_1 - x$, $x_2 - x$, ..., $xn - x$. The quadratic mean gives the "standard deviation" of $x_1$, $x_2$, ..., $x_n$.

The arithmetic and quadratic means are the special cases $p = 1$ and $p = 2$ of the $p$th-power mean, $Mp$, defined by the formula

$$M_p = \left( \frac{x_1^p + x_2^p + \cdots + x_n^p}{n} \right)^{1/p}$$

where $p$ may be any real number except zero. The case $p = -1$ is also called the harmonic mean. Weighted $p$th-power means are defined by

$$M_p = \left( \frac{w_1 x_1^p + w_2 x_2^p + \cdots + w_n x_n^p}{w_1 + w_2 + \cdots + w_n} \right)^{1/p}$$

If $x$ is the arithmetic mean of $x_1$ and $x_2$, the three numbers $x_1$, $x$, $x_2$ are in arithmetic progression. If $h$ is the harmonic mean of $x_1$ and $x_2$, the numbers $x_1$, $h$, $x_2$ are in harmonic progression. A number $g$ such that $x_1$, $g$, $x_2$ are in geometric progression is defined by the condition that $x_1/g = g/x_2$, or $g^2 = x_1 x_2$, hence

$$g = \sqrt{x_1 x_2}.$$

This $g$ is called the geometric mean of $x_1$ and $x_2$. The geometric mean of $n$ numbers $x_1$, $x_2$, ..., $x_n$ is defined to be the $n$th root of their product:

$$g = \sqrt[n]{x_1 x_2 \cdots x_n}.$$

All the means discussed are special cases of a more general mean. If $f$ is a function having an inverse

$f^{-1}$ (a function that "undoes" the original function), the number

$$f^{-1}\left( \frac{f(x_1) + f(x_2) + \cdots + f(x_n)}{n} \right)$$

is called the mean value of $x_1$, $x_2$, ..., $x_n$ associated with $f$. When $f(x) = x^p$, the inverse is $f^{-1}(x) = x^{1/p}$, and the mean value is the $p$th-power mean, $M_p$. When $f(x) = \ln x$ (the natural logarithm), the inverse is $f^{-1}(x) = e^x$ (the exponential function), and the mean value is the geometric mean.

## NORMAL DISTRIBUTION

The normal distribution (also called the Gaussian distribution) is the most common distribution function for independent, randomly generated variables. Its familiar bell-shaped curve is ubiquitous in statistical reports, from survey analysis and quality control to resource allocation.

The graph of the normal distribution is characterized by two parameters: the mean, or average, which is the maximum of the graph and about which the graph is always symmetric; and the standard deviation, which determines the amount of dispersion away from the mean. A small standard deviation (compared with the mean) produces a steep graph, whereas a large standard deviation (again compared with the mean) produces a flat graph.

The normal distribution is produced by the normal density function, $p(x) = e^{-(x-\mu)^2/2\sigma^2} / \sigma\sqrt{2\pi}$. In this exponential function, $e$ is the constant $2.71828\ldots$, is the mean, and $\sigma$ is the standard deviation. The probability of a random variable falling within any given range of values is equal to the proportion of the area enclosed under the function's graph

*Germany's 10 Deutsche Mark banknote depicts a bell curve. The curve's highest point indicates the most common value, which is the population's average.* Photos.com

between the given values and above the $x$-axis. Because the denominator ($\sigma\sqrt{2\pi}$), known as the normalizing coefficient, causes the total area enclosed by the graph to be exactly equal to unity, probabilities can be obtained directly from the corresponding area (i.e., an area of 0.5 corresponds to a probability of 0.5). Although these areas can be determined with calculus, tables were generated in the 19th century for the special case of = 0 and $\sigma = 1$, known as the standard normal distribution, and these tables can be used for any normal distribution after the variables are suitably rescaled by subtracting their mean and dividing by their standard deviation, $(x - \mu)/\sigma$. Calculators have now all but eliminated the use of such tables.

The term "Gaussian distribution" refers to the German mathematician Carl Friedrich Gauss, who first developed a two-parameter exponential function in 1809 in connection with studies of astronomical observation errors. This study led Gauss to formulate his law of observational error and to advance the theory of the method of least squares approximation. Another famous early application of the normal distribution was by the British physicist James Clerk Maxwell, who in 1859 formulated his law of distribution of molecular velocities—later generalized as the Maxwell-Boltzmann distribution law.

The French mathematician Abraham de Moivre, in his *Doctrine of Chances* (1718), first noted that probabilities associated with discretely generated random variables (such as are obtained by flipping a coin or rolling a die) can be approximated by the area under the graph of an exponential function. This result was extended and generalized by the French scientist Pierre-Simon Laplace, in his *Théorie analytique des probabilités* (1812; "Analytic Theory of Probability"), into the first central limit theorem, which proved that probabilities for almost all independent and identically distributed random variables converge rapidly (with sample size) to the area under an exponential function—that is, to a normal distribution. The central limit theorem permitted hitherto intractable problems, particularly those involving discrete variables, to be handled with calculus.

## PERMUTATIONS AND COMBINATIONS

The various ways in which objects from a set may be selected, generally without replacement, to form subsets are called permutations and combinations. This selection of subsets is called a permutation when the order of selection is a factor, a combination when order is not a factor. By considering the ratio of the number of desired subsets to the number of all possible subsets for many games of chance in the 17th century, the French mathematicians Blaise Pascal and Pierre de Fermat gave impetus to the development of combinatorics and probability theory.

The concepts of and differences between permutations and combinations can be illustrated by examination of all the different ways in which a pair of objects can be selected from five distinguishable objects—such as the letters A, B, C, D, and E. If both the letters selected and the order of selection are considered, then the following 20 outcomes are possible:

| | | | | |
|---|---|---|---|---|
| AB | BA | AC | CA | AD |
| DA | AE | EA | BC | CB |
| BD | DB | BE | EB | CD |
| DC | CE | EC | DE | ED |

Each of these 20 different possible selections is called a permutation. In particular, they are called the permutations of five objects taken two at a time, and the number of such permutations possible is denoted by the symbol $_5P_2$, read "5 permute 2." In general, if there are $n$ objects available from which to select, and permutations ($P$) are to be formed using $k$ of the objects at a time, the number of different permutations possible is denoted by the symbol $_nP_k$. A formula for its evaluation is

$$_nP_k = n!/(n - k)!$$

The expression $n!$ (read "$n$ factorial") indicates that all the consecutive positive integers from 1 up to and including $n$ are to be multiplied together, and 0! is defined to equal 1. For example, using this formula, the number of permutations of five objects taken two at a time is

$$_5P_2 = \frac{5!}{(5-2)!} = \frac{5!}{3!} = \frac{(1)(2)(3)(4)(5)}{(1)(2)(3)}$$
$$= \frac{120}{6} = 20.$$

(For $k = n$, $_nP_k = n!$ Thus, for 5 objects there are $5! = 120$ arrangements.)

For combinations, $k$ objects are selected from a set of $n$ objects to produce subsets without ordering. Contrasting the previous permutation example with the corresponding combination, the AB and BA subsets are no longer distinct selections. By eliminating such cases, there remain only 10 different possible subsets: AB, AC, AD, AE, BC, BD, BE, CD, CE, and DE.

The number of such subsets is denoted by $_nC_k$, read "$n$ choose $k$." For combinations, because $k$ objects have $k!$ arrangements, there are $k!$ indistinguishable permutations for each choice of $k$ objects. Hence, dividing the permutation formula by $k!$ yields the following combination formula:

$$_nC_k = \frac{n!}{k!\,(n-k)!}.$$

This is the same as the $(n, k)$ binomial coefficient (*see* binomial theorem). For example, the number of combinations of five objects taken two at a time is

$$_5C_2 = \frac{5!}{(2)!\,(5-2)!} = \frac{5!}{(2)!\,(3)!} = \frac{(1)(2)(3)(4)(5)}{(1)(2)(1)(2)(3)}$$
$$= \frac{120}{12} = 10.$$

The formulas for $_nP_k$ and $_nC_k$ are called counting formulas, because they can be used to count the number of possible permutations or combinations in a given situation without having to list them all.

# POINT ESTIMATION

Point estimation is the process of finding an approximate value of some parameter, such as the mean (average), of a population from random samples of the population. The precise accuracy of any particular approximation is unknown pre, but probabilistic statements concerning the accuracy of such numbers as found over many experiments can be constructed.

It is desirable for a point estimate to be: (1) Consistent. The larger the sample size, the more accurate the estimate. (2) Unbiased. The expectation of the observed values of many samples ("average observation value") equals the corresponding population parameter. For example, the sample mean is an unbiased estimator for the population mean. (3) Most efficient or best unbiased—of all consistent, unbiased estimates, the one possessing the smallest variance (a measure of the amount of dispersion away from the estimate). In other words, the estimator that varies least from sample to sample. This generally depends on the particular distribution of the population. For example, the mean is more efficient than the median (middle value) for the normal distribution but not for more "skewed" (asymmetrical) distributions.

Several methods are used to calculate the estimator. The most often used, the maximum likelihood method, uses differential calculus to determine the maximum of the probability function of a number of sample parameters. The moments method equates values of sample moments (functions describing the parameter) to population moments. The solution of the equation gives the desired estimate. The Bayesian method, named for the 18th-century English theologian and mathematician Thomas Bayes, differs from the traditional methods by introducing a frequency function for the parameter being estimated. Although with the Bayesian method sufficient information on the distribution of the parameter is usually unavailable, the estimation can be easily adjusted as additional information becomes available.

# POISSON DISTRIBUTION

The Poisson distribution helps characterize events with low probabilities of occurrence within some definite time or space. French mathematician Siméon-Denis Poisson developed his function in 1830 to describe the number of times a gambler would win a rarely won game of chance in a large number of tries. Letting $p$ represent the probability of a win on any given try, the mean, or average, number of wins ($\lambda$) in $n$ tries will be given by $\lambda = np$. Using the Swiss mathematician Jakob Bernoulli's binomial distribution, Poisson showed that the probability of obtaining $k$ wins is approximately $\lambda^k/e^\lambda k!$, where $e$ is the exponential function and $k! = (k - 1)(k - 2) \cdots 2 \cdot 1$. Noteworthy is the fact that $\lambda$ equals both the mean and variance (a measure of the dispersal of data away from the mean) for the Poisson distribution.

The Poisson distribution is now recognized as a vitally important distribution in its own right. For example, in 1946 the British statistician R.D. Clarke published "An Application of the Poisson Distribution," in which he disclosed his analysis of the distribution of hits of flying bombs (V-1 and V-2 missiles) in London during World War II. Some areas were hit more often than others. The

British military wished to know if the Germans were targeting these districts (the hits indicating great technical precision) or if the distribution was by chance. If the missiles were in fact only randomly targeted (within a more general area), the British could simply disperse important installations to decrease the likelihood of their being hit.

Clarke began by dividing an area into thousands of tiny, equally sized plots. Within each of these, it was unlikely that there would be even one hit, let alone more. Furthermore, under the assumption that the missiles fell randomly, the chance of a hit in any one plot would be a constant across all the plots. Therefore, the total number of hits would be much like the number of wins in a large number of repetitions of a game of chance with a very small probability of winning. This sort of reasoning led Clarke to a formal derivation of the Poisson distribution as a model. The observed hit frequencies were close to the predicted Poisson frequencies. Hence, Clarke reported that the observed variations appeared to have been generated solely by chance.

## QUEUING THEORY

Queuing theory is a subject in operations research that deals with the problem of providing adequate but economical service facilities involving unpredictable numbers and times or similar sequences. In queuing theory the term *customers* is used, whether referring to people or things, in correlating such variables as how customers arrive, how service meets their requirements, average service time and extent of variations, and idle time. When such variables are identified for both customers and facilities, choices can be made on the basis of economic advantage.

Queuing theory is a product of mathematical research that grew largely out of the need to determine the optimum amount of telephone switching equipment required to serve a given area and population. Installation of more than the optimum requires excessive capital investment, while less than optimum means excessive delays in service.

## RANDOM WALK

A random walk is a process for determining the probable location of a point subject to random motions, given the probabilities (the same at each step) of moving some distance in some direction. Random walks are an example of Markov processes, in which future behaviour is independent of past history. A typical example is the drunkard's walk, in which a point beginning at the origin of the Euclidean plane moves a distance of one unit for each unit of time, the direction of motion, however, being random at each step. The problem is to find, after some fixed time, the probability distribution function of the distance of the point from the origin. Many economists believe that stock market fluctuations, at least over the short run, are random walks.

## SAMPLING

In statistics, a process or method of drawing a representative group of individuals or cases from a particular population is called sampling. Sampling and statistical inference are used in circumstances in which it is impractical to obtain information from every member of the population, as in biological or chemical analysis, industrial quality control, or social surveys. The basic sampling design is simple random sampling, based on probability

*Sampling is known as process or method of drawing a representative group of individuals or cases from a particular population, such as a jar of jellybeans.* Shutterstock.com

theory. In this form of random sampling, every element of the population being sampled has an equal probability of being selected. In a random sample of a class of 50 students, for example, each student has the same probability, 1/50, of being selected. Every combination of elements drawn from the population also has an equal probability of being selected. Sampling based on probability theory allows the investigator to determine the likelihood that statistical findings are the result of chance. More commonly used methods, refinements of this basic idea, are stratified sampling (in which the population is divided into classes and simple random samples are drawn from each class), cluster sampling (in which the unit of the sample is a group, such as a household), and systematic sampling (samples taken by any system other than random choice, such as every 10th name on a list).

An alternative to probability sampling is judgment sampling, in which selection is based on the judgment of the researcher and there is an unknown probability of inclusion in the sample for any given case. Probability methods are usually preferred because they avoid selection bias and make it possible to estimate sampling error (the difference between the measure obtained from the sample and that of the whole population from which the sample was drawn).

## STANDARD DEVIATION

In statistics, the standard deviation is a measure of the variability (dispersion or spread) of any set of numerical values about their arithmetic mean (average; denoted by $\mu$). It is specifically defined as the positive square root of the variance ($\sigma^2$). In symbols, $\sigma^2 = \Sigma(x_i - \mu)^2/n$, where $\Sigma$ is a compact notation used to indicate that as the index ($i$) changes from 1 to $n$ (the number of elements in the data set), the square of the difference between each element $x_i$ and the mean, divided by $n$, is calculated and these values are added together. The variance is used procedurally to analyze the factors that may influence the distribution or spread of the data under consideration.

## STOCHASTIC PROCESS

A stochastic process involves the operation of chance. For example, in radioactive decay every atom is subject to a fixed probability of breaking down in any given time interval. More generally, a stochastic process refers to a family of random variables indexed against some other variable or set of variables. It is one of the most general objects of study in probability. Some basic types of stochastic processes include Markov processes, Poisson processes (such as radioactive decay), and time series, with the index variable referring to time. This indexing can be either discrete or continuous, the interest being in the nature of changes of the variables with respect to time.

## STUDENT'S T-TEST

Student's $t$-test is a method of testing hypotheses about the mean of a small sample drawn from a normally distributed population when the population standard deviation is unknown. In 1908 William Sealy Gosset, an Englishman publishing under the pseudonym Student, developed the $t$-test and $t$ distribution. The $t$ distribution is a family of curves in which the number of degrees of freedom (the number of independent observations in the sample minus one) specifies a particular curve. As the sample size (and thus the degrees of freedom) increases, the $t$ distribution approaches the bell shape of the standard normal distribution. In practice, for tests involving the mean of a sample of size greater than 30, the normal distribution is usually applied.

First, a null hypothesis is usually formulated, which states that there is no effective difference between the observed sample mean and the hypothesized or stated population mean (i.e., that any measured difference is only caused by chance). In an agricultural study, for example, the null hypothesis could be that an application of fertilizer has had no effect on crop yield, and an experiment would be performed to test whether it has increased the harvest. In general, a $t$-test may be either two-sided (also termed two-tailed), stating simply that the means are not equivalent, or one-sided, specifying whether the observed mean is larger or smaller than the hypothesized mean. The test statistic $t$ is then calculated. If the observed $t$-statistic is more extreme than the critical value determined by the appropriate reference distribution, the null hypothesis is rejected. The appropriate reference distribution for the *t*-statistic is the *t* distribution. The critical value depends on the significance level of the test (the probability of erroneously rejecting the null hypothesis).

For example, suppose a researcher wishes to test the hypothesis that a sample of size $n = 25$ with mean $x = 79$ and standard deviation $s = 10$ was drawn at random from a population with mean $\mu = 75$ and unknown standard deviation. Using the formula for the *t*-statistic,

$$t = \frac{\overline{x} - \mu}{s/\sqrt{n}}$$

the calculated *t* equals 2. For a two-sided test at a common level of significance $\alpha = 0.05$, the critical values from the *t* distribution on 24 degrees of freedom are -2.064 and 2.064. The calculated *t* does not exceed these values, hence the null hypothesis cannot be rejected with 95 percent confidence. (The confidence level is $1 - \alpha$.)

A second application of the *t* distribution tests the hypothesis that two independent random samples have the same mean. The *t* distribution can also be used to construct confidence intervals for the true mean of a population (the first application) or for the difference between two sample means (the second application).

# GLOSSARY

**Bayesian estimation** Technique for calculating the probability of the validity of a proposition based on a prior estimate of its probability and new relevant evidence.

**binomial distribution** A common distribution function for discrete processes in which a fixed probability prevails for each independently generated value.

**biometry** English biometric school developed from the work of the polymath Francis Galton.

**catenary** Curve formed by a perfectly flexible chain suspended between its two fixed extremities.

**combinatorics** Concerned with problems of selection, arrangement, and operation within a finite or discrete system (also called combinatorial mathematics).

**confidence intervals** Interval estimates of population parameters.

**distribution function** A mathematical expression that describes the probability that a system will take on a specific value or set of values.

**eugenics** Selection of desired heritable characteristics to improve future generations, typically referring to humans.

**hypothesis testing** Draws on data from a sample to make conclusions about a population parameter or a population probability distribution.

**interval estimates** Estimate that includes a statement concerning the degree of confidence that the interval contains the estimated population parameter.

**isomorphic** Being of identical or similar form, shape, or structure.

**nonparametric method** A statistical method requiring fewer assumptions about a population or probability distribution.

***p*-value** Measure of how possible the sample results are, assuming a true null hypothesis. A smaller p-value indicates less likely sample results.

**partition** Division of a set of objects into a family of subsets that are mutually exclusive and jointly exhaustive.

**Philosophe** Any 18th-century French writer, scientist, and thinker convinced of the supremacy and efficacy of human reason and nature.

**point estimate** Value of a sample statistic used as a single estimate of a population parameter, without statements regarding the quality or precision.

**probability density function** A function whose integral is calculated to find probabilities associated with a continuous random variable.

**qualitative data** Provide labels or names for groups of comparable items.

**quantitative data** Measure either how much or how many of something.

**regression** A process to determine a line or curve best representing the general trend of a data set.

**regression to the mean** A model in which progeny tend to have the same variance as their parents.

**residual** The difference between the observed value of $y$ and the value of $y$ predicted by the estimated regression equation.

**sample space** The set of all possible outcomes of an experiment.

**statistical test** Assesses whether observed results give reasonable assurance of causation, rather than merely random fluctuations.

**stochastic process** A process in probability theory involving the operation of chance.

*t* **distribution** A family of curves in which the number of degrees of freedom specifies a particular curve.

*z*-**score** Represents the relative position of the data value by indicating the number of standard deviations it is from the mean.

# BIBLIOGRAPHY

## GENERAL WORKS

Ian Hacking, *The Emergence of Probability: A Philosophical Study of Early Ideas About Probability, Induction, and Statistical Inference* (1975, reissued 1991), discusses the history of probability and its interpretations in relation to a broad intellectual background, up to about 1750. Lorraine Daston, *Classical Probability in the Enlightenment* (1988, reprinted 1995), considers probability theory in the 17th and 18th centuries and how it was understood as the mathematics of good sense. Ian Hacking, *The Taming of Chance* (1990), covers statistical ideas of regularity and order, set against a background of scientific activity and bureaucratic intervention, in the 19th century. Theodore M. Porter, *The Rise of Statistical Thinking, 1820–1900* (1986), examines statistics as a strategy for dealing with large numbers, its emergence in bureaucratic social science, and its extension to the natural sciences, and his *Trust in Numbers: The Pursuit of Objectivity in Science and Public Life* (1995) scrutinizes numbers, calculation, and objectivity, understood as administrative tools. Gerd Gigerenzer et al., *The Empire of Chance: How Probability Changed Science and Everyday Life* (1989, reprinted 1991), contains essays on the development of probability and statistics, from its roots in gambling and insurance to its relations to science and philosophy, and on to more recent applications in polling and baseball.

## PROBABILITY THEORY

F.N. David, *Games, Gods, and Gambling: The Origins and History of Probability and Statistical Ideas from the Earliest Times to the Newtonian Era* (1962), covers the early history of probability theory. Stephen M. Stigler, *The History of Statistics: The Measurement of Uncertainty Before 1900* (1986), describes the attempts of early statisticians to use probability theory and to understand its significance in scientific problems.

## STATISTICS

Overviews are provided in David R. Anderson, Dennis J. Sweeney, and Thomas A. Williams, *Introduction to Statistics: Concepts and Applications*, 3rd ed. (1994), an introductory treatment with modest mathematical prerequisites; Judith M. Tanur et al., *Statistics: A Guide to the Unknown*, 3rd ed. (1989), containing a variety of statistical applications on topics of interest to the general reader; David Freedman et al., *Statistics*, 2nd ed. (1991), an innovative treatment of a variety of topics at the introductory level; and David S. Moore and George P. McCabe, *Introduction to the Practice of Statistics*, 2nd ed. (1993).

## GAME THEORY

The seminal work in game theory is John von Neumann and Oskar Morgenstern, *Theory of Games and Economic Behavior*, 3rd ed. (1953, reprinted 1980). Two introductions that require only high school algebra are Avinash K. Dixit and Susan Skeath, *Games of Strategy* (1999); and Philip D. Straffin, *Game Theory* (1993). Applications of game theory are presented in Nesmith C. Ankeny, *Poker Strategy: Winning with Game Theory* (1981, reprinted 1982); and Karl Sigmund, *Games of Life: Explorations in Ecology, Evolution, and Behavior* (1993). Histories of game theory can be found in William Poundstone, *Prisoner's Dilemma: John von Neumann, Game Theory, and the Puzzle of the Bomb* (1992); and E. Roy Weintraub (ed.), *Toward a History of Game Theory* (1992)

# Index